T0285135

GUNS,
GIRLS, AND
GREED

GUNS, GIRLS, AND GREED

I WAS A
BLACKWATER
MERCENARY IN IRAQ

MORGAN LERETTE

A KNOX PRESS BOOK
An Imprint of Permuted Press
ISBN: 979-8-88845-088-8
ISBN (eBook): 979-8-88845-089-5

Guns, Girls, and Greed:
I Was a Blackwater Mercenary in Iraq
© 2024 by Morgan Lerette
All Rights Reserved

Cover art by Conroy Accord

Permuted Press, LLC
New York • Nashville
permutedpress.com

Published in the United States of America
1 2 3 4 5 6 7 8 9 10

For Shelby Belle. You were no help editing this.

CHAPTER 1

Fuck. I think I shit my pants. A white car's barreling toward me. It's within fifteen feet. I hear the shot of a rifle. My rifle. My bullet. I hear the front-passenger tire burst as my bullet impacts. Pop. Love that sound. I wait for the car to explode and push jagged shrapnel through my open window, through my face, and splatter on the gunner behind me. I doubt he'll care. He'll be dead too. Car bombs are all the rage in Baghdad in 2005.

No explosion. The driver's lucky I had my barrel pointed toward the ground. By the time I saw him, it was too late—for him and me. Still, instinct kicked in. I switched my rifle from safe to fire, shot a round, and flipped it back to safe as we finished our turn. No time to dwell on the past.

George: What the fuck?
Me: Me?
George: I had him.
Me: Fuck if knew. He was close.

George is the top gunner in the Hummer. I'm behind Jacob, the driver, with my window down, face and rifle pointing to the enemy, which is anyone not us. Locals. Fuck them. My life's more important than theirs.

My worldview's a twelve-inch square window looking out of the back seat of a Hummer, the equivalent of blinders on a combat horse. I didn't see the car until he was about to run into our convoy. I shot.

George had a better view. The driver was slowing down. George didn't shoot. He didn't need to. I saw a threat, I shot it. If it's between a random Iraqi and me, I'm going home to see Grandma, who loves me. As far as Blackwater, The State Department, and the Iraqi's care, I'm expendable.

George: He was stopping.
Me: Fuck him. Should've stopped faster.
George: Yeah. Oh well.

We enter the Green Zone and park. I drop my kit, pistol, and rifle in my room, take a shower, and chug a Gatorade to hydrate. It's May in Baghdad. It's balls-hanging-below-my-knees hot. I hate this place. Why Saddam Hussein wanted to rule it is beyond me. He was King Shit of Turd Hill. Doesn't matter. I'm here for adventure and money. I'm getting plenty of both.

I grab the key to a Suburban and drive to a beer stand near camp. Cases of Amstel and Carlsberg are stacked waist high on wooden pallets in the blistering sun. Bottles of hard liquor sit on a table under an umbrella. I give the local twenty dollars and take two cases of Carlsberg.

I eat an early dinner and drive to the palace pool. This is where we party. Saddam spent his oil revenue making his palace fit for a king. It's now the US Embassy. While he's rotting in a prison somewhere, I enjoy his excesses.

The pool area has a brass fountain, palm trees, and grass. The water flowing from the fountain to the pool is sky-blue. Military chicks lay out here to get a tan. War pigs. Desert beauty queens. Baghdad beauties. Call them what you will. While in country they're "hot" based on the lack of other women. Military folklore has it upon landing home, a male soldier on the plane says, "How does it feel to be ugly again, ladies?" Stateside I wouldn't fuck them with George's dick and Jacob pushing, but the scenery's refreshing compared to the Blackwater camp with five hundred dudes.

We don't have a mission tomorrow so tonight we get fucked up. Why not? Seeing the sun go down is a blessing. Tomorrow I may be blown up by a rocket. Maybe an IED punctures the armor of my Hummer and rips my kidney apart. If I'm not wearing a colostomy bag at the end of the day, it's a win.

I park, unload the beer, and dump it in an ice chest, but there's no reason to wait until it gets cold. It tastes terrible after being in the sun. Skunky. If I wait for it to chill, it may taste marginally better but that's thirty minutes away. I pound one.

> George: Where the fuck did you get that shirt?
> Me: My closet.
> George: You make five hundred and fifty dollars a day and can't find something better than a dirty-ass brown t-shirt? Come on.
> Me: What's wrong with my shirt?
> George: You're a white trash hillbilly. That shirt smells like Circle K hotdogs and food stamps.
> Me: What's wrong with Circle K hotdogs? You look like your mom tried to abort you.
> George: Nice. Good one.

This is a normal day in Baghdad working for Blackwater as a private security contractor. Every day's a combat mullet—business in the front (by day) and party in the back (by night). I pour a Captain Morgan and Coke. Alcohol in the pool area is communal. George sips scotch from a red Solo cup when Jacob arrives.

> Me: Where the fuck you been?
> Jacob: Had to hit the gym.
> Me: Why? You look like a bag of smashed assholes.
> Jacob: We can't all be flabby pieces of shit like you in that white trash shirt.
> Me: Why does everyone hate my shirt? Is there a fashion show and I missed the radio call?

Jacob grabs a beer, pours it in a red Solo Cup and we tap plastic glasses to cheers. Before taking a drink, we tap them on the table twice in honor of the people we've loved and lost in combat. I hand the Suburban keys to someone not drinking. I doubt I'd get a DUI even if I drove the vehicle into the embassy's front door but there's no reason to chance it.

This is my life. Adventure then party. Rinse and repeat.

CHAPTER 2

You've heard about Blackwater. I venture you have a negative view of us. That's fine. It's a view we cultivated and nurtured. It's well deserved. It didn't start that way, not for me. I wanted to help rebuild Iraq, protect diplomats, and make a shit-ton of money in the process. I was successful with the latter two. I'd like to think I did some good for the people of Iraq on an individual basis. Maybe a few. I doubt it but it helps me sleep.

July 2004. I'm at the airport in Amman, Jordan after spending a night at the Bristol Hotel which is the closest thing to a frat house I've experienced. The night consisted of muscular dudes getting wasted, ordering hookers, and screaming in the hallway. I got in late the night prior, took a shower, put on the awesome bathrobe in the closet, and slept for a few hours before dragging my bags and tired ass to the lobby. I get on a bus that smells like ninety-proof, with a bunch of "operators" and some old farts. One has a sleep apnea machine. We're Blackwater contractors—ready to win this war doing…who knows what. We'll learn upon arrival.

I board a plane that looks like it was flown in Vietnam. I'm told it's a casa bird, a turbo prop plane with the upper and lower wings connected by struts. The plane is for cargo so it can be flown with the back door open or closed. It's haboob—dust storm–season when airports close for days or weeks. We have a tight window to land in Baghdad. I sit in the seat closest to the pilots. We take off, ascend to altitude, and start a comfortable flight to Baghdad. I don't bother to buckle in. I take out my laptop, place it on my knees, and play Minesweeper. I click aimlessly until I hit a mine, then I wonder, how does this game work? This defines my life for the next eighteen months.

When landing in a combat zone, pilots do a corkscrew maneuver where they circle to descend, like a corkscrew going in a wine bottle minus the booze. At the last minute, the pilot flattens out to land. This makes the plane a harder target to shoot down. If the aircraft flies straight to a landing strip as in normal plane travel, it's a tasty target for an RPG as the terrorist can see the probable glide path.

As I click random boxes on my laptop, I question my life decisions. How did I get here? Flying to an active combat zone isn't how I pictured my life at twenty-three. I've done my military time in the Air Force and did a pump to Iraq at the outset of Operation Iraqi Freedom in 2003. Growing up in small town USA, I should be roofing houses or framing duplexes like my uncles. Instead, I'm in this crappy plane, playing Minesweeper, assuming I'll be delivered home in an aluminum box like the one I flew home next to carrying a US service member as I left Iraq in 2003. Ah yes, this is Tony's fault. My good Air Force buddy, a former Force Recon Marine, sold me on the money, being a mercenary in Iraq, and the adventure. His words echo in my head like a fart hitting my pant leg.

Tony: Morgan, do you want to grow old and tell your grandkids you were a banker and made millions on Wall Street or do you want to have cool stories to tell?

This is my cool story. It's time to test my mettle, to prove my high school guidance counselor wrong when she said I was better suited for working construction than going to college.

I never consider the pilots of this plane are Blackwater employees—as crazy as me but with less to live for in their older age. They fly it like they stole it. Without warning, my laptop lifts off my legs. The plane plummets. We're going down. Crashing. I'm dead. The G-force is suffocating. My face hurts. I catch my breath and pray. Forgive my sins, Lord: The execution photo, the steroids, the time I hit the garage wall with

Grandma's car and blamed it on her. I'm relieved I got the prayer out before dying. I should've been pouring concrete today in Cottonwood, Arizona. Instead, I'll be dead before my first paycheck. Fuck.

Like a jolt, we level off. The smell of alcohol coming from the cockpit makes me think the pilots took the corkscrew maneuver a bit too seriously the night prior. The co-pilot unbuckles and walks to the back of the plane, lets down the cargo door, hooks a harness from his body armor to a metal loop on the plane floor and opens a box. I peek out the back door. The landscape below is tan, barren earth. He hands me an AK-47 like the stewardess on a Southwest flight handing out pretzels. How do I work this thing?

He walks to the cargo door and pulls a fully automatic M-249 machine gun from the box, loads it with a belt of .556 ammunition, and sits on the edge with his legs dangling in the air like a five-year-old on a swing. What the hell did I get myself into?

We land without incident and roll to a stop at Baghdad International Airport (BIAP). The co-pilot unhooks and exits with the pilot. They walk around the plane as I put my AK in the box. We unload bags and the boxes of ammunition I didn't notice we had. So much ammo, more than the Iraqi Army has at their disposal. I hear cussing.

Pilot: Fuck. We cracked the strut.
Co-pilot: Really? Where? Fuck. We're going to be stuck in this shithole until parts arrive. I told you not to dive so hard, asshole.
Pilot: And not do the best part of flying into By-opp?
Co-pilot: I didn't bring clothes! Goddammit.

I let this sink in. They dove and banked so violently—with passenger onboard, me—that the strut connecting the upper and lower wings cracked, and they're mad because they can't get back to Jordan to sleep in a nice bed at The Bristol Hotel and fuck a hooker. The assholes are stuck there for two weeks waiting for the part. Good.

A bongo truck pulls up to the plane with three small SUVs in a convoy. I've never seen anything like it. It's a cab on top of six tiny wheels with a large bed, a poor man's cattle truck driving cows to slaughter. Seems appropriate. We were told the vehicles in Iraq have armor. This is a lie. These are soft-skinned European vehicles I've never heard of with names like Tata and Peugeot. We load our bags in the truck. I'm handed a Kevlar vest, an M-4 rifle, and a single thirty-round magazine of ammunition. A combat load is seven magazines—two hundred ten bullets. This is a shitshow, but after the military, it doesn't faze me. The Air Force sent me into Iraq with a single chest plate with the option of choosing to put it in the front or the back of my Kevlar vest so I know this war isn't well-planned. Before we start our trek, we walk to a pallet of Coors Light and load five cases in the truck. The pilot's standing there.

Me: Who runs this airport?

Pilot: The Iraqis. They're new.

Me: New?

Pilot: The people who ran it were part of the regime, so these are all new people. None of them know what they're doing so US contractors run it.

Me: So, it's a clusterfuck?

Pilot: Yep. We fly and let them know when we're landing. Iraq has been sanctioned for so long, no one has any idea how to run an airport. Thankfully, no one flies in, so we don't run into other planes. We radio in before we descend. It's the only place we can get American beer in Iraq, so it's not all bad.

This place is anarchy—people walking on active runways and cars driving across them. They took down the "Saddam" part of Saddam International Airport's sign, so it reads "International Airport," which is true because we flew in from Jordan. It should say "Death Trap" considering the flight.

I put on the vest, grab my rifle with its single magazine, and stand near my assigned seat. A man old enough to be my grandfather is the convoy leader.

Grandpa: Keep your heads on a swivel. If we're attacked, pick a target and shoot. Doesn't matter if someone's there or not. This keeps the enemy's head down. Drivers push through the attack unless the vehicle's disabled. We'll tow the vehicle or hold in place and fight if we can't drive on. Got it?

I have no idea what he's saying so I nod.

Grandpa: Take orders from the team members. I know you're badasses, but they know the route and what to do if we get attacked. Got it?

I keep nodding.

Grandpa: Load up in the cars. No magazines in your rifles until we get out of BIAP. I'll let you know when to lock and load. Got it?

I nod again and turn to the hunk of shit (HOS) SUV. It's dark red with dents from top to bottom like the thighs of a Waffle House waitress. Does AAA operate in Baghdad? At this point, I'm more worried about a mechanical breakdown than an improvised explosive device (IED).

Grandpa's speech is called a mission brief, the standard for every run. The old fucker's on point. He's a knowledgeable, hardened combat veteran. We drive from BIAP to the area known as outside the wire (OTW) or "The Red Zone" to contrast where we are going which is called "The Green Zone." Still no bullets in my rifle. Why can't we load? Before we hit OTW, we stop, and Grandpa emerges from his vehicle.

Grandpa: Make a show of it, boys. We're headed to Indian Country. Lock and load.

This is our cue to disembark and load our rifles. As we're loading, we aim them at red oil barrels filled with dirt, clearing barrels, which were created for dumbasses who can't load or unload a weapon without firing it (i.e., military officers).

Grandpa thrusts his penis toward his rifle while loading. So awesome. His is more sophisticated than mine, his rifle not his penis. Mine is inadequate, story of my life. I wonder if his reference to Indians is directed to Native Americans or Indians from India. Dots or feathers?

I'm behind the driver. This is an important position. The driver can't shoot and drive so my coverage area is wider than most. I have from twelve o'clock (the direction we're driving) to six o'clock (the area behind us), a 180-degree field of fire. More like a 155-degree field of fire as I can't shoot through the driver. I could, but everyone would be pissed as we crash and burn to death.

The passenger seat holds the tactical commander. He tells the convoy where to drive and has a field of fire from twelve to three. The dude behind him has from three to six. See how that works? It's a clock for dumb rednecks like me to know where to shoot.

I get comfortable behind the driver as he starts the HOS SUV.

Driver: There's an armored plate by your feet if we get in the shit. You can hold it up to the window to protect you.

What I want to say is: Seriously, bro? How the fuck am I going to hold a slab of ceramic to block my face when a bomb explodes? How do I know when to grab the plate? Does anyone think my arm and hand are strong enough to stop a blast and keep my brains from being splattered on the gunner behind me? This is ridiculous. Instead, I say,

Me: Thanks for the heads up.

It's seven and a half miles from BIAP to the Green Zone. We're traveling on the Route Irish, the most attacked highway in Iraq. Oh well. Too late to puss out now. It's hot as fuck. Two million degrees in my estimation since my eyes are boiling in their sockets. Sweat dribbles down my back to fill my ass crack. My torso and pelvis are a sloppy Vietnamese jungle within minutes. Adrenaline courses through my veins. I'm ready to slay the Indian terrorists. (He must've meant Native Americans. I'll see their ceremonial feathers poking over the walls that protect the houses on the route.) My head moves from right to left. I'm a one-eyed dog at a sausage factory looking at every sausage by swiveling my head. My rifle goes where my eyes go. I look absurd. The driver is going eighty mph and my eyes are watering from the wind shear. Or maybe they're sweating. I'm from Arizona, but this place is a new level of hot. My rifle twitches left and right as I scan the terrain. No feathers.

My asshole's puckered so tight I find it hard to walk later. If I knew this is how we'd play ball, I would've shoved coal up my ass to make a diamond. The driver blasts heavy metal music. Why's the music so loud? Listening for gunshots would make more sense. Maybe I'm getting old. Young kids' music is terrible. Hell, Grandpa running the convoy is hip enough to enjoy the screaming, ear-bleeding music so why can't I? Dude humped his rifle while loading it. So awesome. I'll never be as cool as him as we drive down a rather normal road, save for large craters every few miles where a car bomb blasted people into chunks day earlier.

We arrive at the Green Zone. The entrance is a serpentine obstacle course of barriers, huge concrete blocks on each side of the road offset by ten feet and across from each other. This ensures vehicles slow down as they arrive at the gate by making them wind around each barrier like a snake. We stop at the first checkpoint. An Iraqi Army guard looks at us, realizes we aren't terrorists, and sends us down another slalom where we find a US Army military policeman. The driver shows him a badge. "We have some new guys. Going to our team house with them." The MP raises the gate arm and we pass.

We drive through two traffic circles with large bronze statues and take a right into a neighborhood to the team house. The driver and the TC leave the vehicle, grab the cases of Coors Light, and walk inside. Grandpa marches to the first vehicle and yells, "Unload your bags then come on in. Someone'll be here to get you shortly." Then he goes inside. So cool.

We create a chain to unload bags, stack them in a pile, then head inside. It's air conditioned. Sweet, sweet AC. A team house guy tells us there's beer in the fridge. I crack a Coors Light. It's gross after sitting in the Baghdad summer sun, a taste of the Rockies if the river were full of decaying animals and sewage. First run in Baghdad complete. Cheers.

***

The Green Zone is the utopian society where Iraqis and Americans live together in harmony. At least that's the theory. Every military unit has a walled off compound so it's a litany of bases in a base and allows the locals to smuggle in explosives under the auspices they live there. Contracting companies bought up local houses as staging points for operations. Some "normal" Iraqis live here but it's primarily the transitional Iraqi government officials and their families. The US Embassy is here. The US made the colossal mistake of handing over Iraq to a supposed representative government so as not to look like an occupying force. In the middle of combat operations US forces had to defer to a diplomatic mission trying to rebuild Iraq. That's why I'm here—Blackwater protects diplomats… whatever they are. I'm told they're important and we're paid to protect them. If they're so VIP, why're they in this dump to begin with?

The US military invaded Iraq in 2003 to free the shit out of the people. With combat operations "ending" in June, 2004, Iraq is now a sovereign nation. This caused the US to shift Iraq from a Department of Defense (DoD) operation to a Department of State (DoS) action. We're here to enable the shit out of them to build a government. DoS has never taken on a diplomatic mission on this scale, so they hired Blackwater Neanderthals, myself included, as protection teams. We protect diplomats traveling OTW to coach and assist the new government. This'll expedite rebuilding the nation, or so I'm told.

There's never been a DoS mission in an active combat zone so the Diplomatic Security Unit they employ was unprepared to complete its mission. Part of this is due to limited manpower and those who are here are blubbering vaginas who refuse to leave the Green Zone. Prior to taking this job, I recall a DoS employee on the news stating if he was sent to Iraq, it was equivalent to "signing my death certificate." Blubbering vaginas.

GUNS, GIRLS, AND GREED

Ironically, after I arrived in Iraq, a diplomat in the Green Zone ate a rocket while taking a shower. Imagine it. He's washing his bean bag with a nice pink loofah when a rocket flies over the wall, lands in the shower, and kills him. The next moment he's being dragged out the shower naked in a body bag, still holding his pink loofah. Bummer.

***

The team house personnel have grown tired of us drinking their beer, so they drop us off near the Blackwater compound at the US Embassy. I'm with Robert, an Asian guy named Dave, and someone who's forgettable because I forget his name.

This is a sweet setup. It's a palace, like the stuff you see in movies. Saddam walked these halls naked whipping people with electric cords to show dominance. It's awe inspiring. Floor to roof marble. Painted, hand-carved wood ceilings. The US ambassador sleeps in Saddam's old master bedroom. The rest is office space, a cafeteria, and a bunch of military officer's micromanaging the war from the comfort of a *fucking mansion*. This war is lost.

Each wing's cordoned off by military units. Even in combat it's a dick measuring contest, each branch of the military trying to get the biggest area to show supremacy. Added to that is the alphabet soup of government agencies, FBI, CIA, DIA, NSA, and WTF. They want credit for success until it turns bad and they blame the other agency (WTF). But hey, the one with the best view from the palace wins today, right? Sadly, the view is a dumpster fire we call Baghdad, and each agency is fighting for the high ground to watch it burn.

Behind the palace is a pool with a diving board. It's glorious. Surrounding palm trees and a brass water fountain make it feel like a resort. I look over this wishing I was a ruthless dictator with a sweet mustache. Want a mustache ride? No? Kill her and dispose of her body, please.

In contrast to the opulence of the palace, the south side of the embassy has a circus tent with concrete bunkers surrounding it. This is where I live. I walk my bags to the tent as my sloppy, sweaty, butt cheeks rub together and toss my bags on an empty cot near the entrance. No one wants to be close to the opening and the heat it emits. A random guy tells me how to get to the bunkers when rockets and mortars land. Thanks, bro. I have no plans for self-preservation. I'm exhausted. Ready for death. This piece of coal in my ass is starting to chafe.

A railroad car converted into eight shitters sits behind the tent. It smells like a sewage plant and seminal fluid. The tent reeks like a dog park, piss marks territory. Fifty men live here. Why would they walk to the bathroom when they can stick their pecker out a slit and whiz? My cot is oceanfront property at Piss Beach.

I'm thankful it's short-term housing. I'll get assigned a railroad car converted into two bedrooms with a toilet and shower in between. They're building a Five Hundred-Man Camp south of the embassy for Blackwater. It's called the Five-Hundred-Man Camp because it'll house five hundred of us. Creative.

We walk to the embassy to get ID cards. They take my picture and produce an ID within five minutes. I look how I feel, like the poster child for buying Trojan condoms. It's a white-trash mug shot. I love it. It'll be my death photo when this war ends me and the State Department talks about my heroic actions in assisting the effort to help the people of Iraq. Or it'll be the photo used when designating me a war criminal. Either way, I'll look good.

The ID badge gives me access to the entire embassy compound. Next to my face on the badge is a red square with an imbedded black "W" which means I can walk around with my weapon loaded. This is called the "Coveted Red W" even though it's a red square with a black W— nothing in Iraq makes sense. I put the ID in a combat purse with clear plastic on the front to display it, and place the string around my neck so it presents on my chest like a medallion Flavor Flav would envy. When an Army lieutenant colonel asks me why I'm walking aimlessly through his area, I tap my badge. This allows me to wander the halls staring at the ceiling in awe. It's like cutting the bathroom line at Disneyland. I'm a character at an amusement park.

GUNS, GIRLS, AND GREED

I take my new badge to the Blackwater compound east of the pool. It's an old building, a patio with picnic tables, and a tent. The sun is going down. If every day is this long, I'm going to volunteer to walk the streets of Baghdad alone hoping to be kidnapped. I'm exhausted and I don't have a weapon. I may as well be naked as I sit at the picnic table. It's still so hot, I debate stripping off my clothes to cool off since I'm naked without a firearm anyway. My shirt and pants have white salt stains on them. I look down wishing the salt stain around my penis was bigger. I'm a grower not a shower.

Two people bring out a wooden box and set it near me. They point to an open door.

> Dude 1: Grab your shit. Load what you want. When you're done, put it back. I'll be back in fifteen to secure it.

Dave, Robert, and the nameless dude grab ammo boxes of .556 rounds. I grab body armor. We walk to the tables and open the wooden box. I damn near cry. Brand. New. M-4. Rifles. Fuck my ass. They are beautiful. Untouched. Pristine. Pure like a baby. Mine. All mine. I grab one and hold it to my chest like a newborn suckling my milky bosom. Later in life, I watch my child being born. I'm not sure it beats seeing a brand-new rifle. Don't tell my wife.

I begin to load ten thirty-round magazines in minutes before the treasure is taken from me.

> Robert: Jesus, you can load ammo. How do you do that?
> Me: I push in the bullet?

I'm on magazine seven while everyone is on their second. I'm using the speed loader I found in the ammo boxes. They're popping each round out of the casing and manually feeding them into a magazine. That hurts my dainty fingers, so I place a speed loader on each magazine, place the ten-round cartridge in it, and smash the bullets against the table. This allows the casing to fall to the ground as the bullets feed in the magazine. Grandma didn't raise no fool.

I hear a slam on the table next to me and see a 9mm Glock with three magazines. I fill them with ammo. My fingers hurt with each round. Why don't they make speed loaders for pistol ammo? I'll to need to lotion up after this, so my delicate skin doesn't crack.

I load the pistol with a magazine, pull back the slide to seat a round, and secure it in the holster on my belt. I'm a bona fide BAMF (badass motherfucker). Grandma's proud. Fifteen minutes later, someone comes over to write the number sixty in blue marker on the buttstock of my rifle. I want to slap his mouth. You don't blemish my baby. You don't tug on Superman's cape. You don't spit into the wind. You don't pull the mask off the Lone Ranger and you don't touch my baby like a Catholic priest. Mine is the sixtieth rifle issued in Iraq by Blackwater.

Pissed off, I walk behind the patio and, bless my soul, there's a statue of Saddam's head. It's bronze and perfectly replicates him from the shoulders up, scaled to ten feet. It lies face down, but I can see his amazing mustache. I piss on his face aiming for his flavor-saver. The smelliest piss of my life. I vow to piss on his face for good luck before every run. He seems like the kind of guy who deserves to have a golden shower from an American patriot.

I walk to the tent behind the patio where "operators" watch TV and cruise for girls on Myspace. I'm not sure what being an operator entails, but I know it's not me. Based on the names I hear in the tent—Caveman, Hook, Stitch, Dickface—I'll need a cool name to be classified as an operator.

Sitting behind a computer is a massive human with a beard Zeus would be jealous of. He's typing with one hand and has a spring grip forearm strengthener in the other. He's either really into fitness or preparing for a Baghdad date night. Based on his forearms, I hope it's the former. The scuttlebutt is he's former Army Special Forces and has a cool name which sounds like an anime character. He's a kung fu ninja so lethal he can't fight in the UFC. I believe it based on his python forearms.

Operator names are called "handles," and they're all the rage. They are used in case the enemy cracks the encryption on our radios. We hear there's a bounty on Blackwater contractors but if a terrorist figures out who "Morgan" is after breaking encryption, they deserve to…know my name? Note to self: if someone tries to give you a handle, don't respond or it'll stick with you forever. Most are degrading.

In a military deployment, the first thing you're told are the Rules of Engagement (ROE). Not here. We're told through the grapevine we don't have any because our mission is transporting diplomats by any means necessary. Platitudes of not making enemies arise but if we get in trouble, Blackwater will get us out and claim diplomatic immunity. This is backed up by the State Department passports we have.

I'm assigned to Templar 12, the sixth team in Baghdad, with Dave, Robert, and the twat on our flight who needs a sleep apnea machine not to die in his sleep. We're a mishmash of humanity named after the Knights Templar; an elite fighting force sworn to protect Christians during the Crusades—the original mercenaries for a cause. Their mission was protecting Christians against Muslims, which makes the name appropriate until a politically correct diplomat realized its historical significance and forced us to change Templar to Raven. Diplomats…winning wars since nineteen-oh-fuck-we-lost.

Templar 12's led by a former Army Ranger who was in Somalia. At least, that's what he tells us. Like prison, there's a rule stating any person who leads with how awesome they are and what they've done is a shithead. They're called "funk fakers" because they tell everyone they have the funk: legitimate combat experience when the US hasn't been in a real war in thirty years. They have no funk, so they fake it. It later comes out that the team leader, who can't wait to tell everyone he was in Somalia, hurt his arm and got sent home before *Black Hawk Down*. Funk Faker. There are a lot of these people in Blackwater because they rarely screened candidates and kept horrible records. Stories of them hiring former military recruiting assistants and air conditioner repairmen would come out later. This may be why their executives were later indicted for weapons violations and pled guilty to lesser charges of not keeping proper records.

I connect to the internet and email Grandma, so she knows I'm alive. The Asian guy, a former Marine and nauseatingly intelligent, sits next to me. He's toddler tiny. He pulls up a scholarly article on the geopolitical effects of Iranian influence in the region and how they affect political changes via trade. I watch a cat play piano and make small talk.

Me: I'm Morgan.
Asian: I'm Dave.
Me: Dude, I expected you to have an oriental name.
Dave: Oriental? What am I? A rug? Soup?
Me: Huh? I'm fairly certain you're not a rug.
Dave: Oriental is soup.
Me: Or a rug?
Dave: It's offensive.
Me: What should I call you?
Dave: Dave.
Me: Yeah, but if oriental is offensive, what exactly are you?
Dave: Asian. I'm Korean. It's Asian. My dad was a ROK Marine.
Me: Rock Marine?
Dave: ROK, Republic of Korea.
Me: I was imagining a rock on a beach.
Dave: No, fucker. R. O. K. ROK Marine.
Me: No shit. So, you don't want to be called Oriental? Learn something new every day.
Dave: Idiot. I'm starving. Let's eat.

Two things are clear to me. One, to be a badass, I need a Myspace account and to grow a beard. Two, I'm a dumb redneck. Who knew Orientals were called Asians?

Dave and I walk to the cafeteria. We're best friends now that I offended him. First day in Baghdad is complete. We head to the circus tent to get some sleep.

CHAPTER 3

Templar 12 is half staffed so we do driver training at the Cross Swords monument until the next group arrives which is delayed by the casa bird being broken. Blackwater doesn't get paid for people sitting in Jordan and the contractors are paid two hundred and fifty dollars a day compared to five hundred and fifty dollars in Iraq. Both want to be in country. Blackwater gets tired of paying people not to work so they send them commercial.

Dave and I go to the bazaar, which is a Middle Eastern farmers' market minus fruits and veggies, and located on a main street with houses behind it where the locals live. There's a hodge-podge of locally made crap: rugs, plastic shit, and lingerie, which is odd to me as Muslim women are only allowed to wear black ninja pajamas with a hood over their face and a hole for their eyes. I walk to the back of the market to a tent where the good stuff is hidden. Tea sets, personal pictures, fancy shit made of marble. It must've been looted from the former regime. My eyes are drawn to fancy china plates and cups, not the oriental stuff. I see a fifty-dollar price tag on a plate with Hitler's face. It must've been owned by a regime member.

Grandma has a plate collection she hangs throughout her kitchen and dining room. This is the perfect piece to round out her collection. I'll invite the family and her church friends over and say, "Grandma, this plate with a ruthless dictator reminded me of you." We'll all laugh as Grandma blushes. She'll hang it at the center of her collection. Her church friends will admire it at Bible Study.

I need to cash a check so I can buy it. The market for Hitler plates seems tepid. I have a couple days to come back for it.

As I exit the bazaar, I'm bombarded by children trying to sell DVDs of pirated movies. Many were still in US theaters when I left. Their quality is awful—they're made by a guy holding a camera in the theater. We play these in the Blackwater tent. I hear people clearing their throats and laughing while subtitles show in a random language.

The ringleader of the kids assumes I'm interested in a more risqué selection. He thrusts fifteen DVDs in my hand as I walk. I can't help but look at the covers. Normal porn, midget porn, clown porn, German shepherd porn, classic porn from the '70s where the women have bushes that start above their belly buttons, and new porn sans bush. You name it, he has it. I pull out my wallet and hold it upside down to show him I have no cash. He's visibly angry.

Porn Kid: You don't want porn? You faggot?
Me: Dude, go away. Wait, how do you speak English?
Porn Kid: Fucking faggot. Like little boys?
Me: Bro, get lost. I love the ladies.
Porn Kid: Faggot, fuck you. You want to fuck me?
Me: No, thank you. I'm in a committed relationship. I left her at home but I think she may be the one. I don't know. I can't wait to get home and…
Porn Kid: Faggot.

How does he know such good, filthy English? I'm told by Dave that the cash they get is given to terrorists because US currency is fungible. What the fuck does fungible mean? Come on, Dave. Talk to me in English.

I never get the Hitler plate. The bazaar is blown to smithereens by a suicide bomber a couple days later. Four DynCorp contractors are killed along with several innocent Iraqi civilians trying to make a few bucks to feed their families. The suicide bomber walked up behind the contractors and detonated. The closest contractor had his body blown off. That isn't a grammatical error. His body was blown off his legs. His boots and legs stayed intact standing on the ground with his body no longer attached. The loss of contractors is sobering. I'm bummed about the plate.

As a fun aside, two Blackwater contractors who arrived in country that day were at the bombing but weren't informed the Green Zone was a harmonious society. They assumed anything outside the embassy compound was OTW. When the bomb went off, they kicked in the nearest house door, cleared the rooms, and went to the next house. After kicking in a second house door, they realized no one was shooting at them and walked to the embassy. This illustrates how little private military contractors (PMCs) understood about the mission and ROEs.

**

It's my sixth night in Baghdad. There's a rumbly in my tumbly, and I'm blasting mud out my ass so violently, I contemplate suicide. For the first time in my adult life, I'm woken up because I shit my pants. I walk to the bathroom behind the circus tent with a shitty crack. I realize why the bathroom smells so bad. The Baghdad Bug has ravaged many souls (and jejunums) in this enclosed space. I regret eating the chicken curry at lunch the day prior.

I sit down and cut my underwear off with a sweet knife I bought before joining Blackwater. It can't be saved. Better to cut it off than pull it down and get shit on my thighs and calves. I download God knows what. I haven't eaten in thirty-six hours. I lean over my knees as raw sewage pours from me. This is the worst day of my life.

I finish, wipe, stand, and walk to the exit. I hold my head high and take three steps. Nope. Not done. There's more. Thankfully, it's the middle of the night. Every stall is open. I drop my shorts and backpedal to the nearest stall to shit yellow bile. I do this three times. My asshole hurts so bad, I resort to wiping forward hoping I won't get a UTI. On iteration three I look at the toilet paper and my asshole's clinging to it. I've wiped it off my body. I make eye contact with it. It looks like a burn victim, and begs me not to banish it to hell. The pain of each wipe is equal to giving birth.

I walk to my cot, lie on my back, and doze off. I dream I've died. I'm in a pine coffin as pallbearers consisting of my family walk me to the top of a grassy hill. Who let Grandma carry me? She's too old to carry my body. They reach the top. It looks like Montana. There's a hole dug for me. Using orange and black braided ropes, they lower me in the ground. They fill the hole and plant a tiny oak tree in remembrance. The roots maneuver through the soil as the tree grows. They break through the coffin and dig into my stomach. I'm trapped. I flail around trying to escape the coffin as the roots dig into my stomach and rip it apart. I can't escape. I suffer as the roots become larger and dig deeper into my torso. I scratch at the coffin ceiling trying to escape. The weight of the soil refuses to let me. I gasp and lurch…awake.

I race to the bathroom to shit. Fuck this place. Fuck the chicken curry. Fuck my asshole, which has been flushed down the toilet multiple times. I walk to the tent, grab my shower kit (a bag holding my loofa, towel, soap, toothbrush, razor, etc.), and walk to the shower. My asshole can't take any more wiping. I'm going to rinse it off and hope for the best.

I open the first stall and start the water. It's hot. Water never cools off here because the water tanks are fastened to the outside of the trailer. I get in, bend forward, and rinse my hole. It burns like a midget poking my asshole with a tiki-torch. My stomach clenches. My bowels loosen and I resign myself to the inevitable. I shit in the shower. Like a tiny broken baby. I waffle stomp the chunks down the drain.

I get in bed in time for rockets to start landing in the Green Zone. Is this going to be my alarm clock for the next six months? Fuck it. I'm close to death. I may as well grab my pink loofah and wait for it. I have pink toiletries because I learned in the Air Force everything is stolen on a deployment unless it's pink.

A rocket lands close enough to shake the tent. Bring it. I lie in bed, scared to death but don't want to be the pussy who runs to the bunker while everyone else is cool as a cucumber. Plus, if I try to run, I'll poop my pants. Bring the death.

The next rocket makes the ground move and my ears ring. I decide to live. I sit up and look at Andy. He got in yesterday. We both freeze. His eyes are huge. I assume he notices my eyes are similarly big. The sleep apnea machine contractor runs out the tent. Pussy. Now we can leave because he's the coward.

Thankfully, Andy's lucid enough to grab his cigarettes before we run out. Priorities. We smoke and laugh.

Kyle! That's the name of the other contractor. He's a police officer, and this is his second contract. He worked for DynCorp in Kosovo and is a bit of a tender heart. Cops are trained to de-escalate a situation in a litigious environment and save lives. In contrast, military dudes are trained to kill and hope we don't have a paper-pushing asshat question it later. Cops never fully fit in, but Kyle's solid because he contracted before, so I look to him for guidance. He saved my life in the bunker by asking me why I'm being such a bitch and lying in bed.

I explain my dream and my anus-ectomy via toilet paper. After three cigarettes and an absence of rocket impacts, we walk to the tent. Kyle strides to his bag, grabs a bottle of pills and hands it to me. Imodium A-D. Being a seasoned contractor, he came prepared.

Kyle: This'll help.
Me: Help what?
Kyle: Help you stop shitting your pants so you can work.
Me: You had me at "stop shitting your pants."
Kyle: Shut up. Don't take them all or you'll block up the bad stuff in your system. Read the directions.
Me: My hero!

The dosage is two pills and one after each loose stool, not to exceed four in a day. The pills are tiny, like mouse crap. I take four and four more throughout the day assuming the directions are for wimpy US poops and not ruthless Iraqi dictator revenge poops. Within twenty-four hours, I'm plugged up.

Later, I learn the amount of fecal matter in food in Iraq is extremely high. This is due to US contracting firms hiring locals to cook which is part of the agreement with Iraq and, like Sizzler, cheaper than hiring cooks with good hygiene. The locals wipe their asses with their bare, left hands, rinse them with water, and then handle food. Did you hear me mention soap? Exactly. How can we win a war when this is the mentality of the normal population? I'll never eat chicken curry again.

***

We've formed a team and it's time for our first mission. Funk Faker's decided we need a test run the day prior at six in the morning. I'm good with that. Each driver's given a Garmin GPS shaped like a pyramid to put on the dashboard. Maps of Baghdad aren't available. The idea is each team risks their lives to track routes and downloads the GPS data to a computer. We'll know which streets are open later. It's a shitshow but it's all we've got. We plot our route on a paper map and hope for the best.

I fire up the GPS and, under armored glass, it refuses to find a satellite. So much for mapping Baghdad. We leave the north gate, cross a bridge, and get hopelessly lost. It's fine. We find the Tigris River and drive south along it until it juts east before circling back west. From the map this looks like a penis. It's affectionately called "the schlong." The 14th July Bridge is located on the northern shaft of this geographical anomaly. We cross it and enter the Green Zone, reeking of failure but alive.

Funk Faker does a map recon. We fire up the Suburban's and head out at nine a.m. Traffic's miserable which is a blessing and a curse. The blessing is there are cars on either side of us to absorb an IED blast. The curse is it slows us down so we're target for an ambush.

Funk Faker's in the passenger side seat trying to micromanage the navigation of the convoy. Kyle's the Tactical Commander (TC) in the lead vehicle trying to navigate but Funk Faker's asserting dominance. The Charge of the Light Brigade echoes through my brain until the door gunner opens his door, trying to keep traffic back. A car refuses to heed his warning. He says something awesome like "I'm going hot" and fires a warning shot in the ground. That was fucking cool. Shit just got real.

We find our drop point for tomorrow's mission and circle back to our compound. Funk Faker tells the door gunner to fill out an incident report—the guy's the equivalent of watching porn and busting a nut as the camera focuses on the dude's orgasm face. I lay in my bunk processing the run and begin to understand our ROEs and mission—get people from Point A to Point B and don't die. If you shoot, write a report no one reads. Easy day.

***

I've been in Baghdad a couple weeks. We've figured out which of the roads are functional. The Garmin GPS idea's a waste. We're driving to the Jordanian embassy so a guy I've never heard of can meet another guy I've never heard of to do something to help no one. As we drive along a random road, a kid, probably seven years old, smiles and waves at us. It makes my heart happy. Maybe I'm making a difference?

We arrive at the Jordanian embassy at nine a.m. It's a two-story house on a random street with a cinder block fence. The heat's stifling and the proximity to the river adds humidity to create a hellscape no human should occupy. I've sweat through my underwear, pants, shirt, and boots standing guard by a random door that hasn't been opened in thirty years. My body armor shows white salt stains.

Two people are on the embassy's roof doing overwatch. One's Funk Faker and the other is his lapdog who claims he was an Army Ranger but never finished ranger school. In a lapse of judgement, I radio up and ask if he wants water. No idea why. I hate them. I wouldn't piss in Funk Faker's mouth if his teeth were on fire, but I grew up in a desert, and being parched is a downer. He accepts my offer of cool fluids. Of course, he does. Asshole.

I walk to the back of the Suburban and grab two bottles of water from the cooler. They feel amazing on my bare hands. I need to get them to the roof via a solid steel ladder. I've got this shit. I climb. Four steps up, my hands hurt. It's hot but in the words of my ex, I've had hotter. I ascend three more steps. Do I smell ham? In a Muslim country? The smell must be my hands. They're about to blister. This isn't good for my love life.

I jump ten feet to the ground and take the walk of shame to the Suburban to grab gloves. As I head back to the ladder, my stupidity hits me in the mouth, and I realize I can throw them up. I toss four frosty bottles of water, twice what I was going to bring up, yelling, "Heads up. Incoming water." I wait for a "thank you" over the radio. No thank you arrives as I resume my post.

The principal concludes his meeting and we drive back to the Embassy where Funk Faker has us complete a US Army After Action Review (AAR). This should take thirty seconds—we drove, we protected, we came home alive. Instead, it takes an hour because we must do the obligatory Three-Ups (what went well) and Three-Downs (what we can do better) the Army preaches. I'm an Air Force dude so none of this makes sense. It's going to be a long six months.

***

I walk to my new room behind the US Embassy and start the shower. I've got athlete's foot. I've had it before but what I have now is Lance Armstrong foot; athlete's foot on steroids, filled with lies, and unstoppable. It's two p.m. as I walk to the team tent. Within minutes I can feel sweat slosh in my leather boots. Is this possible? I'm sweating through my skin, socks, and the skin of a dead cow. I'm soaked from head to toe. I could piss my pants and no one would notice. I enter the tent, see JR, and immediately bitch about it. He's a legit retired Army Ranger and the one who tells us Funk Faker is truly a faker of the funk.

Me: Fuck, man. This can't be normal. I sweat through my underwear and pants. Look at my cock. It looks like I pissed my pants.
JR: Your cock is too small to see. You must be Irish. You still wear underwear?
Me: Still?

JR: I stopped wearing underwear years ago. One more thing to wash and it doesn't stop sweat from going through pants.

Me: Good point.

JR: My mom found out I stopped wearing underwear.

Me: You're forty-two years old. How does your mom "find out" you stopped wearing britches? You were so proud you had to call her?

JR: Britches? Are you ninety?

Me: Boxers. Briefs. Thongs. Who cares?

JR: No, butthole. I brought my girlfriend home to meet my parents when I was in Ranger Battalion. My mom did our laundry. After she folded it, she pulled my girlfriend aside and asked if she missed my choners. My girl had to tell her she never knew me to wear them.

Me: Choners? Are you ninety?

JR: Fuck off.

Me: Mom checking up on your underpants. That's adorable.

JR: You may be the most annoying human I've ever met.

Me: Fair. Since you're imparting wisdom, I'm getting extreme athlete's foot. Bleeding and shit.

JR: It's probably your weak genes. Piss on it.

Me: Yeah, man. Fuck it.

JR: No. Seriously, piss on it.

Me: To show dominance?

JR: You're delightful. The acid in piss kills fungus. Piss on it for a couple days. Should clear up. They taught me that in Ranger school. Works great.

After our run, to avoid pissing on myself, I walk to the post exchange (PX) to get Tough Actin' Tinactin. Local children hound me to buy porn as I walk. I give them a dollar to leave me alone, refusing to have my sexuality questioned today. Then I notice the kid has *Team America*, the greatest war movie ever made and illustrates the insanity of the GWOT. I've watched it in the Blackwater tent and must own it. It's how I envision Erik Prince petitioned the Bush administration to hire Blackwater.

It also clears up the age-old question of how puppets procreate. I point at it and tell the kid to give me the DVD for my dollar. He refuses. I give him a second dollar and take the movie.

I walk in the PX and the shelves are bare. No athlete's foot cream. I buy talcum powder even though I've been using it and it hasn't helped. My feet are cracking and bleeding through my socks.

I get to my room, take off my boots and socks, pour Gold Bond on my feet, and walk around in shower shoes for the remainder of the day. This'll dry them out.

I wake the next morning with my feet stuck to the sheet. Who knew dried blood was like Krazy Glue? I resign myself to piss on my feet. Baghdad has humbled me. I walk to the shower with my pink towel, pink soap dish, and pink toothbrush and hop in. I piss the most dehydrated urine on my feet. It looks like orange Gatorade and smells like ammonia. It burns like alcohol on an open wound. This better work, JR.

It doesn't. The next day, I wake again with my bloody feet stuck to the sheets. My bed's a fucking murder scene. The smell of piss makes it a scat film.

Me: The fuck, JR? I pissed all over my feet yesterday. My bed looks like *The Shining*!
JR: Piss on them again. Needs a couple days.
Me: Dude, it hurts when I piss on them.
JR: Weakness leaving the body via your pussy feet.

I walk to the shower and piss on my feet again. It burns like gonorrhea. As I'm getting dressed, I put so much Gold Bond in my socks and boots, they puff smoke as I walk. I try this for three days. It doesn't help. This place shouldn't be populated by living organisms. I call Grandma and she sends me Tinactin. A few days later, I get it and slather it on my feet like a hooker applying lube. Within twenty-four hours, I'm healing. I never piss on my feet again. I never go back to wearing underwear either and begin shaving my body hair in hopes it'll help me stay cool.

CHAPTER 4

The Iraqi elections are today. We ferry diplomats around Baghdad to voting locations so they can verify this is a free and fair election. They walk the grounds looking important as I sit in my Suburban. I'm driving the follow vehicle (the last one in the convoy). My mission is to drive to a polling station, park, and open the hood of the Suburban so it doesn't overheat. Real adventure.

We load up and drive to another voting station. As we approach the barbed wire surrounding the entrance, a car gets too close to our convoy, so Robert opens his door, points his rifle and yells, "*Imshi*!" This means "go away" or something. It's not important enough for me to ask. Aside from a few bursts of adrenaline as we drive and get our daily dose of rocker fire, life in Blackwater is anticlimactic. Now when I hear rockets impacting, I roll over in bed, find the cold side of my pillow, and go back to sleep. If it's my time, I prefer to die comfortable. I'm becoming numb.

My Suburban's fully armored save for the top and bottom. The weight of the protection takes a toll on the door hinges. Robert's door never fully closes because the latch doesn't seat. He has to hold it shut with his left hand while holding his rifle with his right. On our move to a third polling station, he forgets to grab it and the door flies open when I take a corner. Robert reaches for the door to close it.

Robert: Fucking door! Slow the fuck down.
Me: Hold the door, man.
Robert: Hold my rifle and fuck off traffic? Slow down, asshole.
Me: We all have jobs and mine is driving.

I gently hit the gas pedal of our sarcophagus. The roads are restricted to the population. Only Iraqi and US military traffic's allowed on election day. The diplomats' limo driver, John, drives like he's leading the pole in a NASCAR race. Speaking of NASCAR, I'm wearing my Jimmy Johnson #48 Lowes Chevrolet hat.

We move slowly on the deserted streets, which is great for spectating. Locals hold up bluish-purple index fingers as we pass. The news has the free people of Iraq showing off a blue finger and touting a free vote.

Me: Hey, Dave. You're cultured and shit. What's with the blue fingers? Did they eat blueberries and scratch their assholes?

Dave: Seriously?

Me: I'll admit the blue is likely not from blueberry asshole. The rest of the question is serious.

Dave: Once they vote, they dip a finger in ink.

Me: To like sign with a fingerprint?

Dave: No, man. So, they can't vote again later in the day or at another location.

Me: Damn, that's smart.

It occurs to me there's no national identification or voter registry here. In 2002, Saddam got reelected with 100 percent of the vote. Seems legit. I wouldn't vote against the guy for fear of him raping and killing my family, although he can have my absentee father. That guy's trash. After leaving my mom with three kids to pursue the fine art of drinking and drug abuse, he could use a little Saddam slap and tickle.

***

I feel obligated to give the backstory on dear old Dad. This sums him up. When I was sixteen, he wanted to fight me. We went outside and I took him to the ground, stood over him with my fists clenched and said, "If you try that again, I'll beat the shit out of you." He lunged for my balls yelling, "I'll rip off your nut sack. I never lose a fight because I fight dirty." Classy dude. I should have been smart enough to never contact him again but smart isn't my modus operandi.

He never changed. When I turned twenty-one, I decided to take my girlfriend to meet him. I needed to see if the guy was worth an iota of emotional investment after popping in and out of my life for two decades.

We arrived at six p.m. and parked on the street. He lived in a crappy brick apartment building that was once a motel. It was a dump. The neighborhood matched it. Yellow grass, dirt, and spots of green weeds like chicken pox completed the front yard.

I knocked. My dad opened the door and hugged me. Not terrible start. He half-smiled and I noticed he was missing his front tooth. That was new. We both pretended I didn't see it. We entered the house to a cloud of cigarette smoke and sat on the couch. My dad offered me a beer, not abnormal since he's been offering me booze and hard drugs since I was thirteen. I declined. He grabbed a brew, filled a glass mug with ice and poured the beer in it. Not unusual to me but my lady was visibly uncomfortable. We wouldn't stay long.

Five minutes into the visit, my dad lit up a Marlboro Red and our conversation turned to Billy Joel. What else would we talk about? But I got Billy Joel mixed up with Elton John because I wasn't hip to eighties rock. My bad.

Me: Billy Joel just came out as gay.
Dad: No way! Not a chance he's gay.
Me: I promise. It made the news.
Dad: Don't you talk about Billy Joel like that.

I was confused. I liked "Crocodile Rock." I didn't care if he was gay. But my father was offended by this, like Billy Joel was family and I was insulting his son to his face although I was his actual child.

Me: It's no big deal.
Dad: *It's a big fucking deal!* Don't…

31

Me: I'm just saying, he's gay. What's the…

My father punched me in the mouth. A right hook to the chops out of nowhere. I tasted blood near my left molar. Okay. Now it's a big deal.

Me: You fucking punched me?
Dad: Don't you ever talk about Billy Joel like that.
Me: Listen motherfucker, take that cigarette and stuff it in the hole where your front tooth used to be.
Dad: Fuck you. I'll kick your ass.

I stand up.

Me: Don't bother. We're going.
Dad: *You disrespect me in my house!*

We left with my dad screaming at me. This was great. We bonded. Yay. I didn't say a word as I walked to the street. I opened the passenger door of the car for my girlfriend and walked to the driver's side, licking my mouth. Still bleeding. My dad kept yelling from his door.

Dad: You cunt! The best part of you dripped down your mom's leg when she gave birth to you. You came from my balls!

I sat in in my seat, closed the door, turned the ignition, and drove off. We arrived at a red light and I looked at my girlfriend. She's upset. Odd.

Her: What was that?
Me: I don't know. The guy loves Billy Joel?

We laughed. She reached over and touched my hand on the gear shift. It was a sweet moment.

Her: You turned out good. You told me stories, but I had no idea.

Me: My grandfather raised me. It's probably why I'm not working construction or in jail right now.

I never spoke to my father again. He called a few times, but I sent him to voicemail where he berated me for having his last name, promised to kick my ass the next time he saw me, and called me a cunt. I played these for friends, and we laughed. I send him World's Greatest Dad coffee mugs annually on Father's Day.

CHAPTER 5

Templar 12's assigned to protect the Regime Crimes Liaison Office. It's a cool mission. We protect the team gathering, documenting, and transferring evidence to Iraqis to use against Saddam and his inner circle for crimes against humanity. We drive to local courts in Baghdad when it's needed for trial.

Our primary run takes us to a small base north of the Green Zone. It's connected to a detention facility holding high value individuals (HVIs). Saddam's hanged here years later though he was not imprisoned here. Some days the location's called Camp XXX. On others it's called Camp America. It changes weekly. Makes sense considering who's housed there. We call it "the camp of many names" to keep it simple.

The gallows consist of a twelve-foot-high metal platform with stairs leading up to it on both sides. The platform has a trap door, lever, and a noose. A viewing area faces it.

A sign in Arabic is attached to the wall next to a scale. This tells the executioner how long to make the rope: too short and the neck won't break and too long may cause the head and spine to rip out of the body. No one in the viewing area wants to see that.

How awesome is this? The damned get to see how long their rope is before they walk the stairs to the noose as people watch from the comfort of their white plastic chairs.

When the trap door swings open, it smashes into the stand and makes a deafening metal-on-metal clang. It's so loud that when a hanging happens, the people living near the base get pissed off and shoot at

US and Iraqi soldiers. To mitigate this, prison leadership decided to glue a mattress on the bottom of the door to dampen the sound. Innovation.

***

Today I'm in the rear vehicle with Ranger Funk Faker. He's an asshole. I threw him water and he still hasn't thanked me. He calls me Lazy Air Force Fuck like it's my handle. He thinks I shouldn't be in Blackwater because I never got cool guy training. I can't blame him but I have a combat deployment under my belt, which is more than he can say. We'll never get along, so he tries to make my life hell while petting Lapdog who's equally unqualified to be here. Why he thinks criticizing me as I drive him around is good policy is beyond me. It's like telling his wife she's fat. He's not going to win.

I ignore it. I know how to play the game. He never buckles his seat belt, but I do. After he harangues me, I wait a couple minutes and slam on the brakes. He lurches forward. I watch his face smash into the armored windshield. Blood pours from his mouth as his teeth lie on the dash like Chiclets. Fuck. Now I have to clean that.

I'm fucking with you. He flops around the passenger seat and looks at me pissed in his self-righteousness. I smile on the inside, ignoring his scorn.

The driver of the lead vehicle drives like he's retired in Florida, letting cars into the convoy, which could blow us to bits. Why would he care? He's smoked for thirty years and be dead in five. He was in my training class and I hate his guts. Funk Faker yells over the radio, "Stop letting these fuckers in our convoy."

Florida Retiree: Roger that.
Funk Faker: (To me) What the fuck's he doing up there?
Me: The guy's ninety. Move me to the lead vehicle. I can drive without letting cars in the convoy.
Funk Faker: Next run you take lead.

This is a win-win. I drive aggressively, which makes the convoy run smoothly. It gets me away from Funk Faker, which allows his spine to avoid long-term injury. Where's the thank you for the water, motherfucker?

Why do I hate the lead driver? Because he's a pussy and can't be trusted. He's a former Ranger instructor (RI). They're Rangers who teach because they couldn't be trusted in a battalion or in combat. During training, this guy was roomed with a "Batt Boy," someone who served in Ranger Battalion and isn't a shithead. When the RI left for dinner one day, his roommate and another former Ranger pulled a prank on him. Ranger 2 took the RI's pillow into the bathroom and shot a cute little baby load on it.

Ranger 1: Really? That tiny-ass load? You can do better.
Ranger 2: What's wrong with my load?
Ranger 1: He deserves more.

Ranger 2 dabbled in online porn when he got out of the Army, the kind where he beat off while staring sexy faced into a camera for gay porn sites. He took the RI's second pillow in the bathroom and shot a man-sized load on it. Upon returning from dinner at Cracker Barrel at four p.m., the RI got a great night's sleep laying his head on the seminal fluid of two American heroes. Such a great story. I get choked up thinking about it.

The reason I hate him is because I witnessed his cowardice. On our final day of training, in Moyock, North Carolina, I was on RI's team as he led the principal, the guy we were protecting, into a building. I peeled off the formation and posted at the main door with Hog Slayer (Jack) as the principal walked in. RI posted at the bottom of stairs leading to the second floor and was tasked with leading the response if anything went south.

I heard a gunshot. Action time. I pushed into the room with Jack and heard "The principal's been kidnapped" from the second floor. RI stood frozen like an ice cube at the bottom of the stairs, confused, looking around instead of barreling up the stairs to free our principal. Jack and I ran past him, cleared the stairwell, got to the landing on the second floor, and popped through a door to see a man holding a gun to the head of our principal. Jack moved to the right of the door to get out of the fatal funnel, the opening everyone needs to come through. I popped through and moved to the left of the door.

Me: Put the gun down!
Jack: Drop your weapon.
Terrorist: I'll blow his fucking brains out.
Me: Drop your fucking gun.

I'm not Hispanic but understand we're in a Mexican standoff. How awesome is this?

There was enough space between the terrorist and the principal to get a shot, but it would've been tight. My adrenaline spiked. We yelled for what felt like thirty minutes for him to drop his weapon, but it was less than ten seconds. The terrorist lifted his pistol, aimed at me, and shot me in the hand with a sim round. Right between the knuckles. That hurt. I unloaded six rounds on him. He fake-died as we evacuated the principal. Iraq is saved. The war was won.

In an after-action review (AAR), the training terrorist took lead:

Terrorist: Good job. Most people come in guns a-blazin', the principal stands up and gets shot. Were you on the lead team?
Jack: No, we came from outside.
Terrorist: Where was the lead?

We shrugged and stayed silent, unwilling to narc on the blubbering pussy RI. Fucker froze up in a training exercise. *An exercise.* That's why I hate his guts. He's as useless as a paper condom in a rain storm.

CHAPTER 6

It's September and rainy. The roads are packed with cars. George tells me it's because Iraqis are made of dirt, so they shelter from the rain in their vehicles. When water touches their skin, they melt like the Wicked Witch and wash down the gutter. I'm not sure this is accurate, but I like it. It's been a couple months so I'm beginning to realize my ideals of helping this country are washing down the gutter also. Contractors have lots of demeaning names for the locals, including monkeys, savages, Indians, and dirt worshippers. I assume this is because *Deadwood*'s out on DVD and always playing in the team tent.

Nicknames are a part of conflict. It helps dehumanize the enemy and is a great coping mechanism for combatants to justify actions completely against social mores and human nature. Humans have no inherent desire to kill other humans, so they call them inhuman names to distance themselves from their actions. Jap, gook, chink, kraut. Every war has pet names to describe the enemy. I've chosen dirt-worshippers based on George's theory to cope with the savageness of this place. I assumed playing *Call of Duty* would harden me from caring, but the hardest fuckers can't ignore the insanity of what's happening here—even when it's not directly witnessed.

Traffic's thick and the air feels like I'm breathing yogurt. The road's flooded with a line of cars on the left avoiding the flooded lane on the right. All of them have their windows down. I'm thankful to have AC but pissed we're stuck in traffic. We're a target. Contractors drive Suburbans. I see the opening to the right through the flooded lane. Beats sitting here. I crank the wheel and stomp the gas. The other vehicles follow.

Buckets of water splash off my front tires and pour into the open windows of the cars. I feel like the Count on *Sesame Street*, twenty cars, thirty cars, ah ah ah. I look in the sideview mirror and watch the next Suburban do the same. Then the third. With each splash, I see shock and anger cross the faces of the drivers and passengers in the vehicles. It's splendid. We're an assassination crew sending dirt people to the gutters. The entire vehicle erupts in laughter. Hearts and minds, baby. If I can't win them, collect them.

***

The pool behind the US Embassy is where we swim to get cool in the day and drink our livers into submission by night. Every night there's a party, a small camp fire, and people swimming or jumping off the diving board. As usual, Hog Slayer has found a pig to slay. She works for Kellogg Brown & Root (KBR), a US construction company, and a solid nine in Baghdad, maybe a six stateside. She's Asian (Oriental?). She walks off.

> Hog Slayer: I think she has a horizontal pussy to match her eyes. I have to find out if she gets tighter when I push her legs apart.
> Me: I'm fairly certain this isn't true but let me know. She's seen more meat than a butcher, dude.
> Hog Slayer: Who cares.
> Me: This is why you're the Hog Slayer.

How does someone get such an endearing name as "Hog Slayer"? His given name is Jack. He was in my Blackwater training class. I didn't socialize much with the class, but he was the exception because he was my age.

We went to Virginia Beach one Friday night because we had the next day off. He's handsome, which helps him hit on women. Plus, he can talk. It's a lethal combination targeting every vagina in a bar. We went to a pool hall and he pounced on a brunette like she was a wounded gazelle. She didn't bother to escape as he dragged her to a couch. She had brought a friend, and Jack called me over to distract her. She was beefy. I walked to the porn couch, complete with black, flaking leather, to make small talk with the beast as Jack made out with the gazelle. I wasn't even into talking with her, so I decided to kill any attempt at conversation right off the bat. I said the first inane thing that came to mind:

Me: So, uh, karate is awesome, right?
Beefy: Um, sure.
Me: I love a nice karate chop. Helps me tenderize steaks.
Beefy: You can't be serious?
Me: I'm not. I have to jam. Have a great night.

No way was I jumping on the fat-chick friend-grenade so Jack could get laid. I didn't know him well enough to chance suffocation by obesity.

The next morning, I was eating continental breakfast at our hotel. Jack walked in looking like a cat dragged him there, licked him to health, and left him for dead. He made a waffle, slathered it in butter, and drowned it in syrup—the perfect hangover remedy.

Jack: When did you leave last night?
Me: About the time you started to take that girl's bra off on the porn couch.
Jack: I brought her friend over for you!
Me: For me to regret I got an STD from?
Jack: She wasn't that bad.
Me: She looked like a pig waiting to be slaughtered.
Jack: Ha. I took that chick home.
Me: Here?

I look around hoping she's not behind me after I insulted her friend.

Jack: Her house. I grabbed a cab back here. Cost me fifty bucks.
Me: Sorry?
Jack: It was worth it. I was too drunk to get hard. It was like she was playing pool with a rope man, so she started blowing me.

Me: How was that worth it?

Jack: I shot my load.

Me: I'm confused.

Jack: You never blew your load with a limpy?

Me: I don't think that's physiologically possible.

Jack: It is, dude.

Me: No shit.

Learn something new every day. Jack is now forever known to me as Hog Slayer. He fucks every pig he can find. His philosophy is to go down on every girl. Meet. Connect. Clam dive. This makes the ladies fall in love. When we got to Iraq, I called him the Butcher of Baghdad after seeing him slaughter the war pigs.

Enough reminiscing. Back to the pool. It must be Friday because most of the team have the day off.

Jack: We're headed to the pool. Come on.

Me: It's a bit early to start drinking.

Jack: We're going to play water polo.

Me: I'll pass. You guys are swimmers. I'm at best a tadpole.

Jack: Shut up. Let's go.

We walk to the pool and take it over in force. No swimmers allowed. All those pussy-ass military people can wait until we're done. We set up goals on each end using orange cones we steal from the palace. There's a lifeguard on duty but he gives up trying to tell us not to dominate the pool. He has no authority, and we're intimidating dudes with our shorty shorts and large pectoral muscles.

I was on swim team in elementary school so I'm accustomed to water, but I neglect to realize the people I'm playing with are former Navy SEALs and Recon Marines. They live in the water and are extremely competitive. They're fish to my duck-billed platypus.

I grab the ball in the deep end ready to score a meaningless goal. Two hands grab my shoulders and push me under to the bottom of the pool. They hold me there. And hold me. I look up to see a muscular dude calm like a fish. I look at him, my eyes explaining I'm pescatarian. His eyes are fixated on the ball. Why do I have this fucking ball in my arms? Is it worth drowning over? I release it. He swims off chasing it like a Labrador. I push to the surface and gasp as I swim to the shallow end. I'll play goalie back here.

Afternoon turns to evening and alcohol magically appears. No one bitches about who bought the booze or hordes it. We share knowing someone else will bring the next round or we'll all be dead so there's no reason to fight over it.

We drink. Heavily. The beer tastes like piss. Doesn't matter. It's better than no beer. There's Jack Daniels, Captain Morgan, and fine scotch, which is too fancy for me. I buddy up to an Amstel after ingesting more rum and coke than my liver can handle.

Brian, a retired Army medic and drop-dead alcoholic, is polishing off a European beer. He's hammered. I know this because it feels like I'm looking into a mirror. He dumps his beer on me so it looks like I pissed my pants. The crowd laughs at me about how I just pissed my pants, but I play it up like a proud four-year-old. I trust Brian so there's no reason to blame the guy.

Earlier in the week I was sitting in the back seat of the "ambulance," a Suburban yoked out with medical gear, with Brian, our medic. He's tasked with saving lives. I smelled beer on his breath.

Me: Brian, did you have a drink this morning?
Brian: I had to take the edge off.
Me: Awesome.

We drive through a tunnel and hear gunshots. Brian starts yelling on the radio.

Brian: We're taking fire!
Me: Fuck.

We're trapped in a cement coffin taking fire in the vehicle with zero firepower. In a sadistic way, I'm glad the half-drunk medic's here.

Convoy Leader: That's us.

Brian: Fuck it is! That's AK fire.

Convoy Leader: That's us. You're in the tunnel and the sound
    is echoing.

Brian: Roger.

Brian calms as we exit the tunnel with clinched butt cheeks. I'm pissed he freaked me out. That's life. As we drive back to the Green Zone I recall an E-7 in the Air Force pulling his Baretta on a fisherman near our private beach in Oman and scaring the shit out of everyone. Nothing's atypical when you've been enlisted. At least Brian's highly trained. If blood is pouring from my body, Brian will fix me, drunk or not. I have little choice in the matter. If I trust him to save my life after taking the edge off, I trust his spilling a beer on me is an accident. No reason to make a scene.

We're trashed, drunk but refusing to stop. One of the Blackwater crew does a front flip off the diving board. We cheer. This night is approaching epic status.

Not to be outdone, another climbs up and does a back flip. The entire crowd quiets. The show's on. It's a dick-measuring contest now. Thankfully, my dick's shriveled from cold beer so I have nothing to show.

Another muscular man climbs to the top to perform acrobatics into the pool. Cartwheels. Handsprings. Handstand to a front flip. Amazing feats of athleticism are produced by the minute. Then someone who had a couple too many tries a front flip and belly flops. We boo until the next man executes an exquisite belly flop. We cheer. For the next ten minutes, everyone gets a cheer. Belly flops get the loudest ones. The competition heats up.

Someone steals a bike, climbs up the diving board, and rides it into the drink. We cheer noisily. The bike remains at the bottom of the pool as he comes to the surface. The crowd yells for him to get it. He dives but can't retrieve it. He's booed mercilessly.

A Recon Marine jumps in, grabs it, and lugs it to the surface to cheers from the crowd. We applaud as he drags it up the diving board steps, does a wheelie, and rides off. He leaves the bike at the bottom. The competition begins.

Multiple people dive for the bike, which results in a fight at the bottom of the pool. How do they hold their breath for so long? The winner shoots to the surface with the bike to loud cheers. He drags it up the diving board, jumps on and does a bunny hop off the board. Loud cheers.

My teeth are numb, which means I'll be hungover tomorrow. A hulking man walks to an air conditioning unit, pries it from its base, and carries it to the diving board. Sober people attempt to stop him. Not me. I want to see where this is going. Undeterred, he drags it up the diving board and jumps in the pool with it. The Army Military Police are called. I watch the blue and red lights of a police car pull up to the pool. They have no authority over us and half the contractors here are better trained and packing pistols. The other half, myself included, are wasted and wearing shorts, which may burst allowing our testicles to pop out. It's an awkward encounter.

I don't want to be caught in the dragnet, so I enter the embassy to get Pop Tarts for a drunken snack. I stumble to my room as I devour them like a rabid dog and fall asleep in a position that I've named the beached dolphin: legs extended with arms pressed against my sides, palms up. It's the most comfortable position on a tiny bed.

The next day we have an impromptu all-hands meeting about the "Great Air Conditioning Pool Caper of 2004." I'm the only one who calls it that. The director starts to speak.

Director: I got a call this morning that someone threw an AC unit off the high dive. Stop laughing. This is serious. I told them it wasn't a Blackwater employee. (It was.)
Random Voice: Thanks Ben.

The room erupts in laughter and the director yells to get our attention as we look in Ben's direction. That's right, this is serious.

Director: This is serious. If anyone asks, you have no idea who did this.

Random Voice: Fucking Ben did it. We watched him.

Director: Stop laughing! Blackwater's bidding on several contracts right now and shit like this could ruin our chances. I don't give a fuck who did it. All I know is it wasn't any of us so circle the wagons and shut your mouths.

The meeting ends with everyone congratulating Ben on his heroics. I walk by the pool and notice the diving board's covered in yellow tape like a crime scene with a white sign saying "Closed" hung across the steps. It's never used again. Thanks Ben. You ruined it for everyone.

CHAPTER 7

Funk Faker hates my Lazy Air Force Fuck Ass so he sends me to the team house to drive new employees from the airport to the Green Zone, which is constantly being bombed. He thinks I'm expendable. I don't care. It's fun work and it gets me away from him.

Funk Faker: You're going to the team house for the week.
Me: Sounds good, dude.

He's not happy to be called dude.

Funk Faker: You may as well try to stay there.
Me: Dude, I agree. They make a lot of runs, dude-man, and I'm
    happy to work.
Funk Faker: Be here tomorrow at zero six hundred and they'll
    come get you.
Me: Awesome, dude. I look forward to it, el Duderino.

He's seething when we split. Good. Fuck him. He's as worthless as a Beanie Baby.

I'm assigned as rear gunner in the same busted-up SUVs I rode in when I arrived in country. I have a squad automatic weapon (SAW), an M-249 fully automatic machine gun, which normally has a plastic two-hundred-round drum attached to the bottom. The ammo is loaded in the top so it can pump out rounds at a lethal rate. In contrast, I have a para-SAW, same nomenclature but a shorter barrel and collapsible butt-stock. It has a small drum made of fabric and holds thirty to fifty rounds.

It's lovingly referred to as "the nut sack." I sit in the back of the SUV with no back window playing with my para-SAW and its amazing nut sack. I marvel at its lack of hair.

We arrive at the airport to grab new guys. There are ten people. We have seats for nine. Some poor bastard is going to have to sit in the back of the bongo truck.

My buddy Tony's on the flight. He was my roommate in Phoenix after we got out of the Air Force. When he was talking about joining Blackwater, I tried to talk him out of it. Four Blackwater contractors had just been killed in Fallujah in March 2004. Their bodies were mutilated and dragged through the streets before being hanged from a bridge over the Euphrates.

As we drank beer, he talked about the money, so much money. I mentioned the death, so much death. His rebuttal was the adventure, so much adventure.

I couldn't convince him not to join. Likewise, he was unsuccessful convincing me to join. Then one day that May, my phone rang at six a.m. I was dead asleep. I answered the phone, reached through the receiver, and strangled the person on other end with my bare hands.

Me: (Pissed off.) Hello.
Random Caller: Steve Jackson from Blackwater Security Consulting.

I'm jolted awake.

Steve: Your buddy TONY gave me your phone number and said you'd be interested. We fly you out to North Carolina for training. You'll be paid two hundred and fifty dollars a day for training, and then it's five hundred a day when you get in country, plus ten percent bonus when you complete your contract. How does that sound?
Me: I'm in.
Steve: You fly out tomorrow.

Me: Wait. I'm in college and need two weeks to finish class, then I can fly out.

Steve: Who gives a shit about college when you can start making money?

Me: Too close to stop now. Two weeks. I'll be there. Promise.

Steve: I'll send an email with the information and contract.

He hung up. He was either the worst salesman or the best. I just signed up for a dangerous job based on a three-minute call. As the magnitude and abruptness of what I had just signed up for hit me like a brick in the face, I lay back on the comforter my grandma bought for me when I was in tenth grade. Blue checkers. I refused to replace it. Not because I was emotionally attached but because I was broke.

Tony was two classes before me in training, but his security clearance never came through, a prerequisite for the contract. He got a "noncleared" position in Al Hillah, a city about a hundred clicks (kilometers) south of Baghdad, that pays six hundred dollars a day when I'm making five hundred. Fucker keeps winning at life. He grabs his armor, M-4, and one magazine of ammo. We talk until we're told by Grandpa, "Load up." Tony's the poor bastard without a seat. Grandpa looks at him.

Grandpa: Jump in the back of the truck.

Tony's eyes get huge. Oh yeah. First day in country. I remember that look. He climbs in the back of the truck.

Tony: How the fuck am I going to protect myself?
Grandpa: Drag bags around you.
Tony: The fuck?
Grandpa: Yes, the fuck. Let's go.

Tony shakes his head as he makes a bird's nest with the bags. He pops his head out like a gopher. I laugh so hard I almost shit myself. He's freaking out. Pussy.

We drive to the clearing barrels and Grandpa yells, "Lock and load. We're headed to Indian Country," and humps his rifle. So cool. I laugh watching Tony drag his ass out of the truck to put in a single magazine of ammo and return to his nest like a penguin.

We drive to the Green Zone without an incident. The new guys unload the bags. Tony's told to stay in the truck and hand them down like a bitch. He's having quite the first couple hours in Baghdad. I stick around to bullshit with him and a guy named Steve. They have a million questions. I have no answers but Steve's a cool dude. His teeth are amazingly straight, and I can see them every time he smiles through a five-day beard. I wish I never met him.

***

Getting a security clearance is a problem for many contractors. To work on the Worldwide Personal Protective Service (WPPS) contract, you need a DoS secret clearance. People volunteering to risk their lives for money in an active combat zone make questionable life decisions. This implies we've made absurd choices before. The most absurd concern money, which results in debt and Tony has plenty of that. Hell, he owes me ten thousand dollars. God knows what he owes the IRS.

When Blackwater won the massive contract for WPPS, there were only so many former special operation guys available to fill it. They relaxed their hiring criteria to include guys like me and the guy with sleep apnea. Right place, right time. Blackwater was in the business of making money, not screening people. That was the State Department's job.

Matt Marshall was a former Force Recon Marine in my class at Blackwater. I was the Air Force guy, so I shut my mouth and tried to learn from the BAMFs which included Navy SEAL's, Recon Marines, Army Rangers, and Special Forces dudes. Save for the old farts who smoked two packs a day and went to Waffle House for dinner each night, I was out of my league and knew it.

I was on the pistol range next to Matt. The man could shoot. As we walked to our targets he said "Fuck Air Force, you can shoot." I blushed but said nothing, knowing my invitation to Blackwater was a recommendation from Tony, a legit operator. I could shoot but in the land of operators, I was an Afghani Chia Boy.

We went to lunch in the Blackwater chow hall after the pistol range and Matt sat next to me. I invited Tony over to talk Force Recon with him since they had it in common.

Me: Hey Tony, this is Matt. He's an OG Force Recon dude.

Tony: Great to meet you.

Matt: I was shooting next to Morgan and he's tits on.

Tony: We met in the Air National Guard and deployed to Iraq in 2003. He's solid.

Me: OK. Stop. My penis can only get so erect before it explodes.

Matt: Seriously, you can shoot.

Me: I need to go to the bathroom to finish myself off unless one of you want to help?

Tony: Fuck off.

Me: That's the plan. Do you have lotion?

I left the chow hall while Tony and Matt talked for a bit. Tony never got a security clearance but Matt got his shortly after me and was assigned to Templar 12 in Iraq.

***

There were two steps to getting on the WPPS contract. First was the screen by Blackwater which consisted of submitting your resume and military or law enforcement service record. The military version of this is a DD214 which was standard for a Blackwater application. Second is the US State Department security clearance which consisted of an interview and filling out a form stating where you worked and lived for the last seven years. If you pass the screenings, can shoot, do a PT test, and finish training, you're in.

The trick to obtaining a DoS clearance is to divulge as little information as possible. Deny everything. Tell the interviewer what they want to hear and leave. If you can respond with a single word, that's the correct answer even if it's a lie.

I had my clearance interview during training. I was a clean-cut all-American man blessed to have been birthed in this great country. I was juiced out on steroids, but I wasn't about to tell the interviewer that.

The interviewer was a young lady with red curly hair who was sitting on a tan couch. She was wearing a black sundress with flowers. I fell in love. Agape love. I sat in a metal folding chair. She stood up, walked to me, unzipped my pants, and started blowing me. I tilted my head back. It was amazing; too bad it was in my mind. I told myself an attractive interviewer's a setup. I got my head in the game (sic). Steroids make a man horny in ways that should be illegal. I told myself, "Unfuck yourself, Morgan. You're a saint."

Her: Have you ever done drugs?
Me: Never. (This relationship is going to be built on lies.)
Her: Any outstanding debt? Not car or house debt but excessive debt like credit cards where you could be extorted if someone paid you?
Me: No. (True. Our relationship is back on track.)
Her: Looks like you have DoD clearance. Will we find any differences between our questionnaire and theirs?
Me: No. (Damn it. We're back to the lies. How can we make this work?)
Her: Can you come over here and take off my dress?
Me: Yes. I'm in love with you and want to plant a baby in your tum-tum.

We made hot sweaty love on the sofa. I promise to relive this moment later in my hotel room with Jergens lotion and Kleenex. She'll get the coveted four-tissue cleanup.

In reality, she sent me out and asked for the next applicant. She probably feigns interest in all Blackwater employees. This relationship would never work. She broke my trust and the seam in my pants.

I walk back to class, open the door and Max, who's Filipino, is bound with zip ties. Nathan's holding up his head by his hair. They call me over so I can get in the team execution photo. This is reminiscent of the Filipino contractors brutally murdered in Iraq the week prior. I put on a black scarf and jumped in the picture. Death is funny until I'm plummeting to the ground on the plane ride into Baghdad and begging God for forgiveness.

My clearance processed by my last day of class and I signed a six-month contract. It's frightening but fucking rad. It says:

WELCOME TO BLACKWATER

> The risks include, among other things and without limitations, the undersigned being shot, permanently maimed, and/or killed by a firearm or munitions, falling from an aircraft or helicopter, sniper fire, landmine, artillery fire, rocket propelled grenade, truck or car bomb, earthquake or other natural disaster, poisoning, civil uprising, terrorist activity, hand to hand combat, or disease, etc., killed or maimed while passenger in a helicopter or other aircraft, suffering hearing loss, eye injury or loss, inhalation or contact with biological or chemical weapons (whether airborne or not), and/or flying debris etc.

Fuck it. I don't have much to live for, so I sign it with a shitty Bic pen and mentally prepare myself to voluntarily move to a war zone.

CHAPTER 8

September 30, 2004. Funk Faker calls us to the tent to talk about the next mission. It's a slog. We're burned out because he's running the team like a salty platoon sergeant and treating us like grunts. We signed up to be treated like grown-ass men. He does pre-mission briefs, mission briefs, missions, post-mission briefs, after action reviews, and other shit I don't understand, because I was in the Air Force, where people are treated like adults. We're burned out by the stupidity.

He begins his mission brief. No one cares as he outlines the same route we've taken multiple time. Our indifference consumes the oxygen in the tent. Lap Dog jumps in to save him.

Lap Dog: We are going along this route. It's through a neighborhood. If we get hit, we can bunker in place.
JR: We get it. We've done this run.
Lap Dog: If we bunker, drivers should aim their vehicle for a window of the houses and avoid the pillars.

I've had enough. This is the dumbest shit I've ever heard. I look around. The entire team has the pissed-off face.

Me: Damn, Lap Dog, I was planning on running into a pillar and killing everyone in the vehicle. Fucking spot on advice. Guys, can you also please avoid driving into the river?
Funk Faker: Hey! Everyone has something to contribute. Don't discount his input.

Me: Fuck off. Lap Dog's advice is trash. I know you have a Ranger
    connection but he never finished Ranger School.
Funk Faker: So now it's personal?
Me: Damn right. Let's open this shit up.

Funk Faker looks at the team and the mission brief turns into a
"come to Jesus" meeting. I'm sitting on a limb hoping they back me up.

We sit on the floor as he stands to perform a jeremiad. He lectures
us on how we need to operate better and something or other. Who
knows? He's a dick. Plus, my ass is falling asleep on the plywood floor.
I'm still salty he hasn't thanked me for the water I tossed him at the
Jordanian Embassy.

I shift to my right ass cheek to alleviate the stress on my left. One
of the old dudes on the team speaks up about how Funk Faker's been
treating us like children. Mr. Faker castigates him. My ass hurts and my
face warms as anger moves to my cheeks. Someone needs to tell this
asshole off.

Me: This is why we have low morale.
Funk Faker: What?
Me: You're a fucking asshole, dude.
He's mad.
Funk Faker: What?
Me: Yeah, dude. He speaks up and you chew his ass. We're grown-ass
    men. Leave us to do our jobs.
Funk Faker: From the Air Force guy.
Me: Yes, from the Air Force guy. Fuck off. You're the problem not
    me. We can go outside if you want.
Funk Faker: Fuck you.

I stand to let him know I'm serious. The team jumps to my aid and
we have a mini mutiny. Thank goodness. He would've beaten the hell
out of me. This is the start of my evolution. I'm moving from the egg
stage to the tadpole stage of becoming an asshole. I can swim but I'm
nowhere near being a frog asshole.

Funk Faker tells us we're the on-call quick reaction force (QRF) tomorrow, so we need to be at the tent at seven a.m. and be prepared to sit there all day in case we get called out. QRF is a team that can quickly get in a vehicle and come to the aid of another team if they need help OTW. The meeting ends and we leave. I get a call on the radio. We have a team meeting in an hour. Great. Funk Faker's testing my nerves.

I arrive at the tent and the Blackwater leadership's there. Nick's our new team leader. Nice dude. Former Recon Marine. Someone went higher and got Funk Faker relieved. He's assigned mission-planning with the other bitches.

Nick tells us to check in at seven a.m. If we don't have a mission, we can return to our rooms if we're available via radio and able to report within ten minutes. I skip back to my room knowing we live in a meritocracy.

At eight-ten a.m. I get a radio call from Dave waking me from my slumber. I was at the tent at oh-seven hundred and no one was there so I went back to bed. I'm not impressed.

Dave: Morgan, where the fuck are you?
Me: I'm sleeping, asshole. Why're you bothering me?
Dave: We're supposed to check in at seven.
Me: I was there, and no one showed up so I went back to my room.
Dave: It's seven-ten.
Me: Dude, I have a watch. Leave me alone.
Dave: Last night was daylight saving.
Me: Was what?
Dave: Get in here. We can't leave until you come in.
Me: On my way.

I get dressed and walk to the tent. Everyone's pissed. I'm lectured on being late. I'm not in the mood.

Me: I was here at seven and you fuckers weren't. Figured I missed the message we were getting the day off.

Matt: Day. Light. Saving.

Me: What the fuck is daylight saving?

Matt: The time change.

Me: Why would time change?

Matt: Daylight saving, dipshit.

Dave: Morgan, you've never heard of daylight saving?

Me: I have no idea what you're talking about.

Dave: Time changes twice a year. Anything?

Me: No.

Matt: What kind of dumb fucking redneck part of the world did you grow up in?

Me: Cottonwood, Arizona.

Dave: Arizona doesn't change time twice a year?

Me: Not that I know of.

Nick: Fuck. Everyone's released. Keep your radios on.

Me: Matt, what's daylight saving?

Robert: Spring forward, fall back. The clock changed last night.

Dave: We fell back an hour. Seven is six. Eight is seven and you weren't here at seven.

Me: Why would anyone change time?

Dave: (All smart.) It was started so farmers had more time in the day to harvest crops and saves energy consumption.

Me: Whatever, man. I think it's an oriental thing.

Dave: Fuck off. Let's get breakfast.

After researching, I learn Arizona, Hawaii, and a couple areas in Indiana use standard time all year. I let everyone know this when we meet the next day. I'm not a dumb hillbilly, just ignorant. Matt Marshall tells me I'm the "smartest dumb hillbilly he's ever met." I might be in love with him at this point. He compliments me every time we talk.

Iraq got rid of Daylight Savings Time in 2008. Maybe I did make a difference over there?

GUNS, GIRLS, AND GREED

***

We gather around a fire pit near the pool, a four-foot circle consisting of miscellaneous rocks and bricks with chairs surrounding it. The fire's hot so we've pushed back from it. As it cools, we pull our chairs closer until one of us decides to get off his ass to grab wood. Once it's tossed on, we move back again. As the smoke moves, I move my chair right and left to avoid being smothered. It's a delicate dance.

It's my birthday. I tell no one. The last person who told someone it was his birthday was dragged to the ground and beaten. Then we conducted an Iraqi tar and feather party.

The guy made the mistake of telling his team leader, Max, who told everyone to be waiting for them when they finished their morning run. When they entered the compound, Max jumped him and twenty of us joined in.

Initially, he assumed it was a joke. We grabbed his arms and legs. Not a joke. I grabbed a wrist, which he pulled to his mouth and bit my hand. Not a nice bite, a dog-biting-a-postman bite. He damn-near broke the skin. I moved to the safety of his ankle. We flipped him on his stomach and hog-tied him with duct tape. He was a beaten man. We dragged him to a sand pile, laid him on his side and Max poured water on him. Then we kicked sand on him, aiming for his mouth and nose, an Iraqi tar and feather.

Everyone stepped back thirty feet, and we sent the medic to cut him free. Medics are sacrosanct since they're tasked with saving lives. He wouldn't dare fight the medic. This was the fun part. Now someone will take a beating by the birthday boy.

Medic: Don't fuck with me.
Birthday Boy: Deal. (Looking at us.) I'm going to fuck you up.
Medic: (Looking at us.) You ready?

We nod.

Medic: (To the birthday boy.) You ready?

Birthday Boy: Yes.

He was cut loose. We ran like cockroaches when a light turns on. He targeted the weakest gazelle, grabbed him, and used his body to rub wet sand on him. We watched and cheered.

Grandma didn't raise no fool so on my twenty-fourth birthday, I grab a chair next to the fire pit and tell no one. It's an evening of stories. There's always a new story. The first is from a swinger. He's rotating out of country in a month and has a date set up for his wife to get pounded by a guy whose penis is the size of a Coke can. This is alluring to him.

Me: There's no way a cock can be the size of a Coke can.
Swinger: He's verified on the swinger site and has pictures to prove it.
Me: How do you compete with a Coke can?
Swinger: It's not a competition.
Me: When you bang her after, it's gotta feel like throwing a hot dog down a hallway.
Swinger: It's hot.
Me: You should go to the embassy café and get a Rip-It. They're half the length of a regular can. Take a picture of your dong next to it for the swinger site.
Swinger: It's about watching my girl get fucked by a huge dick.
Me: What if you try to be the funny swinger? Caption it, "It might not be very big around but it sure is short." Chicks dig a funny caption.

The guy next to me, tired of the conversation, removes the magazine from his Glock and pops out two rounds. He tosses the bullets in the fire. What a prick. I was just getting started with this conversation.

Him: Toss a round in.
Me: So, we wait and hope we don't get shot?

Six of us play chicken with live ammunition as the fire heats up. I wait for a slug to blast from the embers and smash into my liver. On the ride to the hospital, I bleed to death. Every bit of logic in my brain tells me to run. This is idiotic. I stay because no one else runs.

I hope it blasts the guy who threw the bullets in. Nothing against him except he's endangering my life. I don't want to eat a fire bullet. He's undoubtedly praying the same ill against me. Think of my eulogy: Morgan was shot in the liver by a fire while drinking beer in Baghdad on his twenty-fourth birthday. A true hero. Bury me next to Ira Hayes.

I remove a round from my spare magazine and toss it in. Fuck it. Russian Roulette. Five minutes pass and we have ten rounds simmering. A blue flame ignites in the yellow fire, they're cooking off, exploding and shooting bullets.

Swinger: The shell casing's weaker than where the bullet's inserted.

Pop.

Swinger: That's the shell breaking. The round's falling in the embers.

Pop.

Me: No worries. (Huge fucking worries.)

Pop.

I stare at the fire, willing it to shoot the man next to me. Bright blue sparks appear when the fire touches gunpowder.

Pop.

We're safe. The guy who wants to watch his wife get plowed by an abnormally huge penis can't get it wrong. Right?

Pop.

I'm twenty-four years old, in a war zone, making more money than I can spend, and this is how I die.

Pop.

I miss home but not enough to go home.

Pop.

***

The filthy terrorists have us scoped-in and are hitting us with rockets and mortar with surprising accuracy. They're sneaky. They build launching pads in the back of trucks, drive to the opposite side of the river from the Green Zone, shoot them, and drive away before US forces can get helicopters in the air to blow them to bits.

Thankfully, they're incompetent. Logan's jogging the perimeter of the embassy, a path surrounded by T-walls (twelve-foot-tall concrete blocks that look like an upside-down T). A rocket lands. This is a death sentence. The blast knocks him on his ass and into a pile of sand used to fill sandbags. Other than his ears ringing, he's unscathed. Terrorists are using the wrong fuses. Rockets fly and land but don't explode. The force of impact is enough to ruin a jog but not enough to kill.

The best way to avoid having jagged shrapnel tear through your body, rip your guts out, and bleed to death, is to avoid being in Iraq. The next best option is to lie on the ground with your hands behind your head to shield your noodle from the blast and open your mouth, so the percussion doesn't blow out your ear drums. Rockets explode up and out like the arc of flower pedals from a stem. Blackwater contractors know this, but it doesn't matter. By the time we hear a rocket, it's too late.

A rocket tears through our tent. Fifteen contractors are on Myspace, watching *Deadwood* and looking at huge dicks on swinger websites when it impacts. I hear it come in and have an oh-shit moment. Blackwater's having a mass casualty event. The guy I'm standing near looks at me and says "Fuck. There goes our internet." Priorities. We run to the tent to assist the wounded. I expected it to be cloth shards but it's mostly unscathed. A guy walks out covered in dirt, unharmed. More filter out behind him. The rocket didn't explode.

One of the men, dirt covering the best Fu Manchu I've ever seen, strides to a refrigerator, grabs a beer, and says, "I don't know who this belongs to, but I need it." He slams it in seconds, grabs a second, and walks away. This is surreal. Like a movie. What a badass.

GUNS, GIRLS, AND GREED

***

I'm not impressed by diplomats, our "principles," (or maybe it's "principals" because they're our "pals?" Yeah. I'll go with that.) They sit in their ivory tower with their fancy college degrees and talk to us like we're primates. Many of them are semi-cordial but most are awful, up to and including the ambassador to Iraq, John Negroponte, who's a dick. The diplomats wear suits and slacks in this hellhole in direct contrast to me in boots and 5.11 jeans. They're self-important but unable to protect themselves, which says a lot about them.

> Me: Good morning, sir.
> Diplomat: We need to go code three to the parliament building.
> Me: Code three in the Green Zone? It's right around the corner.
> Diplomat: Yes. Lights and sirens.
> Me: (Over the radio.) Lights and sirens to parliament.
> Team Leader: In the Green Zone?
> Me: Code three, dude.

Secretary of State Colin Powell's an asshole too. I assume it's because his State Department couldn't carry out the mission without hiring PMCs. He's also probably angry the Blackwater's pay scale encourages soldiers to leave the military, not me so much as the legitimate ones. To his credit, he's amazing with the troops. The general in him never died.

Our presence is something of a paradox. Diplomats build the country and we keep them alive. They win hearts and minds. We protect them at any cost. We're paid for what we may have to do—die protecting a person who's integral to the mission but worthless to us—not what we do. We protect people who help Iraq, but in doing so, piss off every Iraqi. Oh well. Maybe for the next war the hawks in D.C. will have a better plan than "we promise you'll be happy we liberated you. Here are PMCs as a stop gap."

When driving diplomats, the Suburban they travel in is in the middle with a lead and follow Suburban buffering it from the most probable points of attack. An explosion will blow us to pieces but the diplomat—sipping iced tea and talking about the socioeconomic impact of the price of bananas on the people of Nicaragua—is safe.

When we park, one of us stands in front of the door where the principal will exit. At that moment, his purpose is to take a bullet for the principal. Once the principal exits, we create a diamond around him or her, so each field of fire is covered. There's always someone between the principal and the potential enemy. We walk them to the meeting and take up positions to protect them. If the poo-poo hits the fan, we can extract them or fight.

This happened in 2004 in Najaf. Blackwater was protecting a diplomat when the building came under attack. A Marine was wounded, and no military helicopter would intervene due to the raging battle. When the military wouldn't, a Blackwater helicopter flew in to evacuate the Marine, saving his life and resupplying ammo. This is the example PMCs use when espousing their value while ignoring the Blackwater contractors who were murdered, burned, and hung from a bridge which led to the fight for Fallujah and the deaths of eighty-two US Marines.

Speed is our friend. We want to be on the road as little time as possible. The biggest threats are IEDs, which are easy to deliver to a stopped vehicle. We drive fast so we're a harder target to hit.

The scariest threat is a vehicle borne improvised explosive device (VBIED) or car bomb. The most lethal VBIED is a suicide VBIED, where a poor bastard drives into a convoy or crowd and blows up the vehicle and himself. The driver thinks he has an option to not detonate, but there's a remote-control detonator. A crazy ass with a phone will blow it up it if the driver wimps out. This is called a Suicide RCVBIED. Confused? Me too.

We keep traffic away as much as possible to avoid Suicide VBIEDs. We put ourselves between any possible explosive (which can be a parked car or random package on the side of the road) and our principal. We do this automatically.

We're on a run to Camp Liberty, which is along Route Irish. I'm driving the lead vehicle and our tactical commander is a Muslim from

Michigan named Raj. He's here to make money to open a gas station back home. The irony. Eager to learn more about Muslim culture, I ask him about the call to prayer—or *muezzin*—as I push the Suburban to eighty-two mph, its maximum speed.

The muezzin blares from every mosque in the city five times a day to let locals know it's time to face Mecca and pray. It's loud and wakes me up at five a.m. I'm not a fan. Intelligence reports state the call to prayer is also used to let terrorists know it's time to bomb shit.

Me: Hey, Raj. What does the call to prayer say?

Raj: It tells people to pray.

Me: Yeah but what are the words? All I hear is (singing) "Ham and eggs. Ham and a-eggs."

Raj: What the fuck's wrong with you?

Me: It sounds like they're singing about ham and eggs.

Raj: Muslims don't eat ham or pork products.

Me: I see you eating bacon.

Raj: It's delicious. Of course, I eat it.

Me: So, what's the literal translation of the song? Are they all the same?

Raj: Each mosque plays a different song. It could be a new hymn every day or different. It doesn't matter. It just needs to happen at the same time. Prayer time.

Me: No shit. Could we translate it so when they sing (singing) "Kill the Americans, kill them a-all," we can warn people?

Our conversation's cut short by a crater in the road from a car bomb the day prior. I'm driving too fast to avoid it. I take it head on as I yell to the gunners in the back, "Hold on to your dicks." How that specific phrase comes to me in that precise instant is a mystery. In the rear-view mirror, I watch the gunners lift off their seats and crash their heads against the roof.

Raj: (Over the radio.) Crater. Go left.

Robert: Hey, fucker. I smashed my head on the roof. My back's going
  to hurt tomorrow.
Me: Ha ha. Old fucker.
Robert: Fuck you. Watch the road.
Me: Maybe you're too old for this war stuff.

We arrive at Camp Liberty and the principal goes to his meeting.
Dave and I sit at a picnic table talking to one of the principal's minions.
He's young, twenty-five and wants to go Burger King. Yes, this base has
a Burger King. We refuse to take him. We aren't a food taxi. The conversation turns toward college.

Minion: Did you go to college?
Me: Yeah, I took classes at Coconino Community College.
Minion: (To Dave) What about you?
Dave: Yes.
Minion: Where?
Dave: Tufts University.
Minion: Really? Why're you doing this job?
Dave: Huh?
Minion: That's a great college. I went to Bowdoin. Why are you a
  security contractor and not working for the State Department?
Dave: It pays better.

I never knew fancy colleges were a thing. I know of Harvard but
that's it. Apparently, Tufts and Bowdoin are good colleges. I listen to
Dave bitch about the minion for days after our encounter:

Dave: Fuck that guy. My education's better than Bowdoin. Snooty
  asshole. Probably got rejected by Tufts.
Me: What's a Bowdoin?
Dave: I make four times what he's making as a State Department
  bitch. Acting all hot shit about Bowdoin. Fuck him.
Me: What's a Tufts?
Dave: That guy can suck my jumbo dick.

Me: Ha ha. Jumbo dick. You're Asian. I know you aren't packing heat.

Dave: Fuck you, fuck him. Jumbo's the Tufts mascot.

Me: Fuck him, not me. I don't want to be fucked by that tiny dick of yours.

CHAPTER 9

'm assigned a mission in Arbil, Kurdistan, for a conference about war crimes. Dave's tapped to go also, which is good since he's cultured and shit.

Kurdistan has the largest displaced population in the world. The Kurds are autonomous due to the no-fly zone established by the US and coalition forces after the first Gulf War. The Kurds are self-governed and united in their hate for Saddam, Chemical Ali, aka Ali Hassan al-Majid who orchestrated the Anfal campaign of genocide against the Kurds in the eighties, and Sunni Muslims.

Kurdistan starts north of Kirkuk, which has a massive oil field that Saddam used as a revenue source. After Operation Desert Storm, the Kurds prepared to take Kirkuk with Peshmerga forces, their local army. Peshmerga means "walking the line of death." This insurgency was thwarted by regime troops using helicopters to slaughter the resistance.

We fly into the international airport in Arbil. Northern Iraq is beautiful with mountains and green vegetation, whereas southern Iraq is barren, flat, and dusty as hell. Armored SUVs are staged on the runway for us. There must be thousands of these across the country because every time I go somewhere, they appear. We pass a Christian church on the way to a three-story building. We escort the principal inside and wait by the vehicle in the parking lot.

Peshmerga soldiers approach us and ask to see our weapons. I make sure there's no ammo near the M249 before they crowd around to take pictures. One of them holds a hundred-year-old, polished wood, bolt action rifle. It's a musket in the land of automatic weapons. I hold it and have Dave take my picture. If shit goes down, I'm following the guy with the musket because he's either lethal or insane. Either way, I'm pushing him toward the gunfire before running like a coward. One of the Peshmergas comes up to me like we're bosom buddies.

Him: Assyrian.
Me: Sure, man. Syrian.
Him: No no no. Assyrian. Christian.
Me: Go Jesus!

He shows me a keychain with an Assyrian symbol. It has a star as a nucleus and red and blue squiggly lines protruding from it like octopus' arms. He insists I hold it. I pretend to be impressed. Wow. Colors. Keys can go on here? No shit? This is a mistake. He tells me to keep it. No, thanks. He insists. No. Take it back. He refuses. Oh well, I take it and put it in my pocket. Dave looks at me.

Dave: You have to give him something.
Me: What? Fuck that. It's a key chain.
Dave: It's the culture. They give you something and you give them something.
Me: I'll give him his key chain back.
Dave: That's rude. You accepted it.
Me: The fuck am I supposed to give him? I don't have shit on me.
Dave: Figure it out.
Me: I'll grab an MRE from the truck.
Dave: No, dude. It has to be something personal. You can't give him constipation in exchange for his gift.
Me: Serious? All I have is sunglasses.
Dave: Do it.
Me: What? They cost fifty dollars. That key chain is worth dick.
Dave: Culture, dude.
Me: Fuck you and your culture stuff.

The Peshmerga dude knew what he was doing. He must've smelled the culture on Dave before approaching me (no cultural odor) to give me worthless shit. I hand him my sunglasses. He rushes to his buddies to show them off. Asshole. Now I have no sunglasses and I'm standing in the sun while Kurdish leaders badger our principal to admit Saddam committed war crimes and the Sunnis cannot have any position in the new government. He can't say anything even if he agrees because he's a diplomat and any comment made could be later used as leverage against the US.

Me: Hey, cultured Dave, watch my shit. I need to take a dump.
Dave: Okay.

I point at a soldier.

Me: Hey, dude, where's a shitter?
Soldier: ?
Dave: Toilet. Everyone knows toilet.
Me: Toilet, bro. Shitter. Loo. Water closet. Any place I can go so I
    don't shit my pants would be great.

He points to the second floor of the building. I trudge up the stairs, turn the corner, and enter a bathroom. It smells like Satan's breath. I walk out to decide if I can hold it. Nope. I've got a turtle head poking out and haven't shat my pants in weeks. I brace myself for the stink. Is it better to breath in the stench through my nose or mouth?

The toilet's a hole in the floor with a ceramic insert. Areas on each side of the hole are where I assume my feet go. How do these people shit, stand up and hope it falls out? I unbuckle my thigh holster, drop my pants, pistol and all, and squat. Hell yes, I'm getting cultured.

This lasts half a turd before the weight of my body armor makes my legs shake. I lean against the wall to alleviate the stress on my hips. My legs tremble as I push out the monster into the hole, sort of. It teeters between the ceramic bowl and the abyss. I stand to give my legs a rest and look for toilet paper. I see a hose and a green flowerpot. Great. No

GUNS, GIRLS, AND GREED

one stocked the TP. I walk around the bathroom. The good news is my olfactory glands no longer register the stench. The bad news is nary a sliver of paper is to be found. I need a big brain to tell me how to wipe my ass. I walk my shitty ass down to Dave.

> Me: There's no shitter paper. Just a flowerpot and a hose.
> Dave: The hose is to fill the flowerpot, then cup your hand to hold water and use this to clean your ass.
> Me: Bare hand to shitty ass?
> Dave: Yep.
> Me: Would you do it?
> Dave: Hell no. I shit before we left.
> Me: I'd rather chafe. Wait, fuck yeah! We have MREs in the car. They have TP.

It's third-knuckle toilet paper. The paper's so thin that when you wipe, you end up with a finger in your ass up to the third knuckle. I grab an MRE, tear into it like a starving lion, and grab the small pack of toilet paper.

> Me: Watch my shit. I'm taking the walk of shame back to the toilet.
> Dave: Okay. You use the hose to wash your turd down.
> Me: Not today, Dave.

I wipe my ass and toss it near the turd hanging on the edge. I refuse to wash it down. They can enjoy that American monster. I'm done with this place. Thankfully, we leave that evening and return to Baghdad before anyone can call me out on leaving a turd in the toilet.

At our nightly mission brief we're told Templar 12 is going on a five-day excursion to Kurdistan the next day.

We're sent to pack and told to be ready to leave in the morning. I pack ten days of clothes and four rolls of toilet paper.

Ten of us jump in a Blackhawk early the next day. Helicopter rides are fun. We lift off and I watch the earth shrink as we fly north over the city. The houses are smashed together. Many are large due to having three generations living in them. Power lines spread across the roofs connect them like roots. I doubt they have code inspectors here or if they do, inspectors have great sideline going from bribes.

Out of nowhere, a flash of red, orange, and yellow bursts next to me outside the chopper. We've been shot down! My adrenaline spikes and the hairs on the back of my neck stand up. First the flight in and now this? This is how it ends for me: *Blackhawk Down Baghdad*? We level off. Very odd. I yell over the deafening sound of the rotors.

Me: What the fuck was that?
Dave: Flares.
Me: I think I shit myself.

The flash is the anti-missile system. If it senses a threat, it shoots flares intended to mimic the heat coming off the helicopter. A heat-seeking missile will go after the flare instead of the bird. I live another day.

I'd learn later we weren't being shot at. It's normal for flares to eject when flying over the massive burn pits the US military used to dispose of everything from paper plates to toxic chemicals. The black billowing smoke accomplished two things. First, it made the defense contractor who made flares a ton of money. Second, it would later be linked to cancer and other maladies for those who served in Iraq and Afghanistan.

After thirty minutes, I'm over this helicopter ride. My bag's on my lap due to the high occupancy. I can't stretch my legs. They've fallen asleep, past the uncomfortable prickly feeling to dull pain. Exhaust pumps in the cabin and the stench of burnt fuel scrapes my throat. We have four and a half hours remaining on this flight to play a little game I call: How many hydrocarbons can I ingest?

After a couple hours, we land for a pitstop. The pilot kicks us off the helicopter while fuel is pumped. My legs feel like Jell-O. I'm happy to stand. I do yoga stretches but don't get to finish my downward dog before we're ushered back on to the screaming-hell-beast. By the time we land in Sulaymaniyah, I'm stoked to get in a vehicle. I'm the tactical commander on this trip—a promotion without the luxury of additional pay.

Our mission is to ferry diplomats around Kurdistan to gather evidence for the upcoming trial of Chemical Ali. We drive to the hotel where we'll stay for the next few days.

Perched on a hill overlooking the city, the hotel is where affluent locals hold weddings and vacation. It has two floors. The ground floor consists of the lobby, a large dining area, and a back patio. The second floor has our rooms. The other side of the hill houses the compound of the local leaders.

We stand on a polished wood floor in the lobby waiting for room keys. I have the attention span of a goldfish, so I walk around. I hold back tears when I see the bar. A real bar. Time to get fucked up.

We pair up and are given a single room key. I'm with Dave. We walk to our room, drop our bags and piss in the bathroom sink for no reason. Dave's barely tall enough to reach. It's cute.

> Me: Get on your tippy toes. Don't piss on the faucet. I don't want your piss on my hands when I wash up.
> Dave: Fuck off. I got this.
> Me: Look at the toilet! It has a butthole washer.
> Dave: Why're you in the bathroom with me?
> Me: I saw the hole washer.
> Dave: It's called a bidet.
> Me: Call it what you want. I'm fucking using that bitch tonight even if I don't shit.
> Dave: Sure beats getting TP out of an MRE.
> Me: You better be nice or I'm going to make you wipe me.

We head to the bar and the front desk person walks over to pour drinks. There's a local liquor, which turns from clear to white when poured over ice. The bartender insists we try it. I take a sip. It tastes like elephant piss, assuming elephant piss tastes like black licorice. I close my eyes, plug my nose, and chug it. I'll stick with anything but that for the rest of the afternoon.

The sun sets and the hotel staff are busy putting out an enormous amount of food on a huge table. It looks awful. I feel bad for the people coming to dinner. I go to my room to try out the booty washer. The water's freezing yet satisfying. Now my asshole is wet. Do I use TP to dry it? That would defeat the point. I drip dry.

Thirty minutes later someone knocks on the door. I notice my O-ring's itchy from the washing. It feels like my asshole has chapped lips as I walk to the door and open it. It's Nick, our fearless leader.

Nick: We've been invited to the feast downstairs.

Me: Enjoy, man.

Nick: You and Dave need to put on pants and come down. It's Ramadan. This is the large meal after sunset.

Me: Huh?

Nick: Have Dave explain it. I have to get the others.

Dave explains Ramadan is a month of fasting where Muslims can't eat during daylight. At the end of each day, a large meal is prepared. At the end of the month, there's an extra special feast. This feast is to celebrate our arrival in Kurdistan, but since it's Ramadan, it couldn't happen until after sundown. The table's twelve feet long and filled with dates, random vegetables, and the largest, ugliest fish I've ever seen. Its eyes are baked dry and staring at me. It looks like the three-eyed fish from *The Simpsons* but uglier. I turn to walk back to my room. Nick stops me.

Nick: You're going to sit here. The interpreter is Kurdish and some of his family was killed by the former regime. He wants to treat us to a meal as a thank you for helping them gather evidence to convict the regime.

Me: Nope. That fish looks like Satan procreated with a mermaid. It's the spawn of forbidden love.

Nick: So, don't eat the fish. Eat the bread, dates, and vegetables.

Me: That fish is giving me the stink-eye, man.

Nick: Shut up, sit down, and eat.

I already have a beer buzz.

Me: I'll have liquid dinner.

Kudos to Nick. As the fish stares at me I recall hearing a story about a US general taking his commanders to a dinner where they were served local food. Some of the officers refused to eat so he asked to be excused with his commanders and told them to eat the eyeballs out of the meal as a show of solidarity and act of diplomacy. The officers returned to the meal and ate the eyeballs of the cooked sheep. I have no idea if this is true but I ate some hummus to show I'm all in for our mission.

The interpreter tells us the fish was caught at Lake Dukan. Yep. Not eating it. He explains his family was persecuted by the former regime and many were killed. His immediate family fled Iraq through Turkey and migrated to the US.

When the war started, he volunteered to interpret for the State Department to see justice served. He cries. It's a touching moment and helps me understand the gravity of our mission but I can't stop returning the fish's stare. It ruins the moment.

After dinner, we drink. The interpreter's bombed. Hugging me, he says he loves me. To get out of the conversation, I challenge the bartender to an arm wrestle. He puts up a decent fight. It's adorable. I slam his hand against the bar to cheers from the locals and our team.

Four of us walk to the hotel patio. JR breaks out cigars. In the crisp air, we light them and look at the city below. It's darker here than in Baghdad. I see millions of stars in the sky. I look south to the city lights. Thousands of them. It feels like a vacation for a moment. When this war ends, I'd like to come back with the family and rent a boat to go fishing with my kids.

We begin missions the next morning. I'm hungover but functional. The first stop is a local police station. Our principals walk through the gate as we survey the area. The wall surrounding the station is pocked with bullet holes, so Robert and I decide to take a photo in front of it. To make the picture pop, he takes linked .556 ammo and puts it over his shoulders and across his chest to make an X, Rambo style. We smile big as Dave takes the photo.

The interpreter returns to the vehicle.

Interpreter: This police station was attacked by the regime during the Kurdish uprising after Desert Storm. The police officers were lined up along the wall and shot, hence the bullet holes.

Maybe I shouldn't have smiled for the picture.

Me: Where's the next stop, boss?
Interpreter: A village up the road.
Me: Can you show us on the map?

I open the map, and he points to three tiny dots. We load up the principal and drive six miles down a dirt road to a tiny village consisting of twenty homes. They are crappy, stucco houses, each about six hundred square feet. It's not the Stone Age mud huts I expected, more like fifties-style homes which haven't been updated.

Studying the population, I notice the absence of able-bodied men. Everybody's old or under the age of sixteen. It's one of many villages in the area where regime troops slaughtered military-aged males in 1993 and 1994, wiping out an entire generation of Kurdish males. We walk with the town elder to a bump in the landscape. Everything around it is undisturbed but this twenty-by-ten-foot area doesn't fit in. It's rocky on the surface whereas the rest of the landscape is smooth. Through the interpreter, the village elder explains.

Elder: This is where the regime soldiers dug a hole, dragged all the village men to it, and shot them. They pushed their bodies in and covered it.

Ruthless.

We drive to the next village. Same story but worse. Since it was a nexus for the uprising, soldiers killed everyone; men, women, and children. We stand above an excavated gravesite.

Interpreter: One of the other towns dug up this site. They found a mother holding her child. The child held a red ball. They were both shot in the head.

Me: (Quietly) Holy fuck.

I wonder how the mother and child were shot. The only explanation is the child was shot first. The mother lifted him up and held him, knowing she would receive the same. Awful. This story made international news in 2004. I'm proud to be part of bringing the asshole who ordered this atrocity to justice.

The next day we go to Halabja where Saddam's regime used chemical weapons in 1988, killing anywhere from 3,200 to 5,000 men, women and children and wounded another 7,000 to 10,000 because the town was assisting Iran in the Iraq/Iran border conflict. It's considered the largest chemical weapons attack against a civilian population in history.

It's raining and muddy as we drive through a small village on our route. The streets overflow with brown water. A man in a store chops the head off a live chicken and drains the blood into the water. It's awesome. We're driving slowly enough to watch red blood flow past us in the dirty stormwater.

We arrive at the Monument of Halabja Martyrs, which commemorates the victims of the attack. It's no Smithsonian. It's dumpy but considering where it's built, appropriate. The exterior is designed to look like hands reaching to the sky, delivering the victims to heaven. The fingers are squared, and the right hand is below the left making it seem like a skeleton trying to grab a soul. It's creepy.

We walk inside. Pictures of the attack hang over a display recreating a scene of bodies in the streets. They remind me of papier-mâché art I did in kindergarten, paper covered in glue over a balloon and painted by hand. The walls of the museum, painted by an art school dropout with brushes he bought at a yard sale, depict scenes of carnage.

Me: There are pictures of other areas, not just Halabja?
Interpreter: There were many attacks. This was the worst.
Matt: Why?
Interpreter: That day was perfect weather for a chemical attack, cool and no wind. If it were hotter, the chemicals would have dissipated. If it were humid, the chemicals would've drowned in the moisture. Wind would have blown the chemicals away. Perfect conditions allowed the chemical to linger in the air so more people inhaled it.
Me: This is terrible.
Interpreter: The chemical drowned the victims. As they breathed, pustules formed in their lungs and popped. This flooded their lungs. They lay on the ground gasping for air.

I can think of no worse way to die. We walk the grounds and see statues depicting the attack. One looks like a guy taking advantage of the attacks by humping a woman, but it's a man holding his dying wife. Why didn't they ask a fourteen-year-old what he saw before casting this? Granted, contractors aren't right in the head or we wouldn't have volunteered for this job.

We drive to a small house a mile away. It's square with light brown walls, just a kitchen and three other rooms. No bathroom. Rugs on the floors. This is where a bomb dropped but didn't explode. The translator tells us the after-effects were worse than the attack with high rates of birth defects and cancer. Many of the bombs didn't explode.

Interpreter: A bomb pushed through the roof and planted in the floor. The owner couldn't afford to move so he poured concrete over it and continued to live in it. All his children had birth defects.
Principal: We need to see if we can excavate the bomb as evidence.

I think there's plenty of evidence without this bomb but I'm not in charge. I never hear if it was dug up.

It would take until 2010 for Chemical Ali to be convicted of the Anfal genocide campaign, which resulted in the death of 50,000 to 182,000 Kurds. Prosecutors used the evidence we helped gather. Sadly, he's been hanged. I would've preferred he be put in the small house with the bomb so he can die slowly of cancer. Near the end I'd throw mustard gas in the house and watch him drown in his own fluid. Now that's an apropos death for him. I'm becoming callous.

CHAPTER 10

After five days of depression in Kurdistan, we're back in Baghdad. It's a short trip. We have seven days to get our crap together and then get on a plane back to Sulaymaniyah, aka Sulay. Thank goodness. A plane and not a helicopter.

Since I have a week, I volunteer for a two-day run to Al Hillah. I may as well see as much of this country as I can. Plus, Tony's there and owes me ten thousand dollars. I'd like to get that before we die.

It's two hours to Al Hillah and I'm stuck as the rear-gunner in the last vehicle of the convoy. It's the worst seat. I'm a tall drink of water crammed into a space fit for an eight-year-old. I'm miserable but I'm the odd man out. The team I'm going with is staying whereas I'll catch the next ride back to Baghdad.

As we leave Baghdad, we lose radio communication with our TOC. It's just us if we get hit. Alone. This is expected. A perk of being a contractor is the reduction in bureaucracy. The downfall is we have nearly zero support once we leave the city on long range missions. In contrast, the military will spend hours getting ready for a mission to drive thirty meters but have constant contact with an element that can quickly react if the convoy is hit. The next time we'll have support is when we're close enough to reach the TOC at Al Hillah.

As I contort my body to the least uncomfortable position, the city bleeds away into countryside. I see why this country is the cradle of civilization. Both sides of the highway have swamps, vegetation, and abundant wildlife. This is how people lived in this sun-scorched hellhole. It feels biblical even as my knees ache from being pressed into my hips.

The highway's closed due to excessive attacks so we're the only vehicle on the road. Every overpass we drive under has a small berm of sandbags and US soldiers controlling traffic. Poor guys signed up for war and got traffic duty while living under a bridge like trolls. We have no comms so it's nice to know if we're ambushed, someone's hiding under a bridge who's happy to come to the rescue.

After an hour of being contorted like origami, we get radio contact with Al Hillah. This means our journey is nearly complete. They direct us to a bridge. We cross it and take a hard left. One hundred and fifty feet down a gravel road, a solid metal arm painted red and white rests three feet above the earth. We speak English so they let us in unencumbered. I grab my go bag, a bag packed with three days of supplies, and slink out of the Suburban. It feels good. I need to get the blood pumping in my torso.

I'm assigned a room where I drop my kit and change into gym clothes. I wear a tiny pair of shorts and flip flops to the gym. Nothing beats a bare-chested workout after a long ride in the trunk of a Suburban. I'm rocking squats when Tony comes in. Tony's the type who'd give you the shirt off his back. He's a mix of ruthless badass and genuine human. It's an odd combo. This is why we get along.

Tony: Hey, pussy!
Me: Well, if it isn't the guy who owes me money?
Tony: Fuck sake. You and this money shit. You couldn't put on a shirt?

I pull up my shorts, so my nut sack drops out.

Me: Did I step in gum?

We laugh. I catch him admiring my throbbing legs. The sight makes him light-headed. He nearly passes out.

Tony: I'm in room seven hotel. Come by in an hour. We'll meet up for chow.
Me: You got it. Now go shower, cock face.

An hour later I walk to room 7H. I barge in without knocking and see bunk beds. So much room for activities. Tony leaps up acting stoned.

Tony: The fuck?
Me: Let's eat.
Tony: Get the fuck out.
Me: You told me to be here.
Tony: Get out!

Moody bitch. I walk to the chow hall feeling butthurt and grab a plate. The food's damn good: fresh cantaloupes and pineapples, juicy hamburgers, crispy bacon. It's manna from heaven compared to the slop at the Man Camp, which was always swimming in a vat of fluid: meatloaf, spaghetti, eggs soaked in butter, burger patties in greasy water.

This is a quantum leap up from the Man Camp. It's the regional embassy office (REO). The compound was owned by a regime member or was a vacation house for Saddam. It's large enough to comfortably fit ten families with an amazing view of the river, which can be admired from the wraparound porch on each floor.

I'm demolishing a burger when Tony strolls in like a boss. Fucking doober. He sits next to me with a plate of chicken.

Tony: What the hell? I thought you were going to come get me.
Me: Dude, I tried. You yelled at me and sounded stoned.
Tony: Oh man.
Me: The hell?
Tony: I was jerking off and blasted a load on my stomach.
Me: That's great. Anything else disgusting you want to tell me?
Tony: I remember someone came in and then I woke up a few min-
    utes ago. I must've freaked out because I had load on me and
    bashed my head on the top bunk again.
Me: Again?
Tony: Yeah, it's happened before.
Me: Maybe lock your door before you beat your meat.

GUNS, GIRLS, AND GREED

Tony: I would but I have to do it when the feeling hits.
Me: No, dude. You can lock the door.
Tony: I'm telling you, I can't. I have to spank.
Me: How you been besides concussed?

We talk for an hour and head to the bar on the second floor. A group of us gather near a pool table. We're sizing each other up to see who's doing cooler stuff, a classic dick-measuring contest. Thankfully, mine's tiny compared to the Coke can guy so I have nothing to prove.

Me: How is it down here? Getting trigger time?
Tony: Not much. But we were on a run to a local police station and
    a car bomb blew up the gate. It was fifty meters from us.
Me: Holy shit.
Tony: Metal was raining down on the vehicle. Our gunner was in the
    back with no window and shit was dropping on him. Suddenly,
    a fuckin' chunk of scalp flew down and landed on his 240
    Bravo. It was fucking great.
Eric: Yeah. That hunk of hairy flesh landed on my 240. It had brain
    and hair stuck to it. I didn't want to touch it.
Tony: Ha ha. You had to, man.
Eric: I'm not going to keep that chunk of goo in the trunk with
    me. It looked like roadkill. I had to grab it by the hair and
    toss it out.

I sip my beer in shock but I'm trying to play it cool.

Eric: Fucking gross cleaning my 240 that night. God knows what
    diseases these people have.

We erupt in laughter. How is this funny?
Tony's team frequently goes to the local government buildings. They take Jolly Ranchers so the children swarm around them. I'm ready for a cute story to balance the last one.

Tony: We started giving them candy and then fights broke out. Kids were pummeling each other for a fucking strawberry Jolly Rancher.

Eric: One big kid started to dominate. Little fists flying all over. This kid had five pieces of candy, then he took one from a little girl.

Tony: I got out and grabbed that little fucker and made him give her back the candy.

Me: Good for you. Now go get me a beer, asshole.

Tony: Okay.

He walks off to grab a beer.

Eric: Yeah, dude. Now we bring candy and toss it in the crowd of kids to watch them fight for ten minutes. It's great.

Me: Baby Fight Club. First rule is you don't talk about it.

Eric: Huh?

Me: It's a movie.

Maybe that story wasn't as endearing as I'd hoped now that they admitted watching kids duke it out. Oh well. We walk to the wrap-around porch and admire the view. Tony returns with a beer as we argue over the best Jolly Rancher flavor. I doubt the kids care. He hands me a Heineken. I take a sip. It's ripe, tastes like warm piss cooled off and warmed again to give it dehydrated piss taste. I chug it.

Tony: I take porno mags with me on runs. We have to talk to the Iraqi police and those monkeys don't speak English.

Eric: This is hilarious. Tell him, Tony.

Tony: I open the porno mag and they look. Then I talk to them in English: "Don't pretend you like pussy. You like pussy?"

He points to a non-existent magazine in his hand.

Tony: "You put this on your buddy's back and fuck his ass, right?"

Eric: They always nod and say yes. It's great.

Tony: I say, "I bet his hairy asshole doesn't feel as good as pussy."
Eric: And they always say yes.

We bust out laughing. This shouldn't be funny, but it is.

***

Al Hillah is the modern-day Babylon and the team is going to the historical site tomorrow. I join. May as well check it out.

We stop at the Gates of Babylon. Alexander the Great marched his army through here. It oozes history even though it looks like it was built by a man with a lazy eye. The entire arch is blue with white animals painted on the pillars. These aren't the original gates. Saddam had them resurrected. Based on the dick size of the cows, I assume a child painted them.

I remember the Tower of Babel story from Sunday school. The origin of language was God punishing people for attempting to build a tower tall enough to reach heaven. God said, "This isn't cool," but they didn't listen. They built the tower and God made them each speak a different language so they could no longer communicate to complete construction. Had they listened we'd all speak American right? Then again, had the US not entered World War II, we'd all be speaking German and goose-stepping. I'm excited to see the tower.

We walk the grounds. They're worn down. Statues of lions haven't been maintained in decades. It's sad. All the history and treasure here and not an iota of care to keep it up.

A map shows the location of the Tower of Babel and Hanging Gardens. I don't see anything resembling what I learned about in church or humanities classes. If Iraq ever gets over being at war, every old woman at my grandma's Bible study would love to see this, and they'd be disappointed by how dilapidated it is. At least, it would give them something to gossip about at church.

We return to the REO and I work out. At six p.m. I attend the evening briefing for my drive to Baghdad tomorrow. I'm in the bitch seat. Great. I walk to Tony's room to let him know. I knock, loud.

Tony: Come in.

His bare ass is pointed at the AC unit and he's pulling his cheeks apart.

Me: What. The. Fuck?
Tony: I have hemorrhoids. One's huge. I named him Gummo.
Me: Seriously, pull up your pants. I can see your turkey neck flopping in the wind.
Tony: Ha ha.

He pulls up his pants.

Me: What's a hemorrhoid?
Tony: It's a burst blood vessel in your ass. It looks like a grape. Doc told me I'd have to fly to Germany to get it removed but I don't make any money in Germany. So, I cool it off when I can.
Me: Does that help?
Tony: No, but it feels better for a few minutes.
Me: I'm out early tomorrow.
Tony: It was great to see you. Here's your check, fucker.
Me: Great to see you too, and you're damn right I'm a fucker. Stay safe.
Tony: You too. I'll let you know when I head to the Green Zone.

We hug. The obligatory "stay safe" is odd, like someone saying, "Have a safe flight," as if the passenger has a choice. We have no choice in our safety. An IED on the route could splatter my guts against the Suburban walls and, best case, I live with a colostomy bag for the rest of my life.

The drive back is anticlimactic. The team I'm rolling with does things different. They run a three-vehicle convoy with a "hate truck" following five kilometers behind. If the convoy's attacked, the aptly named "hate truck" can sling bullets at the enemy—spewing hate. They run long-range missions, sans radio communication, so hate truck acts as a mini-QRF which can be used to evacuate the wounded or tow a disabled or tow a disabled vehicle. It's genius.

The road's clear save for two black Mercedes Benz sedans we're approaching. The hair on the back of my neck stands up but everyone else is calm. I pretend to be relaxed. As we pass, I notice the occupants have big beards and body armor tucked under a button-down shirt. They're cool guys on their way to do cool-guy shit. I'm jealous.

CHAPTER 11

Our week in Baghdad turns into four days. Air assets are being diverted for a ground offensive in Fallujah. I have twelve hours to pack for fourteen days and catch a plane. I walk to the Blackwater area to meet new team members. In the short time I was in Sulay and Al Hillah, they created a transient living area in an old hangar and closed our circus tent. I'm glad to be assigned a room behind the pool because it looks like military barracks and smells like a hospital ward. The Baghdad Bug lives on. The new guys consist of:

Jacob: A Recon Marine and the first person here younger than me. He has dark hair and a huge smile; an all-American boy, but he's trying to grow a goatee that no goat would be proud of.

Jason: A former Army helicopter machine gunner. He's in his mid-thirties and smokes like a coal plant. Blond and rugged, he loves two things: porn and Jack Daniels.

Rampage: A former Marine. He's the size of a house with tattoos from his wrists to his…who knows. I don't want to be the one to find out if they reach his thighs. I tell him if he gets shot, there's no way I can drag out his massive frame. He's fine with this.

Andrew: A handsome black former Marine Corps sniper in his late twenties. I immediately fall in love. He's a smart dude, more Yale than grunt, and I'm intimidated by his masculinity.

Vance: Army medic and tanker. The nicest human I've met at
Blackwater and a devout Christian. He's in his early thirties,
soft spoken, and calm. I'm in awe of him.

I look over to see what I think is a man, slumped over a bed frame
with two mattresses stacked on it. He's not breathing but no one cares.
I take note to not care when people are dead in this area. I'm startled
to reality by a jumbo jet landing. Nope. It's the noise coming from this
human porker. He moves, hoists himself to his feet, then flops back on
the bed and stops breathing again. Oh well. Based on his fat content,
he'll make a nice luau pig roast for us later. Then I notice all of him. This
fucking guy has hair all over his body, except his head. Flaps of skin hang
off his back like the titties of an eighty-year-old woman. The fat rolls on
the back of his head and neck look like a package of hot dogs.

Me: Who the fuck is the dead dude?
Jacob: He's a KBR guy. Washes laundry.
Me: Thank God. I was afraid he was on the team.
Jacob: He has sleep apnea. The guy always stops breathing, then
    startles himself awake with a snort so loud it wakes everyone
    up. He dies five times a day. Does the place in Sulay have open
    sleeping areas like this?
Me: No, dude. We're at a hotel. Stop distracting me. I want to know
    more about this pig. Why's KBR in our sleeping area?
Jacob: It's a transient sleeping area. Everyone comes here. He's the
    loudest. Watch him for a while. It's fun. We found him asleep
    on the shitter a couple days ago.
Me: No way.

Jacob breaks out his camera.

Jacob: Here's the picture. We figured it out because he was snor-
    ing so loud.
Me: He was probably pushing out a turd the size of a small child and
    passed out. Can you blame him?

Jacob: Seriously. Every. Damn. Day. I sleep three bunks away from him.

Me: Someone needs to take that hog to slaughter, bro.

Jacob and I are best friends now.

The next day we board a C-130 and sit in the red cargo net seats. I sit next to Matt Marshall and someone takes our picture. The FBI would ask me about this later. We land in Sulaymaniyah. The airport's under construction but hopes to be the connection between the Kurds to the rest of the Middle East. Five armored SUVs are staged for us. There's so much money running through this place, we can land and have two-hundred-and-fifty-thousand-dollar SUVs waiting. It's nuts. I piss on the runway to mark my territory and avoid pissing my pants. Then we drive $1.25 million worth of vehicles north to a hotel in the center of the city. We have an entire floor of a hotel blocked for us. Your tax dollars at work.

We don't bother to check in. We walk to the top floor and take it over. The carpet throughout is pulled surprisingly tight, which makes it the nicest hotel I've ever stayed in. Why do I keep noticing the carpet?

There are fourteen rooms, each with two twin beds, for twenty contractors, including a bomb dog and his handler. We congregate in the master suite to figure out room assignments.

The dog and his handler get one room. Nick gets the master suite, which has a bathroom, a living area complete with a couch and large TV, a small balcony where we set up communication equipment to talk to Baghdad, and a small room like a closet. We also use the master suite for mission planning and watching the only TV channels in English—CNN and the BBC. It's awful. The same news repeats all day.

That leaves twelve rooms for eighteen people. Six get their own room and twelve have roommates. The people in country longest get their own room, which includes Dave and I.

Then something happens where I have an out-of-body experience and volunteer to sleep in the tiny room attached to the master suite so someone can have their own room. What the fuck is wrong with me? I choose to live like a hermit at the nicest hotel I've ever stayed in aside from the Bristol. You can take the trash out of the trailer park but can't take the trailer park out of the trash.

The hotel brings up a mattress and an armoire. It takes up the entire room save for a foot on each side around the mattress. It reminds me of Harry Potter's space under the stairs before he goes to Hogwarts. I regret being gracious, and the living conditions are less than ideal, so I volunteer for every run every day.

We set ground rules. If a door's cracked, you can come into the room. If it's shut, knock. If there's a hanger on the knob, the inhabitant's jerking off. Proceed with caution and a camera.

Dave and I go to the restaurant on the first floor for dinner.

Me: Dude, this menu's in Arabic. I can't read the squiggles.
Dave: Me neither.
Me: I thought you were cultured and shit.
Dave: I speak Korean, German, English, and French, not Arabic.
Me: I speak American, Australian, and English. You only speak one
  more language than me? Cultured my ass.
Dave: Fuck off.

I order chicken kabobs with rice, and he orders something local. We're living the high life. For me it's Miller High Life: the champagne of beers. For him, it's the cultural experience.

***

Like the last mission, we drive to villages in the hinterlands. Many huts are made of mud bricks. Chickens and donkeys roam free. They have electricity but no plumbing, so raw sewage flows between them.

I walk into a dwelling, which has a single light bulb hanging from the ceiling, rugs, and a radio. This is the village elder's house. I radio back letting the others know it's safe for the principal to enter. It occurs to me I'm the canary in the coal mine, sent in to die if it's not safe.

I exit and see a chicken eating the ass out of a dead donkey. Her head is fully engulfed in the anus, pecking away. This isn't hyperbole. The chicken has its face and neck inside a donkey's decaying ass. I take a picture. How do people live like this?

The principal meets the town elder and enters his hut as I walk toward a living donkey. I'm going to ride this bitch. I hand my camera to Robert and tell him to document it for posterity. I get within three feet and it brays. I chicken out.

Robert: Ride that thing.
Me: No way, man. His dick's massive. He'll push me over and fuck me.
Robert: Don't be a pussy.
Me: I'm trying to avoid being his pussy!
Robert: Let me walk over here so it looks like you're close to him.

He takes the picture, which makes me look like I'm close to the donkey without being raped. Good man.

I walk to Matt Marshall, and he asks me to take his picture. There's a mosque with green trim to his left and a lady walking down a hill behind him to his right. Behind him are several red, blue, black, and gray oil barrels on a ledge, while a piece of yellow and red plastic litter is perched on rocks at his feet. I take his picture and hand him my camera. I pose in the same spot, but seconds have passed, so the lady in the red shirt is crossing a make-shift bridge, but the oil barrels in the background and litter in the foreground are the same. That's a lot of detail which the FBI would ask me about later.

There're no military-aged males in this village. It's the same story of regime forces killing all the males. I would've never noticed if the interpreter hadn't mentioned it. Now I can't stop noticing it.

A ten-year-old with developmental disabilities is walking with a crutch made from a piece of curvy wood. An old towel at the top protects his armpit. He obviously has a rough life, but you'd never know it based on his smile. It's contagious. I feel cracks in my face as I break a grin like the Grinch.

***

We return to the hotel. Dave, Jacob, and I decide to walk around town. We're allowed to roam but must be in groups of two or more and carry pistols. It's Thursday. The local market adjacent to our hotel is full. Friday's the Muslim day of worship so they party on Thursday evenings.

I see women. Real women. Tight jeans and sweaters. We stroll around the market looking in shops. Dave sees a rug shop and forces us to stop. He needs a hand-woven rug. He's so refined. I'm sure he has a place picked out for it in his ivory tower.

The shop is ten by twenty feet and has rugs stacked on all walls with a small path in the middle for viewing. The shopkeeper shows us rugs by folding them on top of each other. Dave points to a rug. The man pulls it and lays it on a pile. The rugs are made in Iran. True to form, Dave gives us a lesson about them.

> Dave: You can tell it's hand-woven if you flip it over and the back looks almost identical to the front.
> Me: So why are they so damn expensive?
> Dave: Someone has to spend days and months making them. The top will have a family crest of who made them.
> Me: I can't imagine their hourly rate's high here in Iraq.
> Dave: They're made in Iran.
> Me: Hourly rates can't be high in Iran either.
> Dave: They don't get paid by the hour. They have to dye the wool or silk by hand. Then weave the rug and sell it to merchants.
> Jacob: Why are we in this stupid fucking shop?
> Dave: I'm going to buy a rug, asshole. I want one with a high thread and knot count.
> Me: How do you know that?
> Dave: The knots are at the end of the rug. You can count them. More threads mean more knots. This one is more expensive because it's silk. You can tell because it shines.
> Jacob: Just get your fucking rug so we can scope some ladies.

Dave haggles with the shop owner. He looks at twenty rugs before he finds one good enough for him. He talks me into buying a rug for three hundred dollars because I can sell it in the US for twelve hundred due to the silk inlays and the crest showing who made it. He'd better be right, or I'm going to punch him in the mouth.

We leave our purchased rugs in the shop so we can keep looking at the ladies. We walk three hundred meters down a crowded sidewalk.

Me: Do you love rugs because they're oriental like you?
Dave: Fuck you, Morgan.

I'm going to take this rug home and wow people with my knowledge. Woven by hand in Iran. There's lots of knots in it. They dye the wool to make it different colors. It has silk inlays. I'm cultured.

We're stopped by two girls. They smell like vanilla. I wonder if they're interested in seeing my Harry Potter closet. They aren't but they're interested in taking a picture with Americans.

Jacob and I are six-foot-two white dudes. Dave's a five-foot-eight Asian American. We pose shoulder-to-shoulder with Dave in the middle with a shit-eating grin and wait for them to take a picture. His grin vanishes when he's handed the camera. The girls bull past him, stand in front of Jacob and I, and shoot big smiles. So nice. Dave isn't amused. He takes the picture and the girls walk off giggling.

Dave: Fuck that. I'm American.
Me: The ladies disagree.
Jacob: Did you smell them? This place smells like nothing but they smelled great!
Dave: Fuck you. They should know America has many ethnicities.
Jacob: That smell. Like flowers.
Me: Calm yourself, Dave. Orientals are so dramatic.

We get our rugs and return to the hotel. Everyone's watching CNN as Dave and Jacob go to their rooms. I lay my rug on the floor and tell them about it, the silk, the knots, the handmade shit. No one's impressed. Uncultured rubes.

***

Two weeks in Kurdistan, my pimpled ass. We've been here for sixteen days with no end in sight. We decide to drive to the closest base to get protein powder and edible food since the chicken kabobs and rice aren't cooperating with our digestive systems.

We leave early the next day on the ninety-minute drive to Kirkuk Regional Air Base (KRAB). As we approach, the morning sky lights up with flames from natural gas being burned in the oil fields. It stinks. I'll have lung cancer if we stay for more than two hours. I cash a check since my reserves are low due to my amazing rug purchase. I spend one hundred and fifty dollars on protein bars, protein powder, and American food. We pack up and head back, making a couple stops on the way.

The first stop is the REO in Kirkuk. Nick goes in to kiss ass and we take advantage of the time to head to the chow hall where food is cooked to order. I could live here. It's a small compound with a volleyball court, a great gym, and just enough space to avoid claustrophobia. After lunch we get back on the road. We know we've passed into Kurdistan when we drive through a roadblock consisting of medium-sized rocks in the road and Peshmerga soldiers.

Fifteen miles from our hotel we divert down a dirt road to a US Special Operations outpost. A mile in, I see an LZ and pallets of MREs. These things have no nutritional value but cause constipation, earning them the name "meals refusing to exit." I make a mental note to steal a box.

The compound has a small US military force, Peshmerga soldiers, and dogs. Hell yes. Nothing's pure like a dog. Even in this shithole, the dogs I encounter are happy to get belly rubs. I see one near the house and walk over. He sniffs my hand before I go in for some head pets and ear scratches. He trusts me now, so he rolls over for tummy rubs. I'm stoked, but not as happy as he is. His dong shoots out like red lipstick from a tube. I name him Red Rocket. You know how to get a dog to stop humping your leg? Pick him up and suck his dick. I don't suck his dick, this time. Three litters of puppies overrun the compound. The Iraqis want them gone because they're seen as vermin.

Nick: What're you going to do with these dogs?
Army Special Forces Dude: We'll take them out and let the Iraqis use them as target practice.
Me: The fuck?
SF Dude: We can't have thirty dogs on the compound. They get in our supplies and eat everything. We keep a few to warn us when people are coming.
Nick: Can we have one?

I'm elated. I want all of them. I'll lie down and let them lick my face for hours.

SF Dude: Sure, grab one. We'll kill them off in a couple days.
Me: You guys are savages. How can you be so cold?
SF Dude: Come back for Thanksgiving. We'll have a turkey, a ton of food, and beer. We'd love to have you.
Me: You guys are great humans. I want to have a daughter so you can marry her.
SF Dude: Grab a bag of dog food for the one you pick. You don't want him eating the local food. He'll shit all over.
Me: You're preaching to the choir.

Nick grabs a brown and white dog. This is a horrible idea. We live in a hotel and there's no way to house-train him. He's going to shit all over the tightly pulled carpet. But hell yes. I pet the puppy all the way to the hotel. We're best friends by the time we arrive.

We sneak him up to our floor and everyone's stoked. They spend the next hour playing with him. Then he pisses on the floor. I grab his scruff, rub his nose in it, and put him on the small balcony to show him where to pee. We can't have this dog pissing all over the hotel. I walk in from the balcony, close the glass door, and turn around. Every team member looks at me like they want blood. The dog howls from the balcony. Great timing.

Me: We can't have him peeing on the floor.
Rampage: Fuck that. What's wrong with you?
Me: I sleep here. I don't want it to smell like piss. Feed him dog food. I don't want the room where I beat off smelling like watery shit.

Rampage stands.

Rampage: I'll feed him whatever the fuck I want.

I look at the six-foot-eight, two-hundred-and-eighty-pound monster.

Me: Come on, dude. Please? It's where I sleep. Don't make me whip your ass.
All: Ha ha.

Rampage walks off. The remainder of us debate what to name the dog. The highest number of votes wins.

Andrew: Diablo. He looks like a devil.
Jason: We should name him five-miles. I walked Five-miles today.
Me: That's funny but we may as well name him Awesome.
Jason: Awesome?
Me: Yeah. Jason's fucking Awesome!
Jason: I hate you.
Me: Let's name him Spliff.
Nick: Sulay.
Andrew: I vote for Spliff.
Nick: What's a spliff?
Me: It's a joint. Smoking a spliff?
Nick: We're not naming him Spliff.
Andrew: Let's vote.

Me: Before we do, I have an emotional story why we should name
    him Spliff. When I was a stoner in high school, we found a
    baby bird and named it Spliff. We sent it home with my buddy
    Paul and his cat ate it. We smoked a joint to honor our dead
    bird friend. It was hard on me. This would make it better.
Nick: No.

We vote and Spliff wins. Nick overrides us and names him Sulay.
The pup runs rampant between the rooms to avoid eating dog food.
I walk in Rampage's room (the door is cracked), and he's giving him a
chicken skewer. This is a lost cause. This dog was a bad idea.

The next day we take him to the local veterinarian to get vaccines.
We park on the street near a small storefront and walk in. The vet's
sewing up the asshole of a goat. Why the poor goat's asshole is torn isn't
a question I want answered. I assume his owner fucked him. This isn't
uncommon in Iraq. I'm shocked they have the vaccines. We grab them
and take them to the hotel for our dog handler to administer.

Sulay eventually makes it to the US One of the team members got
our dog handler to sign off that he's a service dog. It cost a ton of money
to get him home. I'm not sure what service the dog possessed. Crapping
on the floor? Stealing food off plates? I'm glad he's able to live a decent
life in the US. He deserves it.

CHAPTER 12

Nick isn't well. The only time I see him is when I walk to the shower through his room. He's grown a beard and hasn't bathed in a week. He smells so bad I'm afraid housekeeping's going to take him out with the garbage.

We're on week four of fourteen days. This is turning into *Gilligan's Island*. Everyone's stir-crazy but Nick's taking it to a new level. The State Department gave us a satellite phone to call home once a week for ten minutes. Each minute costs thirteen dollars and DoS isn't in the business of paying for us to have phone sex at that cost. Nick keeps the phone in his room like a rat hoarding cheese.

I walk in and it smells like a bedpan. Nick's asleep and I don't want to wake him. God knows he could use some beauty sleep. I can't find the phone, so I nudge him.

Me: Hey, man, where's the sat phone?
Nick: Here.

He pulls it from under his body and hands it to me. Yuck, dude. I have to put this on my face.

I've heard Nick talking on the phone late at night. He's married to a Romanian and the conversations aren't gentle. Maybe it's rough phone sex?

Nick: What the fuck do you mean you need more money?... I just sent you cash... What are you spending it on?...

Me: Sorry to interrupt but I need to use the shitter. Can I take a dump?

Nick: Sure… I'll be there soon… Yes, I love you but you're spending a lot of cash. What's it going to?…

I whistle to avoid hearing the conversation.

Nick: Love you too.

I take the phone onto the patio and step in dog shit. Hell yes. The dog's crapping outside. The hotel floor smells like piss and shit so my boot will add to the ambiance.

I call Grandma and Grandpa. They're doing well. It's wonderful to hear their voices. Grandma and I talk while Grandpa listens. At the end of the conversation, he says, "Love you. Bye-bye." This is the best part of the call. My grandfather's the only consistent male in my life worth a damn.

I walk inside in time for our nightly check in. Nick's somehow late although he lives in the congregation room. Rampage wakes him up. He walks out looking homeless. If I were a gorilla, I'd jump him and search for bugs. We all look rough, but he looks like microwaved shit left to cool off on the counter.

We have no runs tomorrow. Just hang out. Jason speaks up.

Jason: Are we going to get out of this place? It's been a month. This is turning into Gilligan's fucking Island.

Nick: I don't know.

Jason: Who knows?

Nick: I have no idea.

Rampage: I didn't join Blackwater to sit on my ass watching CNN and downloading *Bang Brothers* at an excruciatingly slow rate. Can you find out when we go back to Baghdad?

Nick: I haven't heard anything.

Me: Maybe that's because you hang out in your room talking to your wife and squeezing your meat.

Nick: What? Fuck you.

Dave: You've been holed up in there for weeks.
Nick: I'll call down and see. Who wants out of here?

Half the team raise their hands, myself included. Thanksgiving's in a couple days. Nick's upset as he radios down to Baghdad to let them know he has a mutiny on his hands. It'll be a couple weeks to get replacements, but we have hope.

***

The hotel internet is terrible with Rampage downloading sex boat porn, where the girl has sex with a young dude and old dude, and they tell her to wade in the ocean after they're done then drive away. We tell him this is for show, but he refuses to believe it. We've asked him to stop taking the bandwidth, but he has thus far rejected our desires. He's too big to argue with.

Jason has a porn collection Hugh Hefner would envy. He spent his time in Baghdad purchasing every porn video from the DVD kids. Based on his collection, he must've got paid in one-dollar bills and made it rain on them while absconding with their inventory. Jason puts the videos, all one hundred and fifty-plus, in a CD folder. They're categorized: Teen, lesbian, monster-wong, mini-wong, clown porn, midget porn. You want it, he has it.

Jason: Anyone can borrow my porn, but you have to return it before you take another one.
Me: So, if I need to beat my meat to a pornographic version of *Gone with the Wind*, just take it?
Jason: Yes.
Me: Even if you're not here to see what I take?
Jason: Yes.
Me: That's nice. I really don't want you to know what kinky shit I'm into.
Jason: I own it, brother, so you can't be worse than me.
Me: Good point. I'll take *Grandpa Joins a Sorority*.

Jason's like 7-Eleven, always open for business even when there are no customers. He works on the honor system. I realize the end is near when he knocks on my door.

Jason: Do you have my *Old Hippies Fucking* porn?
Me: Gross, dude. Why would you buy that? I can imagine the smell.
Jason: You know who has it?
Me: No, but you never answered my question.

He leaves. The next day he has no choice but to crack down. Someone ruined it for us all. Now if I want a movie, I have to ask. He hands me the porn and replaces it with a name card in the slot where the disc resided. Upon return, he takes the card out, sets it on his end table, and I'm free to choose another. If anyone comes in and their card's in a slot, no porn will be dispensed. It's genius.

***

Thanksgiving's great. I get a three-thousand-dollar bonus for being here. We drive to the special operations compound and, as promised, no puppies. This is sad. Also as promised, they feed us turkey (likely a large chicken as I haven't seen turkey here), all the fixings, and beer. I can't drink because I'm so full, so I sit on a couch and fall asleep.

***

Andrew's smart, handsome, and driven. Instead of watching CNN, he's teaching himself Arabic. He plans to do a six-month contract and then study in Jordan and Syria. He's going places, and I'm honored to know him.

I'm not proud that I had a negative view of African Americans when I was younger. It wasn't conscious. I grew up in a small town with two African Americans in my high school. I heard and repeated racist jokes. When I got older, I worked with Black people, and none of the jokes seemed accurate, but I'd never had a personal relationship with a Black person. Andrew's my first. In a moment of clarity, I decide to make things right. I enter Andrew's room. (The door's cracked.) He's studying Arabic. Show-off.

Me: Hey, man. Have a minute?
Andrew: Sure.
Me: I've never been around Black people. I hate to admit that many
    of the stereotypes I heard growing up resonated with me.
Andrew: Where's this going?
Me: I wanted to say you've broken every stereotype I had. You're
    badass, driven, intelligent, the exact opposite of everything I
    learned in my small town.
Andrew: I appreciate that.
Me: I appreciate it. I'm ashamed.
Andrew: That makes me feel good. I'm glad you told me.

We high-five or something. I leave before it gets intimate. I don't want him trying to make out with me. This is awkward enough.

***

I see Andrew fifteen years later, after he received a graduate degree from Harvard, and he mentions our conversation. It resonated with him, which makes me feel good.

We have a mission. We jump in the vehicles to go to another village. The dirt roads are excruciatingly slow. We've run out of stories, so we start asking hypothetical questions, which always end up as a choice you have to make to save the world or your family. It's ridiculous but we have no other conversation options.

Andrew decides to be the conductor on the crazy train today. We have Dave, Andrew, JR, and me in the lead SUV.

Andrew: If you had to fuck one, would you rather fuck a fat, ugly,
    disgusting girl or a lady man from the Philippines?
JR: Neither.

Me: Agree.

Andrew: No, you have to choose one. The world will end if you don't choose one person to fuck.

Dave: The fat girl.

Andrew: Really?

Dave: If I fuck the dude, I'm gay. I'm not gay so I fuck the chick.

Andrew: Let me reframe the question. The girl's the grossest thing you've ever seen, so fat's she immobile. Pimples all over her body. She smells like an Iraqi trash pile.

Me: The chick.

Andrew: Wait, I'm not done. The dude's a lady man in the Philippines. He has a killer lady body and big fake boobs. You wouldn't know it's a guy until you pulled down his pants.

JR: The girl. Why does the world end?

Andrew: Because it does. Let me get this straight, you'd rather fuck a hose-beast of a woman than a good-looking lady man?

We nod.

Andrew: Fuck that. I'm fucking the lady-man.

Me: So, you're gay?

Andrew: I'm not gay. He looks like a lady and between the two of them, he's more woman than the biological woman.

Dave: But you have sex with a guy, which is gay sex. Hence, you're having a gay interaction and thus gay.

Andrew: No, you don't get it. It's less gross to fuck the dude. So, it's not gay.

Inwardly, I agree. He has a point, but outwardly I can't agree.

Me: You're gay, Andrew. We don't care. You're my boy.

Andrew: Just because you suck my dick doesn't make me gay.

Me: If I wasn't driving, I would suck that hog right now. Get it out.

We laugh as Andrew questions his sexuality. Our job's done. His job's done also.

***

We're off to Baghdad. After six weeks, we've had our fun and our replacements are in flight. We pack our shit and begin the drive to Kirkuk. Dave and I sing "I'm leaving on a jet plane. No word when I'll be back again." I can't wait to get back to Hairy Back Titties and the pool.

Thirty minutes out of Kirkuk, I'm leading the convoy on a four-lane highway with a median strip in the center. We're going seventy mph, travelling in the far-right lane. I notice a BMW going at least one hundred mph in oncoming traffic. It closes in on a car and merges into the other lane to overtake it. The BMW's windows are down, and I think, "The wind must be slapping them in the face pretty hard."

As the BMW shifts, the back-end swerves hard left. The driver overcorrects, and it swerves right. The car moves toward the median, which slopes on both sides into a V shape for drainage. I instinctively brake as the tactical commander bellows on the radio, "Stop the convoy."

The BMW driver overcorrects again and now he's in the median. The car slams into the V and flips in the air with the driver side toward the ground and the passenger side pointing skyward. I should be concerned but it's like I'm watching a movie stunt. This is awesome. I'm ready for the fire and explosions. I'm not sure how, but the vehicle I'm driving stops in the road. I shift it into park.

Dave: Holy fuck.
Andrew: Whoa, man.

As the BMW flips, a doll flies out the back passenger-side window. It lands in front of me. The BMW rolls past us. Another doll is flung out of the driver-side back window onto the side of the road. The car plummets down the steep, rocky embankment.

I'm out of the vehicle. Dave's behind me. The doll in front of us is a three-year-old child. His eyes are open. They're light-colored. Snot pours over his mouth and down his chin. Clear snot.

Me: Medic!

Vance is on him within seconds. I can't look. I run to the second doll. It's a little girl no older than four. She cries.

Me: Holy fuck. This is real!

I'm not talking to anyone aside from myself. I look back at the SUV thirty feet away. Andrew's veiny arm shows a tattoo of a sexy lady in a bikini holding a suppressed pistol and the word "Passion" above her. He's pulling the medical bag from the back of the vehicle, but it's under our bags which make his boobs bounce around as he yanks at the bag. It's a herculean effort to wrench it out but he makes it happen and runs it to Vance, who's giving the first child CPR as Matt Marshall assists.

Four team members run down the embankment to the BMW, Vance cuts the child's pant leg and sets up an IV. He seamlessly inserts the needle into the child's femoral artery. The kid isn't moving. He's ghost-white, his open eyes staring at the sky. Vance rubs his chest to wake him as Matt watches. Vance's good in the pocket.

A pool of blood is near the kid. Five inches in diameter. Dark red against the black asphalt. No blood leads up to it or trails it. The kid's not bleeding. This must be from the driver smashing his head on the blacktop as the vehicle rolled.

Andrew attends to the little girl. She's screaming but unscathed, which is a miracle considering the force that ejected her. The only logical explanation is she was lifted off the seat and deposited on the ground as the driver's side pounded the pavement.

I'm on traffic control. I look down at the puddle of dark blood near me. Blood of the living is bright red. This is nearly black, blood of the dead. Ignore it. Do your job, Morgan.

A man emerges from the embankment. Blood gushes from his head. He won't stop screaming. Really? We're all men here. Screaming isn't helping. The man runs to Andrew and shrieks in his face. Andrew coolly sits him down to stop the blood pouring from his hair to his ear.

Cars and trucks are stopped on both sides of the highway to rubberneck. Jacob and Jason are at the back of the convoy pushing traffic through. Dave motions cars around our SUVs. I wave them forward.

A car stops near Dave. "Go, motherfucker," he yells and slaps the hood so hard it leaves a dent. The driver stares at him in disbelief. I have no idea why my vision is so zoned in, but I see everything up close. The car passes me, and I gesture for them to keep going as they try to get a look at the injured boy. I'm with Dave on this one. Go, motherfucker.

I look back. Four team members lug a body up the embankment on a blanket. The man's brains are hanging out of his scalp. It looks like someone caved in his skull with a bowling ball. Worms escaping a hole. They lay him on the ground and cover him with the blanket. I assume this was the driver. Based on the pool of blood, I'm standing next to his last conscious thought, his last moment of life. That's a hoot. I want to rip the blanket off the driver and kick him in the balls for driving like an asshole.

The bleeding man sits on the dirt crying. He's in shock. Andrew's done a heck of a job wrapping a bandage around his head and tying it in the front like an adorable little bloody bow. His screaming is replaced by two crying women. Andrew and some of the other team members keep them away from the kids so the medics can work.

Shut those ladies up. Fuck sake. Their screaming causes people to slow down to see what's going on. Keep driving, asshole. Nothing to see here. Okay, there is, but not for you.

Peshmerga forces, the local Kurd army, arrive in a truck with a Red Crescent ambulance, the Islamic equivalent of the Red Cross. The Peshmerga truck will escort us to the hospital in Kirkuk. Vance loads the unconscious boy in the back and Matt joins him holding the IV bag. The truck's in front of my vehicle. I jump in the driver's seat and we hit the road. I assume the Peshmerga will collect the body. As I follow the truck, I see Vance working on the kid for the thirty-minute ride. *Please God, keep him alive until we reach the hospital.* Half an hour's a long time when life's on the line.

We arrive at the hospital. Vance cradles the child and Matt holds the IV bag as they jog into the building. We conduct an AAR.

> Andrew: No fucking kit on the med bag. I couldn't get it out.
> Me: Dude, I watched you pull it out like a porn star. It was straight up retard strength.
> Andrew: Thanks, man. That was hard. Our gurneys were under it and there was no way to them.
> Nick: Everyone did a great job. We figured out what needed to be done and did it. That was awesome.
> Me: I need a smoke. Jason, hook a brother up.
> Jason: You don't smoke.
> Me: I do today. If you had a crack pipe, I'd take a hit.

We break up into small group conversations. I think, fuck politicians who say video games desensitize kids to violence and death. Nothing prepares a person to see death that close. Especially kids. They're too innocent for this.

Vance and Matt walk out ten minutes later. We fall quiet, hoping for good news but fearing bad.

> Jason: Is the boy going to make it?
> Vance: I doubt it. The hospital isn't well equipped. He had a pulse when we left, but he's unconscious.
> Me: Fuck that. He's going to make it.
> Vance: I give him a five percent chance.
> Andrew: He's going to make it.
> Jacob: The little girl okay?
> Vance: She'll be fine.
> Me: As will the boy.
> Vance: Well…
> Me: Shut it.

We don't need any more negativity today, Vance. I must assume the little boy is alive. In my head he's a doctor in Kirkuk treating and saving sick children. He's married, owns a farm, and has children. He speaks glowingly about how Americans saved his life. Yep. That's his story.

We're somber as we drive through the hospital gate. We know we'll never learn what happened to the boy. That hurts. His eyes look at me when I don't want to see them. Clear snot all over his little face. Brain fluid. That makes him real when he appears in my dreams.

We joke about death. We know there's a chance none of us makes it home outside of a shiny metal coffin. It's not personal but this is an exception. This death is personal. I don't want to think about it. I refuse to talk about it.

CHAPTER 13

aghdad feels like home. I go to my room behind the pool with sand-bags stacked eight feet high around it. Home. My sheets are bloody from my athletes' foot. That feels like forever ago. Home. My own shower. So nice. I take the hottest shower a five-gallon water tank can give. Home.

The water flows down by body in slow motion, face, chest, stomach, thighs, feet, washing off the trauma of the day. I need a dog to pet. Dogs make everything better. Unconditional love.

I dress and sit on the step to my room. Crisp air fills my lungs. It's early December. I hear explosions. It's fine. I hear people at the pool partying. It's fine. I'm not sure how to feel. Should I cry? My sister tells me a good cry is cathartic. I try but can't squeeze out a tear. I call my Aunt Shirley from my shitty cell phone using a card granting me thirty minutes of time, which translates into no more than seven minutes for international calls.

Me: How's everything?
Shirley: Good. I saw on the news there was a big bomb today.
Me: I didn't hear it.
Shirley: I hope you're safe.
Me: Me too. It's been calm as far as I know.

A bomb explodes in the background but it's far enough away that I don't bother with it. I need a taste of home. Aunt Shirley's level-headed, which is why I called.

Me: Did you hear that?

Shirley: No. Is everything okay?

Me: I don't know. It's getting better. Don't watch the news. It makes it seem like this is a war zone. I'm safe. Just needed a voice tonight.

Shirley: Okay. We love you.

No reason to tell her about the crash. She wouldn't understand. Her voice helps even though it doesn't, if that makes sense.

I hang up, content in my thoughts. I should start smoking. No idea why, other than it seems like the right thing to do. I hear a meow and see a gray cat. I reach down to pet him. He doesn't let me. It's fine. I don't need a rabies shot.

After a couple nights sitting on my step, pondering everything and nothing, he becomes my best friend. I name him Mr. Mittens after he lets me pet him, which only happens after I butter him up with tuna from the PX.

He's sweet. I pet his head. He purrs. I pet his body. He purrs. He does the thing where he walks under my hand, so I stroke him from head to tail. He purrs. I feel the vibration on my palm when all I feel is numb.

I have a stockpile of tuna packs, which come with crackers, mayo, and a nice mint to freshen fishy after-breath. I eat the crackers and feed Mr. Mittens tuna one piece at a time as I pet him. I cut a water bottle near the base and fill it for him. I love his purrs. I'm not a cat person. Somehow his purring cuts through my depression.

I walk to the Blackwater tent for our evening briefing. I'm early so I look through the care packages. One has a flea collar, which I put in my pocket for Mr. Mittens. The idea is for soldiers to wear flea collars to keep bugs off. It's loveable but absurd. I've never seen anyone wearing one. I keep digging in the box looking for a treat but finding random shitty candy. The box has been rat-fucked. Tropical Fruit Jolly Ranchers should never be sent to a combat zone. The local kids won't fight over them.

After our meeting I walk to the PX for tuna. It has Tinactin in stock. Great. Just in time not to help. I buy protein powder and every tube of

Tinactin out of spite and walk back to my room. The five-hundred-Man Camp is open, and I have keys to a room, but I prefer living behind the pool. Mr. Mittens is there. I'm not leaving.

I crack a tuna pack and we have dinner. He's getting fat. This is good. He was thin when we met. I've transformed him into a cat none of the other cats will fuck with. He's the cat that kicks sand in the faces of lesser cats. I'm proud. I feel more connected to this stupid cat than I do to my family.

After a week, Mr. Mittens disappears. He fucking ghosted me. He must've found another sugar daddy with legit ahi, seared. I'm depressed. I walk to the pool and see Jack. He's getting serious with his war pig. We sit in chairs under a tent and talk. His lady-friend thinks it's adorable that I miss a stray cat.

I see Mr. Mittens under a shrub tree. I run to him and he hisses. I refuse to believe it's him until I see the collar. It's him. What the fuck, Mr. Mittens? This is why I'm a dog person. Mr. Mittens runs deeper into the shrub. I'll refuse to be rejected so I get down on my hands and knees and crawl to him. He's being an asshole. Hissing. Hair up. I'm genuinely hurt.

I duck under a branch and see him protecting a litter of kittens. He wasn't getting fat from the tuna. He's a she who was knocked up, using me as a tuna supplier. I understand how it feels to be a guest on *The Maury Povich Show*. I'm not the father but I've been paying child support for weeks. I never picked up Mr. Mittens so how would I know his sex? Should have looked for balls. Thank goodness he wasn't a hooker, or I'd have gotten a chance to answer Andrew's question.

I walk to a pallet of water, grab a bottle, and do the walk of shame to my room. I get a tuna packet and return to the tree, cut the water bottle in half, and fill it to the brim with water. I filet the tuna pack, set it next to the water and leave. Fucking cat stole my heart.

I never see Mr. Mittens again. She was probably euthanized. Traps around the compound lure stray animals to be killed. She ignored them because I was feeding her. Breaks my heart. Oh well. It's a cat. I'm a dog person. Does the life of an animal really matter here?

GUNS, GIRLS, AND GREED

***

All Blackwater contractors are summoned to the helicopter hangar. If it's everyone, it's important. Maybe we'll be fired. Naw, can't be. The State Department has no way of tracking what we do. No rules. No laws. No oversight. It's intoxicating for a twenty-four-year-old young man garnering a huge salary with no adult supervision.

The hangar's situated near the west gate of the Green Zone, a twenty-minute walk from the pool. It's dusk, a beautiful night for a lonely walk. This may be the most isolated place on earth, but I've grown to enjoy the solitude.

Sixty of us huddle in the hanger talking war. We congregate with our teams. I don't know many people as most of my team is still in Kurdistan and our ranks have exploded in the last couple months. I talk to Dave as we wait.

> Me: I may have to move to the man-camp. That was a long walk.
> Dave: Yeah, we have a fire every night and started a no-limit Texas Hold 'Em tournament.
> Me: The food's better at the embassy. What the fuck is Texas Hold 'Em?
> Dave: You should stay there for the food. Texas Hold 'Em is a card game. It's a sixty-dollar buy-in.
> Me: Sixty bucks! No way I'm paying that.
> Dave: You win it back if you know the card combinations.
> Me: Card combinations? I don't even know how to match my belt and shoes.
> Dave: I can teach you.
> Me: My grandpa told me Las Vegas equals lost wages.
> Dave: It's all about probability.

Someone yells and the sound echoes off the metal walls. We look over to see the man, the myth, the legend, Erik Prince, the big kahuna of Blackwater, walking over. Wow. I've never seen him in person. He's shorter than I envisioned but looks stalky. He wears casual clothes made by name brand companies I can't afford. Wait. I can afford them now. He looks sharp.

Erik: Men.

I stand a little taller, suddenly feeling like a man.

Erik: I wanted to get you together to tell you what an amazing job you're doing. There's no way State could do it without you. It's an important job, a dangerous job, and you execute it perfectly each day.

Fuck yes, I do!

He speaks to us for five minutes and I get bored. I have the attention span of a goldfish. I look around the hangar at the frame holding the walls and roof. An explosion jolts me conscious. I watch Erik Prince run like a cockroach toward a bunker as his security surrounds him. The rest of us stand tall. This is a nightly occurrence.

The irony is suffocating: The man who furnishes bodyguards in combat has bodyguards running him to safety. It's not lost on the crowd. Debris rains on the roof like sprinkles on an ice cream cone—a normal night in Baghdad. When the big boss doesn't reappear, we break the meeting and walk back to our rooms.

I'm alone. Everyone walked to the man-camp as I made a line to the embassy. My radio chirps with my new team leader's voice attempting to confirm we're alive. He's new to country and retired Army so he has control issues.

Team Leader: Status check.
Dave: Dave's up.
Me: Morgan's up.
Will: Will's up.

Once every team member has confirmed life, he tells us, "Report to the team tent at zero eight hundred tomorrow." Fuck. He uses military time. That's a bad omen.

***

I'm assigned to Templar 24. It's been five months and I haven't shot at anyone. Bummer. A new team means bitch jobs until we latch onto a mission. Our first run is driving US congressmen around the Green Zone. We don't bother to wear body armor, which means it's a shit detail.

We drive to the landing zone where we met Erik Prince the day prior before he ran off like Huckleberry Finn. It called LZ Washington and it's where helicopters land in the Green Zone. We pick up a congressman who landed at BIAP but was too important to drive Route Irish to get here. He has an entourage of five minions. I'm driving the limo so I have to wear a collared shirt and can't cuss. I'm sporting my least sweat-stained John Deere hat and shave to look extra nice. The congressman gets in the Suburban with his minions.

Minion: Who are these people driving us?
Congressman: They're security contractors.
Minion: Who hires them?
Congressman: State Department. They're usually prior military. Are you prior military?
Me: Yes, sir.

At least the congressman acknowledges I exist while talking about me.

Minion: They're State Department?
Congressman: No. (To me) How old are you, young man?
Me: Twenty-four.
Congressman: (To his minion) I would venture to guess the young man driving us today is making more than you and I combined.

I smile as we drive to the parliament building and park. While the congressman and his minions are inside, the contractors stand around the vehicles shooting the shit. Every conversation consists of one of three topics: Sex, alcohol, or poop. This one consists of sex and alcohol. The main character's Cole. He's a former Navy SEAL, well-spoken, and a massive human.

Cole: I went to Amsterdam on leave.

Me: Did you go to the red-light district where ladies dance in the window?

Cole: Come on. I went to the nice place.

Me: Levels of hookers? Nice.

Cole: They sit me in a leather recliner and in walk twenty women wearing bikinis. I can pick one or all of them. This one girl catches my eye, Vietnamese. Gorgeous.

Me: You got yellow fever.

Cole: You're an idiot.

Me: It's yellow fever because she's Asian. Get it?

Cole: I get it. Anyway, I choose her, and we go to a big room, lit with candles, red satin sheets. She blows me for a few minutes to get me nice and hard, like so hard a cat couldn't scratch it. I'm lying on a pillow. She stands, completely undresses and crawls up my legs. I have no idea why, but I have to strike up a conversation.

All: ?

Cole: I know, but I have to say something. She's holding my cock and squatting, inches from me being inside her, but I must make conversation. I say, "So you're from Vietnam?"

Her: Yes.

Cole: She's so close. My cock is on her lips. I'm almost inside. I have to continue the conversation, so I say, "What part?" She leans forward, eight inches from my face and says, "The place *you bombed.*"

Everyone's shocked and amused. My mouth's wide open.

Cole: My dick went limp so fast. It fell over. I couldn't fuck her. I
 paid and left.
Me: Why'd you ask?
Cole: No idea.

We get the call on the radio to pick up our principals and drive to
the Crossed Swords. If you google Saddam Hussein, you'll see a video
or picture of him at the parade grounds of the Crossed Swords. It's an
architectural marvel.

The base of each monument is filled with Iranian solider helmets
from the Iran/Iraq conflict. They rise to make a brass hand, molded after
Saddam's hands, holding a silver sword. The opposite side has the same
structure and the swords form an arch over a four-lane road. The same
structure is at the opposite end. Tanks, missiles, and soldiers marched on
the road as Saddam fired a shotgun into the air. In his head he was an
ace predator watching his military cross the parade grounds, feeling the
breeze in his mustache as he smoked a cigar. If I were a chick, I'd ride
that flavor-saver for hours before being beaten to death with an electric
cord. I'm classy.

The congressman walks around getting a tour from an army general.
Part of the dog-and-pony show is illustrating how safe Iraq is so we don't
protect him as we would if we were OTW. The politics of losing wars is
not lost on me. Dave and I walk to where Saddam used to stand. Dave
pops in a cigar and waves his arms in the air holding an M-4, like an
Asian Saddam minus the facial hair since he can't grow a mustache. I do
the same and we take pictures.

I want a helmet from the base of the swords. When the principal's
out of sight, I climb the monument and try to pry one loose. An Iraqi
guard comes over and blasts me with not-English.

Me: I want a helmet.
Guard: %^&$%#$#^^#&#^#&.

I get down.

Me: Speak American, bro. I can't understand you.

The guard climbs up the base of the swords.

Guard: $%#^&#%#$$^$.
Me: Grab me one and I'll pay you for it.

I point to a helmet, pull out twenty dollars, and wave it at him.
The guard smiles and hands me a helmet.

Guard: (Arabic) Fuck yes!

The other Blackwater guys reach for their wallets willing to pay twenty dollars to steal a part of history. This isn't the guard's first time doing this. He knows where the loose helmets are. These fuckers will do anything for a few bucks. I want to think they need the cash for their families, but I doubt it. They know they'll be fucked when the US leaves, so they try to make a couple bucks before being blown to bits in a war to save a government that doesn't give two-shits about them. As a PMC, I understand it.

Dave gets a picture of the team at the monument with a sign saying, "Go Jumbos" for his Tufts University alumni magazine. We drive to LZ Washington to drop off our principals and their minions. Feeling snooty I think, *I make more than that minion.* Fuck him. I bet he went to Bowdoin.

CHAPTER 14

I wake up stoked to go on a mission to Camp Liberty. I'm hungover from a pool party the night prior and a greasy Burger King value meal sounds great. As an aside, the people who never see combat get the creature comforts of Burger King and coffee stands while the rest of us share tuna with Mr. Mittens. Four of us are tasked to escort Michael Bolton. The dude can sing and play saxophone. I can't wait to smell his curly locks. It's a thirty-hour gig so I pack a bag with four days of clothes—this isn't my first rodeo. We fly over on the little birds, the Blackwater helicopters painted blue with a white stripe.

The little bird pilots are former special operations dudes and they're legit. The Blackwater helicopters look badass because they are painted distinctly different from the US military helicopters and are known to maneuver in small spaces. I walk to the LZ sporting a baby beard and long hair. I'm trying to look the part of a Blackwater BAMF.

I'm assigned to the lead little bird. The pilot shows me how to tether in by hooking a carabiner to the back of my vest and latching it to a metal loop on the frame. I can stand on the skids, the metal pipes the helicopter sits on, and lean out. Good gunners can lean out to a ninety-degree angle facing the ground, and direct accurate fire. I'm not a good gunner. I sit down and hold my John Deere hat hoping it won't fly off.

We land at Camp Liberty and an Army Private First Class (PFC) comes to the LZ to escort us. He looks at me like I'm special. I look at him, one eye closed, trying to figure out where I can get Gatorade for my hangover.

PFC: How's the hunting?

Me: Do you have Gatorade?

PFC: I'll grab you one. How's the hunting?

Me: I'm not sure who you think I am. We protect diplomats. Is the Gatorade cold? Green's my favorite.

PFC: I know who you are. How's the hunting?

Me: Great, dude. It's great. Hunting's amazing.

PFC: Nice. I knew it. I'll get you a Gatorade. We have red or orange.

Me: Red sounds good.

PFC: The guy over there is Charlie Daniels. He's waiting for a bird.

He points to a bearded chubby guy in a flak vest. It's Charlie-Fucking-Daniels. I grab the team and we run to get a picture with him. He gives us dog tags with his name on them and is sweet as pie. He's on a USO tour, headed to another base for a performance. He's a patriot. If we're hunting fiddle players, I've succeeded in my mission. Now we're off to hunt and protect a dude with a saxophone.

We get into vehicles and wait for Michael Bolton. Mike. Mikey. We're going to be on first name basis. We see him. The dude hasn't aged well. He's old with glasses and a mustache.

Me: What the fuck? That can't be Michael Bolton. Where's his sax, the perm?

Cole: *John* Bolton, not Michael Bolton.

Me: Who?

Cole: He's a national security advisor to the President, works at the U.N.

Me: But we met Charlie Daniels and shit?

Cole: Don't ask him to play us a song, please.

Me: I think I'll ask him to get on his knees and play my skin flute.

Cole: Shut up.

Me: Come on. That's funny.

We ferry John Bolton around to different palaces so he can get his bean-bag kissed by generals who tell him we're winning the war. Hans Christian Andersen predicted this in his 1837 parable "The Emperor's New Clothes."

At the end of the night John Bolton gets to stay in a mansion while we're directed to a small house with mattresses on the floor, no sheets. It's next to a canal and animal cages, which make it an ideal breeding ground for mosquitoes. This is where Saddam kept his tiger collection. We turn on the AC and eat MREs. Of course, the conversation turns to sex, poop, and alcohol. Nothing will beat Cole's Vietnamese hooker story, but George tries.

George is a former infantryman with curly hair and a baby gut. His brain works only on logic, excluding morality. It's refreshing. In one breath he can compare Plato's *Allegory of the Cave* to modern political leadership. The next, he's talking about how he sold weed until he was seventeen years and 364-days-old to buy an apartment complex in Missouri. He stopped dealing to avoid severe criminal penalties. He's Harvard brilliant with no morality clouding his thought process.

George: I love hookers. I've got a rotation.

Me: How does this work?

George: I bring her in, we have a nice dinner. We fuck. She leaves. I treat them nice.

Me: How do you find a hooker stateside? It's illegal, right?

George: Escort services. They advertise as escorts but they're hookers. I've had to go through a lot to find my rotation of four.

Me: You call a number in the newspaper?

George: They run ads in papers and online.

Me: Not in Cottonwood. Tell me more.

George: Some come in with attitude. I hate that. I try to make them cry. Don't come to my place and act all hot shit. You're hot and all, but you're a hooker.

Me: Make them cry?

George: Yeah. I say stuff like, "I bet you were the prom queen. Look at you sucking my dick. I didn't go to prom. Here you are sucking me off to money. What would your dad think if he saw you doing this? You're so much better looking than me."

Me: Brutal, man.

George: Don't come to my house to fuck me for money thinking you're hot shit.

I'll remember this—hot hookers have an attitude—and reiterate it to a friend. To his folly, he won't listen, and we'll get the shit beat out of us as icing on the cake.

We drop John Bolton at BIAP the next day. We stand in a row behind the engines as he boards a C-17. He's fully clothed but may as well be naked, as the sycophants dressed in US military uniforms congratulate him on the success of the war. I suck exhaust into my lungs as he walks to the plane. He takes time to shake the hand of every contractor protecting him.

Bolton: Thank you. I appreciate what you did for me.

Please leave so I can stop breathing in exhaust fumes.

Me: Thank you, sir.

I'm genuinely touched by his words even if it means lung cancer. Most people we protect look at us like we're primates who should be kept in the big-cat cages we slept near last night. It's nice to be treated like a human.

We're told to bring one of the Suburbans back to The Green Zone by latching on to an Army convoy later which sucks because we're exhausted. We could easily bomb down Route Irish and be home in twenty minutes but a one vehicle convoy is asking for trouble. It's eleven p.m. when we arrive at a base within a base within the base where all the generals are losing the war. We pull up to a gate and Air Force Security Forces E-3 stops us.

Me: Don't worry guys, I speak Security Forces. I got this.

Will: We'll all act like you're a bad ass. You're secret's safe with my indifference.

Me: You cut me deep. As a Marine I assumed you're the reason tubes of tooth paste have instructions. These guys scored high enough on their ASVAB to join the Air Force. Plus, I have an active Air Force ID card since I'm still in the National Guard.

Andrew: Vouch for us Morgan! Thank you for your service.

We get to the gate, I show them my military ID, and they look at me funny. Why's an Air Force Staff Sergeant with a beard and long hair driving an armored Suburban? It's secret squirrel shit. They let us pass, tell us to check in with the convoy commander, and we drive 300 meters to a huge line of vehicles.

Me: Are you kidding me? Is this the line to fuck Will's mom?

Will: Ha. That was funny. I'm too tired for a comeback which is what I give your mom nightly.

I park and, after my hubris of pretending to know what to do, Andrew tells me to figure out what we're doing. I walk a line of vehicles with trailers filled with food, water, gas, and other shit to support the war. I find a crowd and meet a bald US Army Sergeant First Class (SFC) trying to wrangle US military, local nationals, and random people like us. Poor bastard. He's tasked with coordinating a supply route across multiple bases throughout Baghdad. I'm no help.

Me: Hey dude. Who's in charge of this cluster fuck?

SFC: Me.

Me: When do we leave and where do you want us?

SFC: Who are you?

Me: I'm Morgan.

SFC: Morgan?

Me: I was told to get in the convoy to The Green Zone. After that, I'll be out of your hair?

SFC: Are you on the manifest?

Me: (we're not) Of course. What vehicle do I need to follow?

SFC: I don't see you on the manifest.

Me: I'll investigate that and get back to you. Just need to run Irish, get through the gate, and we'll take it from there. When do we jam out?

SFC: No idea. Get in line and we roll when we roll. Make sure I get your manifest and where you drop so I can track it.

Me: In line? Is there a convoy leaving soon?

He points to the line I walked by.

SFC: That's it.

Me: You mean the target I just walked past? That's a traffic jam waiting to be ambushed.

SFC: That's the convoy.

Me: Fuck. I'll tuck in behind a gas truck so we can drive through the ambush like Batman.

SFC: Tuck in where you can. Just get me a manifest and where you'll drop out.

Me: Deal. When we hit The Green Zone, I'll let you know we're RTB (Return to Base but it means we've arrived) so you can track us.

SFC: Deal.

I can't believe he buys this but he doesn't care. It's a shit show and he's counting days before going home. He's playing me like a violin and I'm playing him like a skin flute. I walk to the Suburban.

Me: We're fucked.

Will: Why?

Me: We're going to be in this shit show of a convoy driving negative three miles per hour on Irish.

Andrew: Fuck that. When do we leave?

Me: Does it matter when we depart? Say your prayers and write a letter home telling your family you died a hero driving the most bombed route in Iraq behind a food truck.

Andrew: A food truck?

Me: Where do you want us to get in the convoy? Behind a fuel truck? Is a fiery death better than one behind a truck transporting chicken nuggets?

Andrew: Yes.

Me: I think I get your point. A death engulfed in flames is more manly than one where we die covered in hotdogs.

Will: We're going to die.

Andrew: Don't worry. No one cares unless a soldier dies.

Will: Morgan, tuck in behind an Army vehicle.

Me: Will do. Once we hit The Green Zone, I'm going to cut loose of the convoy to the Man Camp. I told the Army dude I'd let him know when they stage but I'm exhausted. I'll drop you guys off then park.

I drive toward the front of the convoy and tuck the nose of the Suburban between two military trucks. We try to sleep for the next three hours as the convoy prepares to move. This reminds me why I hated being in the military.

Someone knocks on window and jars me awake. It's a random Army PFC. I crack one eye trying to avoid the blazing lights behind him.

Me: What's up dude?

PFC: We're ready to roll out. I didn't see you on the manifest.

Me: We just dropped it off a couple minutes ago.

PFC: Roger that. We leave in fifteen mikes.

Mikes equal minutes and I'm bummed the PFC didn't have a snooze to push. We're exhausted.

Andrew: Do you think it's best we don't show on the manifest? Death and stuff.

Me: I did a cost benefit analysis just now in half a second. If we get on the manifest, we'll have to drive to every base in the Green

Zone until we hit the embassy. Then we'll have to check out. This will add ninety minutes on our trip and I'm tired out.

Will: We're ghosts.

Me: The plan is to hit the gate and jam out and get some sleep. If we're on the manifest and don't check out, they'll do a search party. It will make international news as we snooze—I'm a poet and didn't know it. Then we'll be woken up to explain it.

They agree. It's too late to disagree. There are over seventy-five vehicles in this convoy. That's 1.3 percent probability we're hit. I'll take those odds notwithstanding the variable of Big Army firepower in the form of Hummers and light assault vehicles (LAVs) I see lined up to protect the convoy.

We start the slog to the Green Zone going ten mph. Big Army's blocked off the exits to local traffic but that doesn't mean they searched the road for bombs.

Will: We're dead.

Me: Yep. Sorry guys. Should have put us on the manifest.

Andrew: Stuff your ID card up your ass so they can identify your charred remains.

We laugh. Death is hilarious as a coping mechanism.

It takes us an hour to drive to a route that normally take seven minutes. As we pass the gate, I split from the convoy and drive to our beds.

Me: We live! I'll drop you off at the Man Camp.

Andrew: We can take our ID cards out of our ass now?

Will: You can but I put mine in long ways. Anyone want to help me get it out? I'm down for a prostate massage.

Me: That reminds me of a joke.

Them: (Audible groans).

Me: Fuck off. Two deer hunters go out early in the morning after a long night of drinking. One stops to take a shit against a tree and falls asleep. The other kills a deer, guts it, and looks over to see his buddy asleep against the tree so he puts the deer guts under him as a joke and goes to camp. Two hours later the sleeping hunter returns to camp and says "Dude, I fell asleep taking a dump against a tree and woke up to see I shit my guts out."

The other hunter asks "What'd you do?"

(I raise two fingers) The sleeping hunter holds up two fingers and says "Thanks to the grace of God and these two fingers, I got 'em back in."

We laugh as I drop them at the Man Camp and drive to my room behind the palace. Our calculated risk paid off as we arrived before the sun rose so we can doze off for a few hours.

***

This silliness illustrates how PMCs don't play nice in combat operations. Rules don't apply. It also shows the inefficiencies of the military in combat, which led to outsourcing logistics and PMCs—needing them to feed the military men and women conducting operations. There's no panacea, but PMCs have become a government line-item which passes with each budget. It deserves scrutiny.

CHAPTER 15

'm ordered to leave my hooch behind the pool and move to the five-hundred-Man Camp so we're all together. It's a gay porn set, bare-chested dudes walking around in tiny shorts. The chow hall has a no-shirt-no-eggs policy. I blame Will, our tactical commander, for this. He's legit, a former Marine who's been contracting for a couple years. He's a solid hunk of muscle from head to toe like an alligator. When we're not working, he's getting jacked in the gym or obtaining a great tan. Men want to be him, and men want to be fucked by him. I assume women do too, but we live in a sausage party.

Our team leader's a retired Army sergeant major, who spent twenty-five years in the Army, never deployed in combat, and is used to being envied and obeyed by soldiers. He's a shit leader but his experience allows him to take over a team within days of arrival. I don't know his name because he wants to be called Sergeant Major, which is an indicator that he's trash. He proves this on the mission plan for Templar 24's first run. We do three hours of preparation for this five-minute run. He's great at planning. We have seventy-five contingency plans. As far as I'm concerned, the only contingency plan worth a shit is trust your team.

I'm driving. I know where we're going because I've done a map recon, know the area, and I'm the Rain Man of driving—if I've been on the route, I'll remember it forever. It's a gift limiting my brain capacity. I can recall a route from my childhood but not where I left socks in my room because I only have so much room in my brain. We're staged at the northern gate of the Green Zone. An Iraqi policeman pushes open the gate. Go time. I smash the gas and we roll. Sergeant Major's pissed. Over the radio we hear,

Sergeant Major: Why're we moving? No one rolls until I say we roll.

I stop the Suburban halfway between the Green Zone and the Red Zone.

Will: Can we roll?
Sergeant Major: Roll out.
Me: (Looking at Will.) What the fuck?
Will: (Shrugs.) Let's roll.

We begin our run and need to make a U-turn as part of the route. The new drivers aren't hip to the abrupt stops and the limo smashes into the back of us. That hurt. That hurt bad. We pull off to the shoulder and assess the damage. The limo's radiator impacted with its engine and it's dead. Awesome. We're in a shit area waiting to be attacked. I'm beyond pissed. Will calls for us to set a parameter so we can tow the vehicle. I back my Suburban to the limo and latch the tow straps. We're ducks. No, we're worse than ducks. We're five kilometers from the Green Zone with a dead vehicle. We're sacrificial lambs.

I get in my vehicle and hit drive but the dipshit in the limo has his in park. We don't move. I'm dead. I may as well go for it. I yell at Mario:

Me: Get in the driver seat. I'm going out.

Mario jumps in as I run to the limo and tell the diver to put it in neutral.

Me: Don't touch shit. Just steer.

Will's taken command because Sergeant Major's sitting in the follow vehicle barking orders over the radio from safety. Will's keeping traffic at a distance as we unfuck ourselves. An Army convoy shows up behind us as if it's the pot of gold at the end of a rainbow. Like a leprechaun, he walks to them, explains who we are, and asks for them to escort us to the Green Zone.

Will jumps on the side of a Hummer as it merges ahead.

Will: They got us. Jump on the side.
Me: Just hang off the hummer?
Will: Why not? (On the radio). Follow the lead Hummer to the gate. We'll figure it out from there.

I grab on the side of the Army Hummer and we lurch toward the gate. This feels real. I'm an Air Force weenie hanging off the side of a hummer in Iraq like it's normal. The wind hits my face and pushes my long hair back like the ears of a Labrador. I realize I'm not wearing a helmet but it's too late. We limp the convoy back to the Green Zone and the Army escort leaves. After a few pictures, we tow the disabled limo back to our compound. Such a cool experience.

Sergeant Major says we need to have an AAR. Fair enough.

Sergeant Major: Who the fuck started leaving before I gave the okay?
Me: Me.
Sergeant Major: Why?
Me: The Iraqi police opened the gate. Seemed like the time to drive.
Sergeant Major: No one drives until I give the okay.
Me: Sounds good. Are we just ignoring the other shit that happened?
Sergeant Major: We performed as planned.
Will: Okay…

Sergeant Major drones on about what we could do better and how to prepare for our next run ignoring he did nothing to help. It's not a battle I want to fight. If he wants to be the guy to tell us when to stop and go, what to pack, what to look for, that's fine. He can play control freak all day. I'm leaving soon and will be assigned to a new team when I return.

On our next run, again I drive lead and Will's TC. The Iraqi policeman opens the gate. I stay put.

128

Will: Go man.
Me: Nope. Vag maj will have a fit.
Will: Ha. Okay.

We wait thirty seconds. The radio crackles.

Sergeant Major: Why aren't we moving?
Will: We're waiting on your word.
Sergeant Major: Go. I shouldn't have to tell you to go.
Me: You told us at the last AAR to wait for your call.
Sergeant Major: Just go.

I wink at Will as we drive. We complete the mission and Sergeant Major says we need to have an AAR. He can't fathom doing anything outside of Army regulations. It's pathetic.

Sergeant Major: Why didn't you go when the IP opened the gate?
Me: I was waiting on your orders, dude.
Sergeant Major: Don't call me dude. I was speaking to Will.
Will: We were waiting for your orders.
Me: I told you, dude. Sorry. I told you, bro.

He's seething but I don't care. I have a solid reputation as a guy who can drive and TC. He's been here a week and our first mission's a fiasco. I don't trust him. No one does but someone needs to be the asshole, and that's my MO. I set a plan in motion to overthrow this dried up pussy.

***

Most Blackwater employees fall into two categories: old people here to make money and willing to deal with bullshit for a buck, or former enlisted Army and Marines who are used to being bossed around and comply…also for a buck. I'm an exception. I'm a Lazy Air Force Fuck and don't mind getting under people's skin when they make life difficult. I'm here for adventure and prefer to be left alone. The special forces keg is tapped and most Blackwater contractors are dudes like me but older and afraid to die. The fallacy of Blackwater being BAMF's, with me as an exception, is dead. I'm a cog in a corporate wheel. I'm an asshole who refuses stupidity. I have a life ahead of me and can wear a "Combat Veteran" hat to the Veteran's Day parade. I have nothing to prove but my mettle.

I grab Dave and tell him I'm going to the higherups to let them know Sergeant Major's a fuck stick. I can't deal with his insanity. He agrees to back me. We march to the tactical operations command center (TOCC) and tell the local head of Blackwater we need a new team leader. Thankfully, he was in my training class in Moyock and knows we're legit. He's a former Army major and a solid dude. This is a serious compliment as almost every Army major is garbage. I call him Crop Duster.

He was a runner, having run multiple half marathons. Part of the physical training test at Moyock was a mile and a half run. We lined up on the road and were told to turn around in three-quarters of a mile. A mile and a half total. Math is great.

Five people took off like a shot. Crop Duster's in the group. I hung in the middle next to Robert. Someone ahead of us blasted a fart. It was wretched. The kind of fart I prefer to breath into my mouth, so I don't smell it. Once I tasted it, I decided my nose was the better option.

Robert: Who did that? Who farted? You motherfuckers are crop dusting us back here. I don't want to breathe that shit in.

We sucked in the stink for a hundred meters. It was awful. I had no idea Moyock could smell worse than Moyock. For the rest of the day Robert went around asking everyone, who farted on the run. Days after he was still trying to figure it out. It had turned into an obsession.

I knew it was the Army major who "crop dusted" us, but he denied it when Robert asked. I wonder if I should bring this up in our conversation about Sergeant Major. He owes me one for drinking in his fart.

Me: Hey, Crop Duster. My team leader's shit. We've got to drop him. He's going to get us killed or we're going to kill him. Dude micromanages everything. We wear big boy panties. We don't need a brass check after each run.

Crop Duster: Big boy panties?

Me: Thongs and shit. Leopard-spotted britches.

Crop Duster: I get it. I've heard the grumbling. Who wants to take lead on this?

Me: Me.

Dave: Me too.

Crop Duster: Call a team meeting at the pool in thirty minutes. I'll grab Sergeant Major. I expect you both to say the same thing to him.

Me: I will.

Dave: Me too.

Fuck. That backfired. I was banking on Sergeant Major being relieved in private and Will taking over. Nope. We must air our grievances like Festivus. We call a team meeting, sitting in a semi-circle of white plastic chairs facing Sergeant Major and Crop Duster. Aside from Dave and me, the team has no idea what this is about. They look pissed. Crop Duster wastes no time.

Crop Duster: There's word this team thinks Sergeant Major can't lead. Does anyone want to start?

Dave: (Sounding all smart) You're not the person to lead this team. Effective leadership is defined by…blah, blah, blah… In the Roman Army the field general…blah, blah, blah… We're all professional here and you micromanage. I can't deal with the wasted time and energy of being under you as a team leader. We're spending more time planning for runs to places we've gone than on the run itself. You aren't cut out to lead us.

Crop Duster: Anyone else?

Me: Ditto to what Dave said.

Crop Duster: What else?

The team jumps in like a pack of lions on a fresh kill. Sergeant Major leans back in his chair, folds his arms across his chest, and listens to us berate him. I doubt he's been critiqued in years, let alone by some of the youngest contractors in Iraq. I'm relieved I don't have to talk.

It's brutal. This man was promoted to the Army's highest enlisted rank. Now he's told to his face with zero ambiguity, he's incompetent. I can't imagine how it feels to hear from ten people that he lacks leadership when he spent over twenty-five years being told he's amazing. Poor bastard.

After we have our say, Crop Duster takes over. He's a great leader. I admire how he handles business.

> Crop Duster: Sergeant Major, now that you've heard what your team has to say, do you have anything you want to say?
> Sergeant Major: I feel this is unfounded. I can lead this team. We can put this behind us and be an effective team going forward.

Fucker didn't listen to a word. The damage is done. Sergeant Major is replaced by Matt Marshall, the former Recon Marine in WPPS class 04 and on Templar 12 in Sulay. Sergeant Major's moved to the TOCC with Funk Faker to conduct planning. I see him when I retrieve missions. He refuses to make eye contact. His demotion means he's no longer here for adventure. He's relegated to being an old man chasing money. Fucking boomers.

**

With Matt as our leader, we drive to the Iraqi Stock Exchange. I'm not expecting yelling and screaming like the New York Stock Exchange I've seen in movies. We exit the vehicle and escort the principal into a dark structure that looks like an industrial building in the middle of a neighborhood. The place reeks like a complex assault waiting to happen so the QRF meets us there.

I walk inside. It's chaos. It's the New York Stock Exchange in Arabic. People scream at a guy on a platform and he's writing stock bids on a chalkboard. I'm in kindergarten watching my teacher complete the alphabet on a chalkboard as children yell the next letter. It's insanity. I walk out and sit in my Suburban. We have a new guy, Special Forces, on our team. This is how it goes—people rotate out on leave and others take their seats at random. He's new in country but instantly accepted into our herd. He's sharp as a tack and full of stories.

Most contractors are tremendously intelligent, albeit with a skewed worldview compared to academia. Many grew up like me, lower middle class joining the military because they didn't have the funds to go to college. I joined out of high school to leave my small town and avoid working construction for fifty years only to die poor. For many of these guys, their military success is due to their intelligence and work ethic. The smartest are Army Special Forces (SF). Navy SEALs are highly trained but arrogant. Rangers and Marines are great at taking orders and executing a job. All are lethal but with differing egos. As I sit down, I instantly know the subject.

SF: I was stationed in Germany and started hooking up with a local girl. She was a freak.

Me: You better bring it. We've heard some crazy stories you'll need to beat.

SF: This chick is crazy.

Me: I'm listening.

SF: She starts off nice. She's a bit wild the first couple times we hook up but nothing I haven't experienced. Then she starts with handcuffs and being tied up. Pretty normal stuff.

Me: Normal?

SF: Yeah. Then she transitions to being tied up and roleplay. I'm good with this.

Me: Normal?

SF: Not now. She starts to ask for weird shit. She wants me to tie her up and rape her in a fantasy world.

Me: But only in missionary so it's normal.

SF: No, she wants me to tie her up and pretend to break into her house from a window. I tell her we need to have a safe word.

Me: Cucumber.

SF: What?

Me: Cucumber's a great safe word. How often do you use it in a sentence outside of eating salad?

Will: Unless you're using a cucumber in bed.

Me: Good point, but he said this was normal, was she vegan?

SF: We do the rape thing. I tie her up, sneak in a window, and we bone. She doesn't use the safe word.

Me: Cucumber.

SF: Sure, Morgan. Then she asks me to do it again but with a knife. She has me hold it to her throat and fake rape her. It's getting a bit out of hand, but I do it. I point the blade away from her neck.

Me: Of course. You're a gentleman.

SF: Then she asks me to bring my pistol. She's so turned on by the thought, I have to try it.

Me: You're a gentleman.

SF: I'm fucking her from behind and pointing my gun to the back of her head. I've cleared it and there's no magazine. My trigger finger's outside the trigger guard. She's loving it. No safe word.

Me: Cu…

SF: Yes, cucumber. I'm losing my mind, pulling the upper receiver back to make sure there's no round in the chamber.

He illustrates by thrusting his hips and pulling the imaginary upper receiver back.

SF: I couldn't get off. I was so afraid a bullet would magic its way into the chamber.

We're all shocked.

SF: That's the last time we hooked up. I told her I was being deployed to avoid her. Never spoke again.

Will: True love.

Me: That's *l'amore*.

CHAPTER 16

I t's Christmas in Iraq, which sucks a fat dick. We get paid a three-thousand-dollar bonus, three thousand bucks to suck a fat dick. I'd rather be home. Christmas is ruined forever.

The Man Camp looks like Tombstone, Arizona. It's dusty and dirty with nary a decoration except in the chow hall. I went there to eat but the decorations couldn't make up for the abortion they called spaghetti. In hopes of getting better food, I walk to the embassy, alone.

The palace has turned into Whoville. Christmas trees and decorations hang everywhere. Each table has white paper cloths and little arrangements rubbing it in my face that it's Christmas. Soldiers wear Santa hats as they walk the halls talking, laughing, smiling. Each area has Christmas songs playing to make the marble walls and painted ceilings feel more inviting. What a waste of money, taxpayers paying for these idiots to be jovial and lose a war.

It's military tradition for officers to serve their soldiers on holidays. Army brass stands behind the counter as I walk with my plate. The food looks great but I'm losing my appetite as I watch a full bird colonel wearing a cowboy hat slop mashed potatoes around. The next server is a major, the most worthless rank in the military, who's handing out green beans and wearing a Santa hat displaying his oak leaf. This is my hell. I got out of the military to distance myself from these pricks.

I grab my plate and sit at a table by myself. I spread out to make it uncomfortable for anyone wanting a seat. It doesn't work. A group of Army people assume I'm lonely because I'm sitting alone. Five of them decide to cheer me up.

Her: Merry Christmas. Can we sit down?

Me: Sure.

Her: The food looks great. Who do you work for?

Me: KBR. I clean the port-o-potties around the base. I ran into one today that had exploded. Shit all over the walls.

Her: Well, Merry Christmas. We appreciate what you do.

The drop holster on my leg filled with a loaded Glock should be a giveaway I'm no janitor, but at least I stopped the conversation. They talk away to each other. All have rifles they have no idea how to fire. All with smiles. All joyful and triumphant. I sit in silence like the Grinch. I stare at a massive Christmas tree as *Jingle Bells* plays in the background. Christmas is dead. These people killed it.

***

I run into Nathan and he's massive. He's former Navy and a cop from Georgia, complete with the drawl and a penchant to say "man" at the end of most sentences. He's five-foot-seven and his arms stretch his shirt so widely, I'm afraid a button will pop off and take out my eye. I know the juice when I see it, and I want it. My body atrophied with the travel to Kurdistan. It's time to get jacked. I squint while addressing him to protect my vision.

Me: You're huge. What are you taking?

Nathan: I got these supplements online. The protein powder's mixed with…

Me: Shut the fuck up. What are you on? I want some.

Nathan: What are you talking about, man?

Me: You look like the Michelin man fucked a crocodile. Sell crazy somewhere else. I'm all stocked up. What are you on, Deca, Winstrol?

Nathan: Anything I can get my hands on, man.

Me: Ingestion or needle?

Nathan: Both.

Me: You cycling Tuesday, Thursday, and Saturday? Take a couple weeks off after six weeks?

Nathan: No, I get it and use it all that day.

Me: You're going to die. How are you getting needles?

Nathan: I only have one.

Me: Get out of here.

Nathan: Serious. I clean it real good and reuse it, man.

Me: I'll come by tonight and pick your brain.

I know about this stuff. Back home after reading the Blackwater contract, I got juiced to the core thinking I'd need it in Iraq. I didn't know how to use steroids, so I got a two-minute tutorial from a jacked bouncer who sold them to me.

Bouncer: Don't let air into the syringe. Place your thumb on your hip. Point your pinkie like you're at a tea party with the Queen of England. Rotate it to touch your ass cheek. This is the injection spot.

Me: Why?

Bouncer: There are nerves you could poke with the needle and end up a paraplegic.

Me: This is ridiculous. This is how you do it?

Bouncer: Yep, don't deviate from that spot.

When it was time to inject, I heard my sister's voice from the bathroom and became acutely aware I was sitting in the living room in my boxers. I walked to my room, grabbed my hermetically sealed needle and the bottle of Winstrol. I tipped the bottle upside down and filled the syringe, no air. I put my thumb on my hip, rotated my pinky to my ass cheek, and located the injection spot. I grabbed the needle and wimped out. I couldn't do it. How five-year-olds with diabetes do it is beyond me.

To pump myself up, I said out loud, "Goddamnit, little girls inject themselves in the stomach, you fucking snooch. Do this." I gripped the needle like a three-year-old holding a crayon. Three...two...one. I thrust the needle at my butt but stopped short of piercing the skin. Fuck. I needed a better target.

I grabbed a Sharpie and drew a circle on my ass to try again. Nope. Not happening. I do what any grown man would and called my sister for help. I was lying on the bed with my ass cheek hanging out when she walked in.

Sister: What's wrong with you?
Me: I need you to push this needle in my ass. I drew a circle for you. Just grab it and push it in. I'll do the rest.
Her: No.
Me: Yes. You live here rent-free. I need this. Push the needle in my ass. Then leave before we make eye contact.
Her: Fine.

I'm pathetic. Little girls do this every day. *Little girls*. Fuck them. My sister approached with the needle. I watched her move it toward my cheek as I counted, One...two...

Her: I can't do it. I'm leaving.
Me: Get back here. Little girls poke themselves with insulin needles every day. You can do this. Please?

She set the needle on my dresser and left. I heard the front door slam. Fuck it. I grabbed the needle and jabbed it in my ass like a man. Fuck, that hurt. At least I'm as tough as a little girl. Hell yes.

I pushed the juice in my ass and immediately regretted it. Cold syrup thrust into the muscle. It felt like a walnut dove into my cheek trying to hide from a squirrel. Pulling the needle out hurt worse. I vowed to never get fat to avoid diabetes.

I walk to Nate's room that evening so I can get the steroid hookup. His neighbor is a medic. They're both on the QRF. They live in a converted boxcar with a bathroom separating the rooms. I find Nathan naked with a needle hanging from his ass arguing with the medic. Nate's balls are the size of raisins. He must've been serious about getting and using steroids the same day.

Nathan: (To the medic) Push it in for me, man.

Medic: No, I told you not to reuse needles.

Nathan: I can't get new ones. I use alcohol to wipe it down.

Medic: They get dull. You can't reuse the needle. They're one-time-use.

Me: How many times have you used it, Nate?

Nathan: Eight or nine probably.

The needle's inserted halfway. He walks in circles and it wags like a dog tail. That has to hurt.

Nathan: Fuck. It hurts so bad. Push it in, man.

Me: I'll push it in.

Nathan: Just push the needle and I'll push in the stuff.

Me: You look like a gorilla. I think you're using too much.

I push it.

Nathan: (Lurching forward) Fuck, that hurts. Push hard.

Me: (Pushing hard) It ain't moving, dude.

Nathan: Twist it while you push, man.

Me: Fuck that.

Medic: I told you. They get dull.

Nathan: That's why I've been stabbing and twisting.

Me: For fuck sake. I'm done. Twist it yourself.

Medic: (To me) You interested in coming to the QRF?

Me: Does the pope shit in the woods?

Medic: No.

Me: Ignore that. Hell, yes, I want to come over. I go on leave in a couple weeks but after I get back, hook it up, man.

Medic: Will do.

I want the juice but need to find a more reputable dealer than Nathan. He's buying it at the local market. I can't get chicken curry without shit particles. I'm not desperate enough to get steroids and a multiuse needle from an Iraqi.

Thankfully Matt Marshall fills the void. He puts in an order and gets a massive box of steroids for us complete with hermitically sealed needles. He calls us over the radio when they arrive. If a drug dog had been in our mail room, he'd be jacked. A line forms outside Matt's room. I walk in, he gives me the juice, a zip lock bag of pills, tells us how to inject, and I go on my way.

I'm a steroid novice. Matt tells me to inject in a circle—right shoulder, ass cheek, right thigh, left thigh, ass cheek, and shoulder. The pills are for when I stop and will "jump start my balls" to produce testosterone again.

Steroids are testosterone which build muscle and reduce the time it takes to recover from a workout. Caloric intake, regardless of the type, is a must to give the body something to build off. After a week, the body increases estrogen to obtain symbiosis. This is why you cycle steroids—get muscle before your body gives you girl hormones and you lactate. Once the cycle's complete, take pills so your testicles begin creating testosterone again. Rinse and repeat.

I waste no time, inject in my shoulder, and work out. I ignore my body and put as much weight as I can on each machine. The steroids will kick in for recovery. I leave and eat Pop Tarts from the chow hall.

***

As the ambassador to Iraq, John Negroponte has his own security detail. He's out of town so most of them have a couple days off, save for a few on a rotating schedule to stand guard outside his room twenty-four hours a day. Pete's stuck on door guard on the night when Kid Rock is doing a concert at Camp Liberty.

Some of the contractors are going. It's an unsanctioned drive down Route Irish. I refuse an invitation. I like Kid Rock but I'm not willing to risk my life to see him. They load up the vehicles with booze and leave.

They're going to be popular since the Army base is dry. The next morning, I go to breakfast to hear about it.

Taylor: We got to the front of the stage with a bottle of Jack. Kid Rock took a drink of it while he played.

Adam: We got to meet him after the show. He had groupies. We picked off a couple from the herd. Army chicks. We got wasted and drove back here to bang them.

Me: Drunk driving on Route Irish, huh?

Pete: This asshole comes to John's room in the embassy.

Me: You stand guard when he's out?

Pete: So, someone can't put a bomb under his bed, I suppose. It sucks.

Taylor: It's worse when he's here. He tries to ditch us. He has a door in his room going to a bathroom. The bathroom has a second door to another area of the embassy. He'll go in one door and out the other to shake us.

Adam: He went into the shitter the other day and I ran around to the other door so he couldn't shake me. I stood there for twenty minutes and heard nothing. I figured we'd be playing hide-and-seek around the embassy but wanted to make sure he didn't have a heart attack while dropping a deuce. I opened the door and he's reading *Stars and Stripes* on the shitter.

Me: Walked in on the US Ambassador to Iraq while he was pinching a loaf, huh?

Adam: So last night, I bring the Army chick up to the bedroom and ask Pete to let me in so I can fuck her on John's bed.

Pete: I said, nope, no way.

Adam: It would have been epic to bang her out on his bed.

Pete: It would've cost me my job. I told him to fuck her in his room.

Taylor: They argued for five minutes while me and the two Army chicks stood there. I brought mine back to my room and banged her out.

Pete: Me too.

Me: Then you took them back?

Taylor: Fuck no. I took mine to the chow hall at the embassy and left. I'm not driving all the way back to Liberty.

Pete: Damn, that's a good idea. Mine is still in my room. I'm going to fuck her again and do that.

God knows what happened to those girls. They had to get back somehow and there's no regular transports from the Green Zone to Camp Liberty. I imagine them doing the walk of shame with bedhead in their physical training uniform to a convoy sent by their unit through the most bombed route in Iraq and then getting an ass-chewing from their platoon sergeant. Rough. I'm happy to be leaving in a few days. Templar 24's in good hands and I need a break.

***

Our fearless Templar 24 Team leader, Matt Marshall, is an abject liar. He was a Blackwater success story until his lies caught him. He's a con artist. I applaud him for how far he got before being exposed.

Matt was in my Blackwater WPPS 04 class and told me he was a Force Recon Marine. I introduced him to legitimate Force Recon Marines and he fooled them. Turns out, he was a Marine reservist and was other than honorably discharged for not showing up to drill.

He told us he was an Indiana State Police Officer on the SWAT team. He saw my NASCAR hat and said he'd get me pit passes for the Indianapolis 500. This was his modus operandi—find a thing someone liked, affirm it, and make promises no one would take him up on.

In Indiana, he told fellow officers he was a Recon Marine in Desert Storm and got a Silver Star which helped him get on SWAT. A former Marine police officer started asking questions which led to an investigation and Matt quitting prior to being fired. He became a security guard with few career prospects aside from creating a steroid ring.

Blackwater landed the WPPS contract in Iraq and was hiring. He sent his resume and Blackwater licked their lips at his awesomeness. He joined WPPS 04 with me and thirty others.

Blackwater never verified his credentials or checked his DD214. They took his resume at face-value which included such heroic courses as High Altitude, High Opening (HAHO) parachute training, High Altitude, Low Opening (HALO) parachute training, Combat Diver, and a litany of badass schools while being a Marine Corps recruiting assistant after infantry school—which he left off. These are schools the best Marine units hand out sparingly in the time he served when the US wasn't at war. His stolen valor far exceeds saying you're a veteran to get free breadsticks at Olive Garden on Veteran's Day.

He worked with me on the RCLO in Kurdistan and took over as team leader of Templar 24 when we returned to Baghdad in 2004 before running the ranks of Blackwater. In this time, they never verified his service. His DD214 had "burned in a house fire." This illustrates the problems with the US government hiring private firms to vet candidates outside government protocols. The US State Department is culpable for granting him a clearance to work under their contract. It's a confederacy of dunces.

Matt took his stolen valor and created a PMC called Amyntor. He got a Force Recon tattoo which shows true conviction to his bullshit. He's the funkiest of funk fakers.

He met high-level administration officials and pitched government contacts to turn the war in Afghanistan over to private security which made national news. How could someone with fake credentials propose government contracts and put American lives at risk to privatize war? This has a direct line back to Blackwater—they gave him street cred.

You'd assume Erik Prince funded this insanity. He's the Prometheus of using private contractors in combat. You'd be wrong. Matt met a venture capitalist named Paul at a SHOT (Shooting, Hunting, and Outdoors Trade) show in Las Vegas, and dazzled him with chimerical tales of covert operations he did in Syria for the CIA.

Matt said he was a CIA operative, was captured in Syria, tortured for a week, and escaped by hiding in a truck bed under chicken coops. He was on scene when the leader of Al Qaeda in Iraq was killed—Jason Bourne shit. He also proposed creating a "better Blackwater."

Paul didn't have the background to call bullshit and gave him cash on the spot to party under the auspices he was helping a hero.

In subsequent meetings, Matt stated he never worked for Blackwater but was a CIA spy working alongside contractors. On 9/11 he was in Indiana when the twin towers fell. CIA leadership said "we need Matt Marshall" and sent a helicopter to whisk him to Washington D.C. at the same time former President George Bush and his wife were grounded. Matt was that awesome. He was boots-on-ground on September 12th in Afghanistan where he was shot. His story was so compelling, he convinced Paul to fund Amyntor.

Matt's a hell of a liar—the *Inventing Anna* of PMCs. PMCs are dependent on government contracts consisting of red tape that slows the process. With Paul's funding, Matt could lead operations to save kidnapped kids in South America while Amyntor bid on government contracts. Paul funded secret squirrel shit in the interim. It was a balance between playing within and outside the system.

He sent Paul the prayer beads taken from the Musab al-Zarqawi killing telling him he'd called in the air strike and took them off his body as he was dying. Paul gave him $750,000 to save kidnapped children in South America and nearly $3 million in total for "off the books" operations. Amazing, Matt was able to do all this while on a lavish vacation in Miami.

Like most professional liars, many of his stories were based in truth. While in Blackwater, we'd drink beer and tell stories. Matt used these but inserted himself as the operator and used real names and handles of the people telling them. I'm in awe of his memory and hubris.

The missions Paul funded never made the news. When Paul asked about the legality of funding, Matt told him it was top secret Batman shit. Paul confronted Matt and was later sent a groveling email stating Paul was his best friend and how his prior best friend was killed in Syria. He had to carry him miles before abandoning him to be rescued and later recovered his body.

Matt couldn't produce documents because he was at the Mayo Clinic for a brain aneurism. His doctor sent him texts that the ideal therapy was to have a couple of drinks a day, moderate physical activity, and a lot of sex. I wish this was a joke.

Paul contacted the FBI and dissolved Amyntor after pouring $10 million into it. Had it gotten contracts, it would have endangered lives of countless contractors under the leadership of a pathological liar with no combat experience. Pretty much what Blackwater did.

Instead of owning his fabrications, Matt painted Paul as a child molester, sex trafficker, and stated Paul asked him to kill someone. He produced emails and texts to prove it while suing Paul for the $300 million in contracts Amyntor lost. The FBI was able to show Matt created twelve burner accounts, sending messages to himself which were relayed to Paul, to prove his expenditures. The lawsuit was dismissed. Matt took a plea deal (the Blackwater MO) and is in prison.

Am I trying to make you feel compassion for a billionaire who was bilked out of a small sum of money compared to his wealth? Damn right I am. Matt's a con-artist and if it wasn't Paul, it would've been someone without the funds or tenacity to fight back. Stolen valor and stealing money are wrong. Tarnishing the reputation of a man who wanted to do good by calling him a pederast is unforgivable. I hope Matt's holding an inmate's pocket and being sold for cigarettes. His lies could've gotten people killed. That's unforgivable.

***

I was unaware of Matt's fabrications until the FBI called me in 2021 asking if I'd worked with him. He submitted pictures showing him doing spook shit in far off lands for the CIA—the same ones he gave Paul. Many included me wearing my Lowes #48 NASCAR hat. I told the agent when and where the pictures were taken and debunked his claims they were in Iraq or Afghanistan on CIA operations.

A picture that stands out had Matt sitting on a red C-130 cargo net preparing for a CIA operation in Afghanistan. I sat next to him buckling my seatbelt. In an eleven-page sworn statement, I swore he was a liar—this was in 2004.

Fast forward to 2022. Like anal warts, Blackwater's the gift that keeps on giving. A gift I never wanted. I got a call from an investigative reporter asking about Matt. He had a hot lead that Paul's a pedophile committing sex trafficking and asks me to verify Matt's heroics. He describes a picture where Matt's sitting on a C-130 doing clandestine operations in far off lands for the CIA. I laugh.

Me: I know the picture. I'm sitting next to him.
Journalist: Not this one. He's alone.
Me: Text me the picture.

I get the picture on my phone and laugh.

Me: That's awesome. Matt's a turd.
Journalist: What?
Me: Give me a minute. I'll text the real picture.

I find the picture I sent the FBI. It's the same picture but Matt cropped me out. I sing circus music as I wait for it to land. (They used this in the podcast which is hilarious.)

Journalist: I can't wait to see this. Fuck.
Me: Do you have my FBI statement?
Journalist: You worked with the FBI?
Me: I'll email it to you.

He opens it on his computer and, from across the country, over the phone, I feel the blood draining from his face. He notices a picture the FBI used. Matt's standing in front of a mud hut with oil barrels behind him and a lady walking down a hill. I point out mine's the same but the lady's walking across a bridge illustrating they were taken seconds apart in 2004. The journalist has Matt's but was told it was Iraq in 2003 before the war started.

Journalist: He got me. I thought I had the next Jeffrey Epstein. All I have's a liar. I had my doubts about his story but this seals it. He wasn't working for the CIA in 2003 that you know of?

Me: Not that I know of. I was still in the Air Force in 2003. He was in my WPPS 04 class in June 2004.

Journalist: He told me he was in WPPS 01.

Me: I'm dumbfounded. If he'd told people he worked for Blackwater and the cool stuff we did, it would've been enough. Instead, he tried to be the coolest cat in the old lady's apartment. Who cares if he was class one or class four? If he'll lie about that, he'll lie about anything.

Journalist: His story's been unraveling but he says he's going to fight the federal charges. I assume everything you've told me is on the record?

Me: Absolutely. I have no animosity toward Matt but he dragged me into this shit. I'll help for spite.

We conversed for months. I was interviewed for a *New York Magazine* podcast which illustrated the lies of Matt but still painted Paul as a villain. This is garbage. Paul's the victim.

Paul had zero financial incentive to fund clandestine operations Matt "led." He wanted to do good, going as far as to see if Matt could help save the girls kidnapped by Boko Haram in Nigeria in 2014. I applaud that. Paul was sucked into a web of lies like the fly in *Charlotte's Web*. Matt feasted like a remora.

Paul sent Matt misogynistic-sounding messages to a normal person but mimic ordinary conversation between Blackwater employees—boasting about pliable morals with hookers at the Bristol Hotel in Jordan. The mantra "trust me with your life, not your money or your wife" resonates in messages sent to his "best friend" about sexual conquests. If this is immoral, Tinder should be cancelled.

Matt dragged me into his lies and I refuse to be a pawn. He stated he barely knew me and I was paid off by Paul when confronted. He deserves to be called out. How he lied to CIA members and not shit his pants out of fear of being called out is astounding. He's a genius impostor Bernie Madoff would be proud of.

I can't fathom why he lied. We worked for Blackwater and protected the people gathering evidence for the trials of Saddam Hussein and Chemical Ali. Paul likely would've funded him based on this. I suppose people always fake the funk. Matt Marshall's the ultimate Funk Faker.

CHAPTER 17

I leave in February. Tony and Eric are on my flight out of Baghdad. Thanks for telling me the next time you'll be in Baghdad, assholes.

We land in Jordan and are taken by van to the Bristol Hotel. They make us keep the curtains closed so no one can see the Americans. Between the breaks of the curtains, we instinctively look for ambush points. Rooftops. Windows. No one talks. We're unarmed yet hyper alert. It feels like attending a gang-bang without a condom. We arrive at the hotel—the Blackwater staging area for Iraq. It's a last chance for hookers before flying in to Iraq or out to one's wife. Not my style but I don't judge.

We line up for room keys and Eric talks about getting a massage. Sounds good to me. I've never had one. I'm down if it helps work out the stress of being on alert for the last six months. We have four hours before the restaurant opens. I take a shower and put on an amazing robe from the closet and take pictures of myself wearing it like I'm royalty. Then I call the front desk to schedule a massage for three p.m.

The masseuse is a burly blonde Russian gal. Her hands can crack Brazil nuts and bend steel. I'm not enjoying the rubdown. So much oil slathered on me by a strange lady in a strange land. Once she's done, she asks:

Her: Need anysing more?
Me: No, thank you. This was an experience.

I pay her. She thanks me and I walk to my room to shower off the oil. I feel like a snail. I walk to the restaurant and sit with Tony and Eric.

Tony: Did you get a massage?
Me: Yes.
Tony: What time?
Me: Three.
Tony laughs like a pirate.
Eric: I got mine at two-thirty. I fucked her.
Tony: Ha. Did you look at her right hand?
Eric: Why would I look at her hand?
Tony: Because I got mine at two and she beat me off. (Looking at me.) She massaged you with the same hand I shot my load on. (Looking at Eric.) She fucked you with my jizz on her hand.
Me: Oh man. I got the last massage? Fuck you both.
Tony and Eric laugh maniacally.
Eric: You didn't have her beat you off?
Me: I beat myself off after my shower. It was free. Why would I pay for it when I'll be home with my girlfriend tomorrow?
Tony: I paid for it. Oiled hands. So worth it.
Me: Fuck off.

***

I spend thirty days home making life mistakes I regret for years. Home doesn't feel like home. It's a place where people drive slow and Tinactin's on every store shelf. I don't have a home anymore. I remember a guy telling me he'd been on active duty so long that home was where he was stationed. I couldn't fathom it until now. Baghdad's my home.

Mistake one is having too much money. Mistake two is having a girl-friend who knows I have too much money. I decide we should get married, so we go to Las Vegas—where else?—and get hitched. I should've gone to an ATM, got forty thousand dollars in cash, and started wiping my ass with twenty-dollar bills. It would've been a better investment.

We walk into a Land Rover dealership. I'm in jeans and a white t-shirt. The salespeople don't bother approaching me. I'm pissed about this. I can buy any car on the lot with cash. I don't how to act now that I have money for the first time in my life. I don't want to be an asshole, but I want everyone to treat me like I'm no longer the poor kid from Cottonwood. I walk into the showroom and point to a Land Rover Discovery.

Me: I want to buy that.
Salesperson: Excuse me?
Me: Do you take checks?
Salesperson: Let me unlock the car so you can look.

The remaining salespeople take bets on how fast my check will bounce as I write a check on the spot. America is ridiculous.

I don't fit in this country anymore. I'm surrounded by people who have everything they want at Walmart but complain about it. It's odd. The abundance of junk is staggering compared to the sparseness of Iraq. Hell, this place has trees to make toilet paper for ass wipes so no one needs to use a bare hand with water. This is real life but not real if that makes sense.

The best part of being back is fabric softener. My clothes smell like a spring breeze in a field of flowers. In Iraq I drop off my foul-smelling clothes with a local who smells worse than Big Foot's dick. He counts each piece and gives me a receipt as he dumps them in a white bag, which looks like fishnet stockings, so hot. They toss this in a huge vat and wash everything together. When I return for my clothes a couple days later, they're folded in a plastic bag. I can't say they're clean, but they don't smell as bad. But this amazing floral scent, I miss.

I'm ready to return to Baghdad where I can give an honest response to people. These spoiled asses in the US are shocked by my answers to questions about the war. I say, "We should slaughter everyone and salt the earth with their blood. The people of Iraq don't care if we're there.

There's no reason to keep investing in them." This is somehow appalling. If you don't want an honest answer, don't ask.

I'm 60 percent asshole. I'm past the tadpole stage and now an adolescent frog. It'll be a couple months before I transition from a frog asshole to a poison dart frog asshole.

***

On my way back to Iraq, I have a thirty-six-hour layover in Amsterdam. I connect with Charles, a Blackwater guy from another team, via Myspace. He's going to be there at the same time. I catch a train from the airport to downtown Amsterdam and walk until I find a hotel with a vacant room. The city stinks like weed and my room's tiny. The shower's built for midgets. If I extend both arms, I can touch the toilet, the shower, and the bed. I can shit, shower, shave, and sleep at the same time. Very convenient.

Charles and I meet for lunch and drinks. This place is expensive. Afterward, we walk to the Rembrandt Museum. I'm amazed by the quality of the paintings. They look like high-definition photographs. The guy had a thing for fruit, and I'm positive the pear in this painting could be plucked from the canvas and eaten. Now I understand why some paintings are masterpieces. I'm in awe. I'm wearing my good John Deere hat, so everyone knows I'm an art aficionado. Hell, I could be a Tufts.

I take a nap on my tiny bed and when I wake it's dark. I call Charles to meet for dinner and drinks. Roaming around afterward, we stumble upon The Sex Museum. Holy cow. We go in and it lives up to its name. Raunchy. It's like Bubba in *Forrest Gump* talking about shrimp: We've got heterosexual sex, lesbian sex, gay male sex, animal sex, sex statues, sex paintings, sex dolls. Now I understand why some paintings aren't called masterpieces. The statue of Satan sucking his own penis is gross even if I envy his flexibility. You know why dogs lick themselves? Because they can.

I have to see the red-light district to confirm it's real, so we walk. It's an alley with buildings on each side. Each one has a white framed window where a woman stands scantily clad with a red light over the door next to it. Women catcall me. I'm honored. They whistle at Charles. I'm way better looking than him so this must be a ploy to get men to pay for sex.

If curtains are pulled over the window, they have business. Behind each woman is a tiny room with a bed not much bigger than a cot. It's sterile like an operating room, but with jizz on the walls. I can't stop humming *Roxanne* by The Police as I think my tiny hotel room isn't so bad.

I'm not impressed with the talent. Most aren't attractive enough to spend fifty euros on. They're all shapes and sizes, obese to emaciated. Like shelves in a ninety-nine-cent store, I never know what the next aisle will bring, but I know it's shit. There's one exception, a blonde woman in a white bikini. She catcalls us. I turn my head to say something to Charles. He's ten feet behind me staring at her like a fly at a turd.

Me: We're not here to shop, Charles.
Charles: I have to fuck her.
Me: Come on, man. Let's grab a drink. There's a titty bar right there.

I point to a neon sign with a naked lady dancing.

Charles: Nope. I must have her.
Me: You never fuck the hot hooker, man. I learned this from George.
　　They have attitudes.
Charles: I'm going for it.
Me: I'll meet you in the titty bar.

Charles is drawn to the door like a moth to flame. He'll be burned but he can't stop walking toward the light. I walk to the entrance of the strip club and look back in time to see Charles enter the whore hole. We both know she has been fucked so many times he may as well be dipping his dick in a glass of warm water.

Ten euros to get in the strip club. I don't know the currency conversion rate, but it seems steep considering I can buy a hooker for fifty. A beer cost seven more. I'm thirty real-American dollars into this place and not impressed. The talent's more Oklahoma than NYC. I'm not a fan of strip clubs. I can't wrap my head around why they're so popular, so I buddy up to the bar.

A lady dances on a stage behind me. It's four feet off the ground. She's twirling around the pole as skinny Europeans stare at her breasts from pervert row. They toss coins. She dances. Her boobs are nice but throwing coins, the equivalent of one and five dollars, seems demeaning, not to mention expensive.

My beer's half gone when Charles arrives. We scream at each other over deafening techno music. I can't hear him, but his body language and pissed-off expression let me know something went wrong. He's seething. I love it.

Me: What happened?
Charles: Fuck that bitch, man.
Me: Told you not to get the best-looking hooker, dude.
Charles: She's blowing me with the condom on and then lays down on the bed like a dead fish. I'm fucking a dead fish like that big-ass fish in Sulay. She doesn't even take her bra off. I go to take it off and she says, "That's an extra ten euros."
Me: Nice. Upselling.
Charles: I keep pounding away. She sees my watch and comments on it.

He wears a Rolex because all former Navy SEALs wear them.

Charles: I tell her to turn over. She tells me that's another twenty euros. We get into an argument. "I paid you for sex. I'm not paying more. You're my whore. Do what I tell you."
Her: I'm no whore.
Charles: I gave you money for sex. You're a whore.

This has become a moral argument for Charles.

Charles goes into a rant about the conversation he has with the lady of the night. This is awesome. He's doing her voice. This is the best night of my life.

Her: *I'm not a whore.*

Charles: I paid you to have sex with me. We're having sex. That makes you a whore because it's the definition of whore.

Her: You want me to push this button and have someone come in and take that fancy watch from you?

Charles: Fuck you, whore.

Her: No, fuck you.

Charles: I'm fucking you for money. You're a whore.

She reaches for the button.

Charles: I took the condom off, threw it in her face, called her a whore again, pulled up my pants and left. Fuck that whore.

Me: I told you not to go after the hot one. George told me that.

Charles: Fuck you too.

Me: (In a Dutch accent) I'm no whore.

We laugh as we leave the strip place and go to a bar. I power down a beer while he keeps complaining about the whore. I try to listen and not make jokes, not my strong suit. It's late and we're drunk. Time to return to our hotels.

The only map we have of Amsterdam is a tourist map where the buildings are huge, and roads are tiny. I point and Charles leads. We enter a dark alley, Charles first. Ten meters in, he bumps into a guy with long dreadlocks. Charles doesn't notice so I turn to the guy and say,

Me: Sorry, dude.

Dreadlock guy: Not a problem. I appreciate your kindness.

Not really. Instead he kicks me in the stomach. The wind flies out of me as I look up. Four people are running over from an adjacent alley to beat the shit out of us. Amsterdam's the best.

Charles is in a scuffle with two of them. Dreadlocks has me in a headlock so I'm looking at the cobblestone street. Such craftsmanship.

I'm holding the leg I got kicked with and trying to punch my attacker. He tenderizes my ribs with his fists.

I push off, stand up, square up and prepare for combat. He backs away. I backpedal. Charles does the same next to me. We clear the alley and prepare for the next assault. We're in ass-kicking mode. Bring it, motherfuckers. They jog off, yelling. I see my John Deere hat in the alley thirty meters away. I'm pissed.

Me: What the fuck was that?
Charles: No idea.
Me: My fucking hat!
Charles: Go get it.
Me: Fuck you. That felt like ants racing out of the den to whip our asses. I'm not going back in there.
Charles: How does it look?
Me: How does what look?
Charles: My eye.

His right eye is damn-near swollen shut. I laugh so hard my stomach hurts. It doesn't help I recently sustained a violent kick to it. I bend over and laugh more. It's hilarious. I'm pissed off and laughing if there's such a thing, but I can't stay mad. Charles took the brunt of the beating.

Charles: What happened?
Me: You bumped into the dude in the alley and then his friends ran out and kicked the shit out of us.
Charles: I didn't see a guy in the alley.
Me: That explains why you bumped into him.
Charles: All I know is, someone was coming at me. I grabbed his arm and was about to Navy SEAL break that shit in half, then I got sucker-punched in the eye.
Me: Ha ha. You were going to pull some Navy SEAL shit? Get the fuck out of here.
Charles: Serious.

Me: Your eye looks like shit, man. Can you see out of it?
Charles: A little. Fuck this place. I'm going to bed.

I walk Charles to his hotel so he isn't accosted by someone he can't see out of his beat-ass right eye. I walk toward my hotel alone, scared, and pissed about my dressy hat being beaten off my head. "Fucking Charles," I say aloud, laughing as I walk. The locals must assume I'm stoned.

***

Charles and I land in Jordan and hail a cab to the Bristol. I don't order a massage. There's a haboob in Baghdad so we're instructed to be in the lobby ready to go tomorrow. If the dust storm persists, we stay here and make a measly two hundred and fifty dollars per day. I go to my room and sleep.

The next morning, Charles, Robert, and I arrive in the lobby with our bags. It's great to see Robert. I had no idea he was here. The haboob's still kicking ass so there's no flight today. I ask the concierge about things to see in Jordan. He mentions Petra, the Dead Sea, and Mount Nebo. I've heard of the Dead Sea but not the others. I may as well see what I can before I die. I try to rope Charles and Robert into my adventure. Charles declines and goes back to bed to rest his swollen eye and dream about breaking arms with Navy SEAL moves. Robert's game. The concierge calls a cab and we're off to see the world.

It's a long drive. We arrive at a dirt parking lot with signs pointing to a walkway. A Hummer is parked next to us with Jordanian soldiers lounging in it, the spoils of helping the US prior to the ground offensive in Iraq. The cab driver asks for payment. I give him half of what he asks for to make sure he's here when we return.

We walk down a dusty trail and enter a chasm with fifteen-foot-high walls and a winding trail. It's neat but I don't know what the fuss is about. There's an aqueduct running along it. A small area between the trail and the aqueduct provides enough cover for me to take a piss. Robert snaps a picture. I'm the reason American tourists get a bad rap.

As we near the end of the trail, I see it. The *Indiana Jones* theme song blasts in my ears as I walk to a fricking castle carved in the side of a rock. I run to find the Holy Grail. I'm speechless. How was this created with rudimentary tools? Pillars jut up from the ground. The second story is ornate with Romanic architecture. I'm in awe. I walk to the front entrance to look in. It has to be a mansion.

It's a room with a black spot on the floor where a fire once burned. I'm reminded of rednecks with five-thousand-square-foot garages next to their dilapidated singlewide trailer. I move back to take in the front again.

Robert wants to ride a camel. He pays its handler, climbs on, and asks me to take his picture. As the camel stands, I see fear on his face.

Robert: Hold on. Let me put on my sunglasses.
Me: Scared? Don't want to have the world see you're afraid of a camel?
Robert: Shut up.

I take his picture after he pulls the Oakleys over his eyes. The handler walks the camel around in a small circle, so he feels like Lawrence of Arabia. The camel kneels and he dismounts so we can walk the grounds.

Nothing compares to the castle. Kids try to sell us trinkets and we pass a few restaurants until we see a trail leading to another monument. I don't want to make the hike but Robert's adamant, so we do it.

It's three and a half clicks from the first castle and a solid climb. I watch obese American tourists ride donkeys. I wish I was diabetic so I could catch a ride without being judged by people like me. Never mind. I can't inject myself with insulin.

We reach the top. It's totally worth the trek. There's a second huge castle carved out of a mountain. This one's bigger than the first and more ornate. A man stands on top. He looks like an ant. The view from the castle is spectacular in its vastness. We sit and enjoy it in silence. I'm awestruck at the peace in this spot. I've never experienced so much culture in such a short time. Dave's ruined me. I'm a Tufts now.

As we walk back to the parking lot, I realize I've been so busy getting culture I forgot to buy a trinket for Grandma. The taxi driver's napping. We jump in the car and pretend to rob him. I'm joking, but that would've been funny. He drives to Mount Nebo, the presumed burial place of Moses.

Moses was a bit of a rebel. He led his people to the land of milk and honey but got stuck on Mount Nebo because he struck a rock to produce water instead of tapping it. I remember this from Sunday school. I walk to a lookout point after getting a picture pretending to move the circular rock that covers Moses' tomb.

Every Bible story rushes through my mind as I read the sign. It shows distance and direction to biblical landmarks. For forty years the Israelites wandered to get to this spot and look over the land below. It took me an hour. I see the Jordan River (where Jesus was baptized), Jericho (where the walls came a-tumbling down after the Israelites marched around it singing), Bethlehem (where Jesus was born), and Jerusalem (something happened here too, I'm sure). I soak it in, then say a prayer thanking God for my life.

Next stop is the Dead Sea. We walk through a hotel lobby to the beach. Across the shore is Israel. Bible stuff happened there too. I stand next to an elevation marker and get my picture taken at nearly the lowest elevation on land: 1,364 feet below sea level. The Dead Sea drops even further to 1,412 feet below sea level, the lowest point on Earth. It's too cold for a swim so we walk the beach looking at rocks covered in salt. The mineral content of this sea is believed to heal maladies. I buy lotion at the little kiosk in the hotel. If it can cure disease, it has to be amazing to beat off with.

We drive back to the Bristol. I pay the cabbie and walk to my room. I'm exhausted but glad I made the trip instead of sitting in my room all day. Time to get to Baghdad to fuck some shit up. Those memories are going to be way cooler future stories.

CHAPTER 18

It's March 2005. I'm home in Baghdad. Ten Blackwater guys are packing up to leave due to a steroid bust. No one's arrested or punished, just fired. Among them are the Lap Dog and the Special Forces kung fu ninja who was always in the team tent using the hand grip strengthener. They're told to go home for a month and come back on the same contract. No one's tracked. At least not us window-lickers at the lowest levels.

The source of the steroid bust was a KBR worker at the gym. Stevie Wonder could've seen he was juicing as his shirt could barely hold his massive tits. He was having the juice shipped in and many of his customers were Blackwater guys. Once caught, he rolled on them. Amazingly, Nate isn't caught up in the bust. There are advantages in getting supply from the locals.

I watch the QRF tow three Blackwater Suburbans that just got hit by an IED. On one were the injured. They were called out to set security, render medical aid, and bring the convoy back. The Suburbans look like hell with the windows blown out. Every inch of them has a pockmark from IED shrapnel like lethal chicken pox. Every contract who sees them runs over to get pictures with the disabled vehicle as if to show they were in them. I see Jacob.

Me: You looking for QRF people?
Jacob: A couple of the team members are leaving to start a team in
    Tikrit, so there are three vacancies.
Me: Where're they going?

Jacob: Luke and Steve are going to Tikrit. Nathan's doing too many steroids. He fell asleep in a garbage pile at the MOI (Ministry of Interior). We almost left him.

Me: No way. That's incredible.

Jacob: I know.

A few fun facts to set the stage of how ludicrous this is:

1. When on steroids, you eat like a pig and sleep like a hound. The body makes muscle because it's being pumped full of testosterone. To feed muscle growth, one must overeat. To recover, one sleeps sixteen hours a day.
2. Testosterone overwhelms the body, so it produces estrogen to counteract it. Users are emotional and mean. It's a bad combo, like crying while kicking a puppy.
3. An increase in testosterone causes the testicles to shrivel because they're no longer needed to manufacture testosterone. This doesn't stop the production of semen, or maybe it does. I have no idea.
4. Iraqi trash piles are rank, ten-foot-tall hills of garbage, including food in various states of decay. Driving near one makes your eyes water.

Jacob: We sent him to scope out the compound and take a defensive position. We couldn't get him on the radio when the principal was ready to go. We almost left without him.

Me: How'd you find him?

Jacob: We sent the lead Hummer over to the area. He didn't see him. On his way back he was spotted sleeping in the trash. We voted him out that day.

Me: Vote me in bro. I'm good in the pocket.

Jacob: I'll put your name in for voting.

The QRF's the best of the best with a vote-on/vote-off team. You must have your shit together to get in, but connections help. Dave and

I are voted on to the QRF that night. I'm stoked. We're told to report to the pool for a send-off party for Steve and Luke.

The QRF is used to escort convoys. The team has an ambulance Suburban and two Hummers decked out with massive amounts of armor. To get the armor, the team's been dropping by the Army bases in the Green Zone with bottles of Jack Daniels. The armor magically appears the next day.

They're retrofitted with massive bumpers, an airhorn, and a siren. The windows roll down so gunners can ride with their rifles and faces out of the vehicle. It's wild.

Iraqi drivers seem unable see the Hummer as we blast airhorns and sirens. It's the job of the top gunner to watch the front over the driver and have a three-hundred-and-sixty-degree view around the vehicle. When traffic refuses to move, they throw water bottles and small rocks at cars until they allow us to pass. It seems mean but it's better than popping off a round.

The lead Hummer escorts the convoy. The ambulance and follow Hummer stay behind ready to react. My only time running with the QRF was when I asked Brian if he'd had a drink that morning. It does four to eight runs a day: grabbing one convoy, escorting it to a meeting, then turning around to grab another. More time on the road means a better chance of trigger-time and my finger's itchy.

We control the road. It's like playing God in a lawless land. It's way too much power for a twenty-four-year-old. I drink it in like an aged scotch.

I report to the pool for the going away party/drinking binge. The "Do Not Enter" sign remains on the diving board. By contract, we're required to work six days a week. It never shapes up that way. At times we work thirteen-plus hour days with no day off while other times we get five or so days off if the mission gets stagnant. Tomorrow, my first day on QRF, is a full day off, which is odd for the team.

We get wrecked. It's a call-the-military-police-to-end-this-party kind of night. The MP's arrive.

MP: Time to call it a night.

Max: We're just getting started.

MP: Look, I don't care if you party all night. I'm just the messenger.

Max: Fine. Pack it up fuckers!

Fucking military pussies calling the MPs on us. They could've come out and asked us to keep it down. We would've ignored them but calling the po-po is a bitch move. Poor MP. Imagine a cop going to a party in the US and seeing forty men, some with guns, wasted. It wouldn't end well. But it's just a normal Thursday night here. It ends without incident.

We walk back to camp, stopping to grab Pop Tarts at the chow hall on the way. I put my radio on the charger and get into bed. The room's moving as I fall asleep. I'm wasted.

A couple hours later, I wake to piss. The ten-foot walk to the bathroom is too far so I piss in a water bottle. I sleep through breakfast and don't feel like eating lunch, but I need something in my stomach. I sit up to figure out the reasons why I'm miserable. Booze. Check. Cigarettes. Check. Sleep. Not enough. I'm so thirsty. I grab a water and chug a third of it before realizing it's my piss. Fuck. Great start to my day.

I sprint-stumble to the bathroom, stuff my fingers down my throat, and attempt to vomit. It doesn't work. I brush my teeth, my tongue, my gums until they bleed. Fuck this day. Fuck everything. I grab clothes, get dressed, strap my pistol on my thigh, get my radio and walk to lunch. The QRF is pulling in from a run. Day off today, right? Fuck me.

George: Nice job, fuckup. We called you for an unexpected run. Where were you?

I grab my radio. It's on the right channel. I push the button and listen for a squelch. It's dead. I must not have put it on the charger properly.

Me: Fuck, dude.

Steve: Don't sweat it.

George: Fuck that. You're gone.

I don't know George well and I'm shitting bricks. First day on QRF and I fuck it up. Dave drops his kit and we grab lunch.

Dave: Don't worry. We couldn't get half the team. We grabbed anyone standing around. You're fine.

I don't feel fine. Between the hangover, cigarette breath, piss mouth, and letting my new team down, I'm livid with myself. I'm a Class A failure at life. I vow to check if my radio charging button's lit when I put it on the charger from now on. Small things. I also promise myself to never tell anyone how much piss I drank this morning. So much piss.

***

April 21, 2005. Seven Blackwater contractors die today. This is the day I lose all compassion for Iraq, except for the Kurds. The footage is on repeat on CNN. All of us are gathered for an announcement. The head of Blackwater in Iraq stands on a dirt pile.

Leader: I'm going to give you the names of our seven brothers in a minute.

My heart sinks. *Fuck. Please don't be Tony.* My guts churn. *Please don't be Tony.*

Leader: First, no one is to post anything on the internet. No emails giving out these names. I trust you and I'm going to treat you like men. These are your brothers and you deserve to know.

Shut the fuck up and tell me names. I need names. Just not TONY.

Leader: If any of their families finds out before we can contact them through official channels, I'm going to find out who did it and beat the shit out of you. Then you'll be fired. Do you understand?

We nod as he reads the names. Slowly. *Not Tony. Please not Tony.* Once he's done, I take a huge breath. No Tony. Thank God. I say a prayer for the families as we all stand in stunned silence. This hurts. Bad.

Steve, Luke, and four other contractors are on the helicopter going to Tikrit. The news shows the helicopter falling to the ground as it burns. Within hours, there's footage from the terrorists who shot it down. The guy who fired the RPG is standing out of view as another filthy dirt-worshipper yells, "*Allahu Akbar!*" I see the RPG fly through the air and connect with the helicopter. It feels like I'm watching in real time. These fuckers just made things personal.

Steve was the guy I spoke with when I picked up Tony at BIAP. Such a nice guy. Always smiling. I want revenge. I want to find these terrorist-fucks and torture them with my bare hands. Not nice torture like waterboarding. I want to cut off each of their fingers and make the assholes eat them. I want to beat them unconscious with a hammer, have our medics revive them, and beat them again. I want to nurse them back to full health, give them physical therapy to get back to normal, and then line them up so everyone can take a turn hitting them with an electric cord. I want to Saddam-Hussein them. These fuckers deserved Saddam and his equally evil son Uday.

We gather in George's room and watch a just-released video of the crash site on Gore.com. One of the pilots survived. He's begging for his life as someone shoots him with an AK-47. The video turns to the charred bodies of our friends. We attempt to identify them. We watch it on repeat.

Max: I think that one's Luke.
George: I don't know, man.
Me: Fuck this. I can't tell.
George: Doesn't matter. They're crispy as Kentucky Fried Chicken.

This is us coping. We desensitize ourselves to distance our emotions from the carnage, from the job. So, we joke. I didn't know Steve and

Luke as well as others who were on QRF with them, but it still hurts. We all feel it.

The other dead contractor was on a run to Ramadi with Tony. This is the first time I've heard about an explosively former penetrator (EFP) IED. A metal box is created with one side made of copper instead of steel. The copper side faces the road and explosives are packed in the box. The explosion causes the copper to form a bullet-like projectile with massive force behind it, which allows it to penetrate armor. A regular IED sprays shrapnel, which isn't aerodynamic and is stopped by armor. The Iranians designed the EFP, and it's no fucking joke.

> Tony: The EFP hit the truck, piercing the armor. Part of it hit the contractor's chest, where his M-4 rounds are. These cook off and shoot into his legs, ripping his femoral artery. He hemorrhages blood.

Tony rips open the door to the truck, pulls him from the vehicle, and starts treatment. He's peeling off body armor when he hears a final breath, a huge whoosh of air from his lungs. Tony yells, "Don't you die on me, motherfucker!"

He's dead. I'll never throw bullets in a fire again.

The attack is not without an interesting story. Another contractor in the vehicle is hit with shrapnel that splits his penis down the center and lodges in his leg. They tear off his pants to attend to the wound.

Seeing his hot dog split, his buddy grabs his penis and holds it tightly to stop the bleeding. They're forty-five minutes from a hospital. That brave contractor holds the dick of his wounded comrade for an hour until he gets medical treatment. Months later a contractor on a convoy calls him. The man, call sign Carrot, tells him the doctors saved his twig then he calls his wife to the phone.

> Carrot: Tell him it works, honey.
> Reluctant Wife: It works.
> Contractor in Iraq: Hold on. I need to grab some people and get this on speaker.

He runs to gather others.

Contractor: Okay.
Carrot: Tell them, honey. Come on.
Reluctant Wife: It works.
Carrot: Hell, yes it does. It works great.
Reluctant Wife: Sure, honey. It works great.

Leadership gives us two days off. We attend a memorial where a State Department spokesman talks about the mission, how vital we are, how these deaths are not in vain. I've never seen this guy, and I doubt he knew the dead. We walk out pissed.

George: Fuck that. If I die, you guys better not let any State Department asshole talk about me and the mission.
Me: Agree.
George: I'm here for the money. I don't give a fuck about these people or this mission.
Me: Agree.

I'm numb. My transformation to poison dart frog is complete.

I jump on my computer and send an email to my family, so they know I'm safe. The news is showing footage with big headlines "Blackwater Contractors Dead." I don't want them to worry. I put ten recipients on the email. It's short and I don't include that I knew some of the deceased. "Wanted to let you know I'm safe in case you're watching the news."

I wake the next morning to a single reply from my aunt, "We're safe here too!" Thanks, Aunty. I'm pretty fucking worried you're in constant danger in Cottonwood. I don't bother replying. They don't give a shit. They have lives bitching about the price of skim milk. I don't expect them to not have a life while I'm here, but the fact they don't care cuts deep. I'm sad about the deaths of my brothers and now I'm morose my family doesn't care. My emotion turns to anger. Fuck them. This is the last time I let anyone know I'm dead or alive.

***

The story above was told to me by Tony and I believed him. It's false.

I must tell the real story to right the wrong of causing a widow and those in the attack emotional pain. It sucks to say: Tony's a liar. I would've died for him. You're welcome to decide if I published a lie out of malice or was fed one. I wasn't in the convoy and had no knowledge of what happened. If I made it up, based on what I got correct, I'm an amazing liar.

Tony told me that story when he came to my house in Flagstaff, Arizona after he finished a contract in winter 2006. We drank and talked. I had his possessions—clothes, personal items, and his Recon Paddle—from when we were roommates. The Recon Paddle represented his service and the history of Recon Marines. His Good Conduct ribbon was glued to the back of the handle after he'd been denied it for yelling at a lieutenant and getting his ass kicked by a gunnery sergeant. He trusted it with me. To say we were close is an understatement.

I tried to get in touch with Tony for years to no avail. He's always been a hermit—going silent for months. I had his paddle from 2004–2011 and couldn't bring myself to throw it away. I drove it to his mom's house in Minnesota on my way to Boston in 2011. I cried multiple times on the drive trying to figure out what I was going to say. I felt like I was giving up the last lifeline to my best friend. In hindsight, I was.

***

Here's the real story of the attack:

Al Hilla transitioned from a DoD to a DoS contract so the team was moved to Baghdad for a few days before relocating to Ramadi, an insurgent hotbed after the Marines took over Fallujah. Two of the men were scheduled to go home on April 22nd. They volunteered for the convoy to take their team to Ramadi. The bond of brotherhood overrode their desire for safety.

GUNS, GIRLS, AND GREED

Three Mambas and a flatbed truck left the morning of April 21st, 2005, for Ramadi, passing Fallujah which looked like a decimated town showing the vestiges of combat. They passed it and soon after an explosion slammed into the lead vehicle.

Mambas are built to withstand IEDs. They have a V-hull so an explosion will deflect the blast away from the people inside.

The lead Mamba is incapacitated, illustrating this wasn't a normal IED. The convoy springs to action. The driver of the second Mamba slams into the back of the lead Mamba trying to push it off "the X" or attack spot. It refuses to move. The brake line was punctured by the blast and caused the brakes to seize. It was dead.

The team set security and began to exfil the wounded. They tried to reach Blackwater via radio to no avail. They're alone. Those not doing security render aid to the wounded. Tony was accurate in telling me shrapnel hit someone in the chest which caused his ammo to cook off and sever his femoral artery, but he lied when he said that he pulled the man from the vehicle and yelled "Don't die on me motherfucker." He was on security. I'll never understand why he lied.

They load the wounded and gear into the second Mamba and drop a thermite in the disabled one to ensure it's disabled and they drive for help. With no long-range radio comms, they're at the mercy of finding a military convoy or outpost. After a few miles, they find an outpost and yell to them for help. The Army officer tells them to bring up the wounded and gets a medic to render aid as they're loaded in Hummers for transport to the Combat Army Surgical Hospital (CASH) in Ramadi. By now one contractor is dead and Carrot's losing blood from a puncture in his groin. Others have wounds and head injuries but are stable.

The convoy needs to get to Ramadi so the remaining men load in the Mambas and drive. Imagine driving in a vehicle filled with the blood of your brethren knowing you have no support from the company you work for. Alone again. They come to an Army checkpoint, tell them what happened, and request an escort to Ramadi. The Army obliges and they arrive safely in Ramadi.

They meet the wounded and it's confirmed their brother in arms has died. I can only imagine the mix of sadness and anger they felt. He was leaving for home the next day. Every man on the convoy likely felt they could have done more to save their brother. The truth is combat is Russian Roulette—a gamble of survival.

If these men were soldiers, they'd be called heroes and given awards. They'd qualify for VA benefits and have their medical bill covered for life. Instead, they're contractors—used by the government and Blackwater to wage war and discard. Their only support will come from their brothers in arms as they carry the scars of combat through life—like the men in this attack.

CHAPTER 19

W e're on the road two days after the helicopter was downed. I'm gunner behind the driver, Jacob, in the lead Hummer. It's a wrecking machine. We're in traffic and moving our way over a bridge near Camp of Many Names. My head's out the window with my rifle eighteen inches from the head of a middle-aged lady in the passenger seat of a car when shots ring out. They're ours. Fully automatic 240B. Must be Rampage in the rear turret. I think nothing of it until the lady screams like she's gut shot. She jumps on the lap of the driver, abject terror in her eyes.

Ha ha. Fuck her. I take a moment to feel bad. She's scared. Nah. Fuck her. Wait. I need to feel bad about this. At least a little bad. Fuck her husband too for no reason. These people don't give a fuck about their country. I don't either.

The next day, we're going to a shit-hole ministry building. We take a right onto the bridge to cross the river. The bridge connects the Green Zone to the traffic circle made famous for its statue of Saddam Hussein, which was toppled by US forces in 2003. A soldier put an American flag over his face as a crane pulled it down. It was dragged through the streets as locals hit it with shoes, a gesture of deep disrespect in Arab culture. It's the definitive sign Iraqis are welcoming us as liberators and not filthy infidel invaders. Spot on assessment, Secretary of Defense Rumsfeld.

Traffic's backed up in both lanes. We don't have time for this shit. A stopped motorcade is a tasty target for the people we liberated the shit out of.

Team leader: Morgan. Ray. Go fuck off those cars. We're cross-
    ing traffic.
Me: On it.

I get out excited and scared. This is the first time I've walked the
streets OTW. I was told by a high school teacher that extreme fear causes
the human body to pump adrenaline into the endocrine system elevating
the heart rate. This causes hyperawareness. I casually raised my hand and
asked, "If I'm running from a bear, this chemical reaction would cause
me to pop a boner when I'm running, right?" I was sent to detention.

Now I'm standing on a bridge in an active combat zone. This is
the definition of fear. Nary an erection in my pants, not even a semi-
chub. It's sad.

I kick the door shut like a BAMF and walk toward the car blocking
us. So we can move left to drive into on-coming traffic, the car needs to
move right a couple feet. I tap the driver's door.

Me: Move your fucking car to the right.

He looks at me indignantly and lifts his hands as if to say "where?"
Yes, I see the problem, no room to maneuver. I go to the car in front of
him, put my hand through his open window, and tap that guy's shoulder. He's startled. I point to the right. He gives me the same gesture. I'm
fucking over this. I push his steering wheel to the right and yell.

Me: Move your fucking car!

The car lurches to the right. I lift my rifle, point it at the driver of the
first car, and flick my left hand showing him where to go. I'm stunned
how nonchalant he seems at having a rifle pointed at him. He moves and
the Hummer crosses traffic. Look at us crossing the language barrier.

Ray and I walk down the center of oncoming traffic, rifles up. The
Hummer follows. A driver yields and the one behind him speeds into the
space like Allah opened up traffic. Then he sees me in full body armor,
my M-4 pointed at his chest, and yields.

The pattern repeats down the lane. Each car I fuck off is followed by one speeding up, until they too yield. I get tiny adrenaline spikes with each one. Sadly, no boner. I'm combat impotent. Maybe I've been here too long.

The Hummer mounts the sidewalk, one side on the road and one on the curb. I hop in and go back to watching out the window. We drive against the flow of traffic on the sidewalk to the traffic circle.

At the circle we cross back to our normal lane. In at six, out at twelve, and head to a tunnel that I've affectionately named the Tunnel of Love. Me and everyone else. I'm so original. We hold outside the tunnel until it clears, backing up traffic behind us. A little bird helicopter flies to the opposite side to tell us it's open.

I put my windows up, the top gunner sits down, and we drive like crazy through it. The Tunnel of Love is known to have IEDs hanging from the walls to blow through an open window or hit a top gunner. We emerge, I drop my window, the gunner stands, and we hold.

Steve: Vehicle one is through. Come on.
Team lead: Roger.

We roll forward as the convoy blasts through the tunnel. Once the follow vehicle is in, we gun it, so they don't have to break stride. We're a well-oiled machine.

We drive under a bridge, hang a left, and ascend to the elevated highway. I love the elevated highway. True love. We're planning our wedding. It runs north-south and stands twelve feet above the earth with barriers on both sides to keep cars from flying off. It doesn't always work.

Jacob guns it. We're driving sixty mph with my hair blowing in the wind. Why do dogs like this? Jacob honks the airhorn to move a car. The top gunner throws a water bottle at it. We're being ignored so Jacob gives him a gentle nudge with the bumper. He moves right and we pass.

We approach a hatchback refusing to merge. This is a special treat. Jacob pushes our front bumper into his hatchback door. This causes the window to flex and burst. It's like a movie. Glass flies in the air, hits the top gunner, and falls through the roof onto my shoulder. The gunner's pissed. He gets on the radio.

Gunner: Fuck, man. Stop hitting hatchbacks.
Jacob: Can't help it.
Gunner: Every fucking time I get hit in the face with glass.

We target hatchbacks because they provide instant gratification. On to the next victim. The next car is going fast but not fast enough. We bump it, causing it to swerve right, then left, then right. He hits the barrier and pops up on two tires. The driver puts his left arm out the window. His arm crumples under the roof of the car. It's looks like a Twizzler bending. Hell. Yes.

We arrive, drop our principals, and stick around to escort them back because it's a short meeting, no more than forty-five minutes. An hour later, the helicopter pilots are bored, so they put on an airshow.

One touches down on the wall of the elevated highway then lifts off. The second bird puts only the front skids on the wall. We cheer. Now it's a competition. The first bird brushes the top of a streetlight with a single skid. We cheer louder. The pilots have skills. I'm impressed.

After a thirty-minute show, we head back. Hell yes. Back on the elevated highway. We ascend via an on-ramp and merge into traffic. A red sedan's hauling ass coming at us. The top gunner's yelling at him. "*Imshi, imshi! imshi*, motherfucker!"

The horn blares as he approaches at eighty mph. We begin to merge and my asshole puckers. This dude isn't slowing down. He may be a VBIED or he may be a shitty driver.

My right thumb moves the safety selector to fire. I drop a couple rounds in front of the car. I watch them puff as they impact concrete. My rifle moves higher and I keep shooting. I'm alone in the world. Bullets impact the grill. I'm not looking down my sights, but I know where each round will strike before I squeeze the trigger.

The next round penetrates the engine. The car moves in slow motion. I'm seeing in slow motion but reacting in real time. Bullet in the hood.

It's silent. I can't hear a thing, not the deafening Hummer engine or the wind. I feel Top Gunner slap my shoulder, jolting me to full motion. The vehicle disappears from my view.

Adrenaline's coursing through my veins. I'm shaking a little. I drop the magazine and load another. I'm back in the fight. Combat reload. Still no erection. My teacher was full of shit.

I find Top Gunner when we park and ask why he slapped my shoulder. I'm afraid he saw something I didn't, that I made a mistake. I don't want to know if it was a bad shoot, but I have to ask.

> Top Gunner: I was telling you good shooting.
> Me: That car scared the shit out of me, man. He was hauling ass.
> Top Gunner: Dumb fucker.
> George: How many rounds did you shoot?
> Me: Five. Maybe seven.
> George: You don't know?
> Me: No idea, man.
> George: Do you know where they hit?
> Me: Most of them. The Hummer lurched hard left so I may have put a couple on the ground next to the car.
> George: You killed an innocent child.
> Me: Ha ha. Fuck off, George.
> George: Baby killer.

I walk with George to drop our kit. He's the greatest.

I have no idea if the driver had malintent or just wanted to drive fast. Did I shoot the driver? Maybe I took a life to save many. Or maybe my trigger finger was too itchy, and I scared the shit out of an innocent man. I'll never find out. That's fine even if it sucks a little.

***

Every car in Baghdad is a hunk of shit due to US led sanctions not allowing companies to do business with Iraq. Mess with the bull, get the horns. Cars are pieced together like Frankenstein's monster. We look at

175

each car and focus on the backend. If the shocks are weighed down, it could be a VBIED. Realistically, it's thirty-year-old springs but it gives us a reason to shoot at it. That's nice.

I've heard only certain people were allowed to drive under the Saddam regime, so most drivers are relearning how to maneuver a car. I have no way of confirming the veracity of this, but it seems legitimate. When the regime fell, locals dusted off old cars and jumped behind the wheel.

Three-lane roads are five-cars wide. The Code of Hammurabi, one of the world's earliest set of written laws, was created fifty miles south of Baghdad, and these fuckers can't figure out traffic rules. It's like watching a slow NASCAR race until we come through slaughtering vehicles. Iraqi police are posted to direct traffic but don't enforce the law. We do, with fury and joy in our hearts.

Jacob put up mosquito netting behind his head because he's tired of my spent round casings launching over the seat and landing on his neck. He has a couple burns that look like hickeys. I doubt he wants to explain this to his girlfriend when he goes on leave.

I'm getting good at shooting moving vehicles as we drive. I try to place rounds on tires and fenders. Nothing beats the sound of a tire deflating after it takes a round. I avoid shooting high as most people aren't a threat, just horrible drivers.

We're driving around a traffic circle and I see a white Kia sedan. It's clean, no dirt, no dents. It's the nicest car I've seen here. Jacob's blasting the airhorn but the Kia refuses to merge. We smash into it and the trunk crumples. The Kia's forced to the left on a walkway as we pass on the right. I get a view of the carpet lining the trunk.

I'm sad about this. I feel real remorse. I see shock on the faces of the driver and passenger. I lean my head out to say "Sorry," but it comes out, "Next time get out of our way, motherfucker." I point my rifle at them for good measure. I could swear I was about to apologize. Oh well. Fuck them. I'm an asshole and hate every fiber of this shithole country. I used to be such a nice young man. Grandma's not proud, but I don't fucking care. Looking back, I assume this anger and numbness were my first symptoms of PTSD.

CHAPTER 20

Tony's in Baghdad to escort the body of a buddy of his, Bulldog, home. Like the military, a teammate and friend of the deceased contractor is selected to escort the body. They attend the funeral and, hopefully, bring comfort to the family.

The video of Bulldog's death is on gore.com. The team was on the roof of a government building. Bulldog was looking around with his chin resting on his hand. There's a gunshot. He disappears.

Tony tells me that Bulldog was in a defensive position. Tony asked him if he wanted to be relieved. He declined. When the shot rang out, Tony ran to him. Blood was streaming from his neck, mouth, nose, ears, and eyes. He was shot through the neck. Dead on impact.

The sniper was posted on a neighboring building. He must've known our team would be on the roof because the cameraman is on a different building. Between the sniper and Bulldog is a building under construction. Buildings in Iraq are made like wedding cakes. A slab is set, then hundreds of wooden poles are set into the concrete and then next floor goes on top. The sniper had to find a position to get a bullet through the poles to Bulldog. It was an amazing shot.

Tony and his team members went to the morgue to say their final goodbyes before Tony escorted him to Baghdad for his honor flight. A soldier directed them to the body. Tony lost his mind when he saw Bulldog. He still had dried blood all over his face. He forcefully questioned the soldier, a young African American woman.

Tony: Why didn't you clean him?

Soldier: We only clean soldiers, not contractors.

This pushed Tony over the edge.

Tony: Bulldog was Special Forces in the Army. His dad was an SF
    soldier in Vietnam. Fuck you, you don't clean up contrac-
    tors. You're going to let his father see him like this? He's a
    fucking hero!

He let loose with a volley of racist names before being restrained by
his team and removed. Everyone has a breaking point. This was Tony's.
But what he did is despicable. It can't be excused.

I met Bulldog a couple times. He was a good dude.

After my intro call to join Blackwater, I went to the mall. I needed a
bad-ass watch and a sharp-ass knife for Iraq. I entered a shop owned by a
guy who wanted to join the military but instead collected knives. It was
a one-stop-shop for gear. Heck, I could have bought a sword if I wanted.
I found the perfect watch in the display case, a Casio Sea Pathfinder. It
was blue and brought out the color of my eyes. With it clasped around
my wrist, I was a gangster. All the juiced-up meatheads in Iraq would
be jealous.

I asked to see a knife and scraped it across my forearm. It shaved
the hair. Sharp for killing or opening MREs. I fell in love and put it
on my tab.

I bought concealed throwing knifes, which could be looped on the
back of my belt. I would put these on and when the shit hit the fan, pull
them out and throw them at the terrorist. One would impale his eye,
killing him. I've never thrown a knife, but I've dropped a few washing
dishes, so I'd figure it out in the heat of the moment.

This was ridiculous. There'd never be a time when the poop hit the
fan so violently that I'd have to go hot with throwing knives. I was an
idiot. Bulldog knew this but was nice enough not to call me on my BS.

Me: Hey, man.
Bulldog: Hey, nice watch.

Me: Yeah, I have throwing knives too.
Bulldog: Cool.

That's as substantive as our conversations got, but the death of any contractor hurts.

Tony wants me to join him in Ramadi, which is basically the fabled Indian Country I heard about on my first day. The insurgents moved there when the Marines took Fallujah. The most frightening are snipers from Uzbekistan, who migrated to Iraq to fight the Holy War. They're deadly and are thought to be who killed Bulldog. But hey, it sounds like an adventure. I'll entertain the idea. Plus, the contract pays more.

Tony: Ramadi is fucking crazy, dude. (It's his selling point.) You
    gotta come.

I'm scared shitless at the thought of Ramadi.

Me: I'm liking the QRF.
Tony: Check this out.

He opens his laptop and pulls dash cam video from the week prior. An RPG smashes into the ground near the car and small arms fire erupts. People yell, "Contact right." More gunfire. They drive off. Yeah. Fuck that.

Me: Dude, that's awesome.
Tony: Come down. This stuff happens twice a week. We get a fuck-
    ton of trigger time.
Me: Hell yes. I'll ask to transfer. (Lie.)
Tony: Let me know. I'll tell my team leader to request you.
Me: Not yet. I have leave in a couple weeks. (Nice excuse.)

I'll soon be forced to decide if I want to go to Ramadi.

CHAPTER 21

'm walking to the embassy to get a decent meal. As I approach the entrance, an Army lieutenant colonel (LTC) stands looking at the dark sky and calls to me:

> LTC: Hey, son. You may want to put your body armor on. It's raining lead.
> Me: Huh?
> LTC: Look at the red tracers.

Tracer rounds dash across the sky like red shooting stars to the soundtrack of AK-47 fire. I wonder why the dirt worshippers are celebrating.

Tracer rounds are used to identify where bullets impact when weapons are firing on full-auto. In a belt-fed weapon like the 249 and 240B, they're every fifth round. They glow red due to a small pyrotechnic at the base of the bullet, which burns when fired. They can be seen in the day and can't be missed at night. Every time the locals celebrate—when the national team wins a soccer match, when they vote, when they use actual toilet paper instead of their hand—the sky erupts with red speckles.

The lieutenant colonel has his flak vest on with no ammunition attached to it. He's a white-hot pussy. His belly pushes the vest, so he looks like Winnie the Pooh with a camo gunt (a gut covering his cunt, gunt).

> LTC: It's crazy. People are shooting at us and we're standing here watching.

Me: Shooting at us?
LTC: Yeah.
Me: Ha ha. Come on, dude.

He looks at me funny for calling him dude.

LTC: Crazy, huh?

I walk by him shaking my head. He's serious. He thinks he's in the shit, yet able to watch like it's a sporting event. I'm certain we'll never win here after this thirty-second conversation. Who else has he said this to? How many other military commanders think like this? The war's lost and so is what small amount of respect I had for the military.

***

The flashbang grenade is used to stun. It's a simple concept. It creates a flash of light and a loud bang. You toss one in a room, a team breaches the door, and shoots the stunned individual in the face.

Max gifts me a flashbang grenade; it looks like a silver tube surrounded by a blue cage. The outside casing is reusable. I'm under strict orders to send it to a hilarious death.

It has two pull rings and I'm baffled as to how it works. It seems I'd pull both pins but they're at opposite ends. I'd have to pull one, flip it over, and pull the other. Once I pull the first one, I'm holding a live grenade, which will flash or bang at any moment.

I'm told we'll drive through the local market so we can enjoy the show when I throw out the flashbang. I'm up for a challenge. I'm debating how to do this while holding my rifle as we approach the market. This'll be fun. My definition of fun has changed.

I feel like Neo choosing the blue or red pill as I debate which pin to pull. I'm in the lead vehicle so I'll miss the show, but the back ones will hear and see the flashbang and enjoy watching people scramble. Max is in the last vehicle, which is why he gave it to me. The pervert likes to watch. I pull a pin, toss it out the window and watch it bounce as we drive off.

I imagine women and children running from the grenade, fearing imminent death. The stampede runs over tents filled with lingerie and porno DVDs. The chaos. The carnage. Then they realize no one's hurt and have a good laugh. I'm expecting thank-you cards within days.

When we park, we conduct an AAR and Max asks if I threw the flashbang.

Me: Yep. How was it?
Max: Did you pull the pin?
Me: Yes.
Max: I didn't hear it go off. Did anyone hear or see it?
Collective: No.
Me: Must've been a dud.
Max: Did you pull both pins?
Me: Hell no. I'm not holding that thing and waiting for it to blow my hand off or drop it in the Hummer. You've lost your shit.
Max: You pull both.
Me: While I hold a rifle? Come on.
Max: No, dipshit. You set the rifle down.
Me: Still no.
Max: What should your punishment be?
Me: Punishment?
Max: Everyone gets to punch you in the arm.
Me: How about everyone gives me a blowjob instead? Seems fair. Line up fellas.
Max: Go ahead and punch him.
Me: Whatever you want.

I get punched in the arm by most of the team. Some don't. I'm thankful for that. My shoulder aches for days. Note to self: never accept a gift. Santa isn't real. The pain in my shoulder is.

I must make it clear. I had every intention to drop the flashbang and scare the fuck out of people in the bazaar. I've become numb. I have no sympathy. I want to punish these people for the death of every contractor and military member. If I could gather every person in Baghdad and execute them to get back a single US soldier, I would.

***

If a penis were to steal a priceless painting and I'm the only eyewitness, I could tell you if it was George's. I've seen it so many times, I feel like a Michael Jackson victim. I can describe every freckle and vein. As far as dicks go, it's not ugly but I wouldn't bring it home to meet Grandma even if it had the Hitler plate. I prefer my own.

I walk to George's room and he answers naked. It's impossible not to look over a naked man's body. I'm not sure why. I think it's an instinct to see if they're wearing shorts or boxers, a sock, anything covering their privates. So, I give him a full-length look and there it is. Cute little guy. Then I see it drip.

Me: The fuck? Did you just get done beating off?
George: Yes, why?
Me: I watched your dick drip load on the floor.
George: (Shrugs) Come on in.

I take a large step over his drip and sit down. He puts on shorts and wraps his fingers around my neck. I pretend he's choking me while praying he washed his hands post-self-coitus. He yells, "I'll kill you." This is normal. I stick my tongue out like Bart Simpson being choked by Homer. George then holds an airsoft gun to my head.

George: Don't turn this rape into a murder.
Me: I submit.

It's all fun and games until one day he points an airsoft Desert Eagle at Steve as a FNG (fucking new guy) walks by the window. He assumes he's witnessing an attempted murder and busts in, pulling his real weapon with real bullets out of the holster and screaming at George, "Drop the gun!" Steve and George stare at him, stunned someone would be so callous as to barge in during fun time. This isn't normal but it isn't abnormal.

George has the greatest porn video ever created. It's German. Probably. An old woman slathers her vagina with peanut butter and has a German shepherd lick it off. She says, "Clean it up. Clean it up," in a thick accent. The dog makes it German porn.

My radio echoes at two a.m. to the sweet sound of George saying, "Clean it up," in her voice. It haunts my dreams. That's animal abuse. George's impression of her makes it worse.

Nothing's abnormal at this point. I walk naked in my room and invite people in without bothering to put on pants. Any camera left lying around will get a picture of my healthy hog on it. I stretch it out before snapping the pic to make it bigger.

Jacob leaves his watch in the vehicle, so I wrap it around my cock and balls, take a picture, and send him a ransom email from an account I created. George is there when he gets the email. Jacob says, "That looks like Morgan's dick." George agrees and they call me on the radio to confirm. I wash his watch and return it because I'm a gentleman. I'm not sure what normal is anymore.

I'm coming up on a year in this place. I'm numb to these people. I'm numb to the sound of explosions and gunfire. I'm numb to my family. I've reached a high level of hate and anger with a splash of fuck-everything. It's an intoxicating elixir.

A ray of sunshine hits me as I walk in the PX at Camp Liberty. I see signs in the book section saying the sixth book in the Harry Potter series will be released tomorrow. The actual release date is the following day. No way they fly them in tonight. Not in a combat zone. They're already here. I can smell them. I feel the presence of a sorting hat. I must have it.

I ask a cashier if I can buy it since I won't be here tomorrow and the PX in the Green Zone won't have it. No. I get the manager. I explain my love for Hagrid. No. Fuck. Come on, dude. Don't be all Snape about it. Go grab one. I'll give you fifty dollars. No. Fuck you. Sorry, I didn't mean that. Why is life so hard?

At our team meeting that night I ask the team to make a run to Camp Liberty the next day. I forgot something. They look at me like I have a dick growing out my forehead. I come clean.

Me: I need the new Harry Potter book.
Jacob: No.
Me: I'll never ask for anything again.
Max: No.
Me: I'll buy everyone who makes the run Burger King.
All: Done.

The next morning, we drive down Route Irish, still the most bombed route in Iraq, to get the Harry Potter book. It's ridiculous and yet, here we are. People willing to sacrifice their life for Burger King and *Harry Potter and the Half-Blood Prince*. These are my brothers.

I read the book cover-to-cover over two days. Spoiler alert: When Albus Percival Wulfric Brian Dumbledore dies, I damn near cry. How could such a tragedy happen? How did he get the name Brian? He deserved better on both counts. I walk in the miserable heat to clear my head. I've lost a family member. This is the closest I've been to crying here.

***

I want to rescue every puppy in this God-forsaken shithole. They deserve better. They're innocent. The people...not so much. I'm sitting on the curb near an Iraqi checkpoint at some random ministry building. I notice a puppy, so I pull beef jerky from my vest and give him a taste. He loves it. I pet him. I love it. I keep the jerky flowing and give him all the ear scratchies he can handle. He bites me playful-puppy style. I smell his adorable puppy breath. I'm in love.

An Iraqi police officer manning the checkpoint walks over with a smile. We make eye contact. He assumes we're friends. He's wrong. He kicks the puppy and laughs. I stand up and rise a solid eight inches above him. I grab his shoulders and squeeze. His smile disappears as his eyes widen.

> Me: If you touch my puppy, I'll beat your fucking brains in. Get the fuck out of my face, you heartless fuck. You deserve death. I'll give it to you.

Even with the language barrier, he understands. I point to the dog and continue to yell. Fuck him. Fuck this place that hates dogs. I sit down and coax my puppy back. This may be the only time he gets love in his pitiful life scrounging for food and water. A life absent of love and tummy scratching. I vow to save a dog from this hell if I can. I'd rather save a dog than an Iraqi.

That night we congregate around a room and the Coronas flow like the Mississippi River as the war stories come out. Aside from being part of the Ground Offensive in Iraq and protecting the base where Jessica Lynch was flown to, I'm a poser. I break out my Pat Tillman Story.

I grew up in Arizona. Pat Tillman was a legend to me before he quit football to join the Army Rangers. I was a security guard at the Arizona Cardinals training camp in Flagstaff in 2002 tasked with checking ID badges. It wasn't glamourous but I had a cooler next to me full of bottled water for the players. I'd sneak home four of them daily because they were amazing and free.

Jake Palmer, also an Arizona State University legend, walked to my station with someone not authorized to enter. I stopped them and Jake castigated me. I was making ten dollars an hour, sans the free water, and had to tell his friend he wasn't allowed to pass. I felt like a bag of dirt.

The next day, Pat Tillman was walking by me and asked if I wanted anything from McDonald's. I asked him to grab me a two-cheese burger meal with a Coke and grabbed my wallet. He said "I got you" and walked off. He came back, dropped it on my table, and left. I'll never forget it. His humility was on display even then. I'm honored to have met him in passing even though the burgers had onions on them which I had to scrape off. I was watching the NFL draft in 2004 when they announced his death. The term "hero" is tossed around but a man willing to put his life on the line when he was financially stable is the epitome of hero. His death cut me deep.

The next story was combat cool. A former DevGru operator sipped his Corona and started:

> DevGru: We were doing a training exercise where we had to infiltrate a hijacked plane flight. We went to the bone yard to find a plane to practice. There are four of us on the top by the exit doors. We'd land on the plane and take it down.

I'm in awe of this. It's impossible but they train for it. It feels like me preparing for a night with Jenna Jameson.

> DevGru: We tether in at the top. We have to jump toward the doors at the same time using the other person as our counterweight.
> Me: This is James Bond shit.
> DevGru: I don't know if I jumped early or my partner jumped late. I fell on the wing and broke my back only to see my buddy flying over the plane and smash on the fusillade.
> Me: Jason Bourne isn't real!
> DevGru: Fuck no he's not. I was in the hospital for six weeks and after three months returned to the teams.

I wipe the saliva off my mouth. I'm suddenly aware I'm standing on the shoulders of giants. For as many Funk Fakers are here, there are more legitimate operators.

***

As people return from leave, I get new hooker stories. Jack the Hog Slayer has come back from Florida where he went with his war pig, but they had a falling out. He likes his women like he likes his coffee, without another man's dick in it. Selfish bastard.

Jack met up with his cousin in Fort Lauderdale, Jack's Mecca. They decide to call an escort service after a hard night partying. The picture on the brochure shows young, fit, delicious hookers. They order two and wait in the hotel room, which has two beds. Classy.

Jack: It's one a.m. and we're dead asleep when the hookers arrive. I'm not going to fuck a hooker.

Cousin: We have to bang these hookers.

Jack: It's a solid argument so I walk to the door and see two used up old women standing there. One blonde and one with black hair. They're in their late forties. The blonde has lipstick smeared across her cheek. I'm not paying to bang either of these hookers.

Cousin: We have to bang these hookers.

Jack: I'm convinced. We'll bang these hookers. They come in and get undressed. We start fucking them on separate beds. It's gross but fuck it. Then we bang them on the same bed. We're high fiving doing the spit roast (one in front and one in back like a pig over a fire). We go back to our individual hookers. I'm standing two feet from my cousin.

Cousin: This hooker stinks, bro.

Jack: I know. I can smell her from here. We high five again. It was awesome.

Me: Was the hooker offended you called out her smell?

Jack: Fuck no. She had to have known. It smelled that bad. Never buy hookers in Fort Lauderdale.

Me: Noted.

At this point, my understanding is never buy hookers in Fort Lauderdale, hot ones, old ones, ones in Amsterdam, ones of Vietnamese descent, basically any hooker at all.

CHAPTER 22

We're lost and driving aimlessly in Baghdad. There are places we avoid such as Sadr City and Haifa Street. Those areas aren't fans of the US freeing them and call us occupiers. Steve's being groomed to be the tactical commander, so I get his squad automatic weapon (SAW) today. Dean's driving the lead Hummer. I sit behind him.

Steve's the nicest guy in Iraq aside from Vance, who's still in Sulay. He's jovial and constantly smiles. He wears huge Oakley Heater sunglasses, fit for both combat and church softball. His room smells amazing because he puts fabric softener sheets in his AC vent. I've never seen him angry or frustrated. He's also a ruthless machine gunner. Machine guns aren't point weapons, but Steve can take out the tires of a car while we drive sixty mph. His accuracy is unmatched. I'm glad he's on our side.

However, Steve is shit with a map. I see where we need to go but getting there's a different story. Many roads are closed off due to the proliferation of car bombs. We take a left into a neighborhood. Fuck. Neighborhoods are never good. My asshole's puckered. We turn around.

Dean: Where the fuck am I going, Steve?

Steve's looking at his GPS like he's trying to decipher hieroglyphics. Not good. From the back of the convoy, Max gets on the radio.

Max: Take a right.
Steve: Roger.

Max directs the convoy from the back, which is exceptional considering he has to gauge where the lead vehicle is at any point and tell it where to turn. We get back on the road parallel to the river. We know where we are. We drive north to the roundabout and take a left over the bridge, but the road's closed. Dean's pissed.

We divert east through tall buildings and hanging powerlines. We're above the Tunnel of Love. The top's packed with people so we U-turn to take the tunnel.

Dean guns it down a ramp and obliterates a car by pushing it against a barrier. The windows pop and break as its front-end smashes. The car lurches in an attempt to find room but there's none. That car is fucking dead. The driver could be also.

We hit the roundabout and cross the bridge where I pop-off a nice eight- to-ten-round burst at a car. Just enough to ensure it needs to be cleaned tonight. We park and I hand Steve his para-SAW. He will not be directing the convoy again.

Max: Steve, you're running the convoy tomorrow. Same place.

Me: Here you go, Steve. Your baby's back in your arms safe.

Max: Nope. Fuck that. Keep it. Steve's the TC tomorrow. We're going to make this run until we get it right.

Steve: Sounds good.

Me: I'll clean your baby like it's my own. I'll hold her tight and swaddle her. She'll suckle from my bosom and be put to bed early. She's safe.

Steve's not amused but unable to be unhappy.

Steve: Thanks.

I drag the SAW to my room and take it apart. It's been a while since I played with a SAW and this is a para-SAW, same guy but shorter. I'm a surgeon used to working on adults and learning to operate on children, same guts but a smaller frame. I clean it and put it back together. I jack the charging handle back a few times. Seems like it works. I set it by the bed for tomorrow.

Same run. No problems. No smashed cars. No puckered assholes. I admire what Max did in making Steve get it right. He could've tossed him in a gunner position without complaint but made him grow as a leader. I'm not sure Steve cares but we're proud of him. Live and learn. Mostly live.

I give Steve his para-SAW, and I drive on our next run. Jacob's a genius. The mosquito net's nice and keeps hot spent cartridges off my neck. He's on leave, which is why we're playing musical QRF positions.

Steve's behind me. I'm wearing Groucho Marx glasses complete with fake nose and mustache. The driver of every car I smash looks back to see my stupid face with a huge smile on it. I hope they enjoy my sense of humor.

A car barrels toward us from an adjacent road. I hear the bolt of a 249 pull back. Steve's going to lay down hate. I love this part. Clunk. Fuck.

The 249 is an open-bolt weapon. The bolt stays to the rear of the gun when ready to fire. Combat Safe means the bolt's forward and ammunition loaded. Safety off. To go hot Steve pulls the bolt to the rear position. When he pulls the trigger, the bolt rushes forward, the firing pin hits the bullet, and the bullet leaves the barrel as the spent cartridges fly into mosquito netting. The force of fire pushes back the bolt. When the trigger's held down, it continues to move back and forth until all ammunition is spent.

"Clunk" is the sound of a 249 malfunctioning. The bolt moved forward but no bullet fires. This is caused by either the bolt or the bullet being seated incorrectly. I'm guessing it's the bolt since Steve knows how to load his shit. I, on the other hand, put the bolt in and I don't know my shit, at least not like Steve. Okay. I don't know my shit.

I hear Steve open the top and reseat the ammo. He yanks the bolt and fires again. Clunk. I'm an asshole. I swerve at the car and it stops. Good. Just a shitty driver. Steve's pissed. He's cussing as he transitions to his M-4. I'm mortified. If Steve's cussing, it's bad. We complete the run and as we unpack the Hummer, Dean gets animated.

Dean: Steve, what the fuck? Why didn't you light that car up?
Steve: My weapon jammed.

I'm looking at birds and shit.

191

Dean: How the fuck did that happen?

Steve: I don't know. I need to take it apart and check it out.

Me: I fucked up putting it back together last night after cleaning it.

Dean: You don't know how to put a 249 back together?

Me: I do. I have. I don't know. What the fuck.

Dean: You should have fucking asked. "Clunk" is the last sound you hear before you fucking die.

Steve: Let me take it apart and see.

I walk with Steve toward his room.

Me: I fucked you, man. I took that apart yesterday and must've fucked it all up.

Steve: I'll check it out.

Me: Sorry, dude.

Dean, Steve and I are all in the same lead vehicle the next day. Prior to the run Dean comes over. I feel like an asshole.

Dean: So, what was wrong?

Steve: The ammunition must not have been seated right.

Dean: No way.

Steve: I took it apart and it was put together right. It wasn't Morgan.

Dean gives me the "you're lucky" look. Steve saves my bacon. I'm positive I fucked it up. There's zero chance he mis-seated the ammo, cleared it, reseated it, and it was wrong. Steve's a professional. I'm a faker. He saved my reputation with his humility. I sit in his room nightly watching him take apart that SAW. I have no idea where I messed up but I know I did. It's dumb shit like this, small mistakes, that are the difference between life and death.

***

We all fuck up at some point. We play by big boy rules, which is nice compared to the military which plans, over-plans, and stands around debating if they should plan more. This is the environment Sergeant Major loved for twenty-five years and why I got out. This new paradigm's refreshing.

We set a time to leave and drive off. Each member's accountable to know routes, runs, weapons, and their spot in the convoy—big boy rules. Everyone gets one fuckup and must accept the punishment chosen by the team. My fuckups are well documented but luckily, never get me kicked off the team.

We have a run at 10:00, so I get to the Hummer at 9:30 to prepare. The drivers have fueled up the vehicles. We paper, rock, scissor for spots in the vehicle. I'm behind the driver because I won. The seat behind the driver gets more trigger time so I prefer it. We put Dean behind the tactical commander/passenger seat because he hasn't arrived.

We roll at ten a.m. and Jacob sees Dean in the sideview mirror running behind us. We stop, he jumps in and puts his kit on as we drive. We don't have time to wait for him to unfuck himself.

Dean: I thought we were out at ten?
Jacob: It's ten.
Dean: Ten to the vehicles.
Jacob: Ten is RP. (Release Point, time to go.)
Dean: Fuck, I fucked up. Sorry, guys.
Jacob: Big boy rules, Dean. Figure out what you need to do to leave by RP.

Dean's never late again. He bought the beer at the next pool party. That's the normal penance—buy beer, which is no chump change considering the super-livers of Blackwater contractors.

Max, our team lead, has a nice fuckup. We're driving through a roundabout when a car barrels toward us. He pulls his pistol and shoots the mirror off the Hummer. It's never replaced.

As atonement, Max shows us his sex tape. It's unpleasant. First, I assumed it would be a theatrical presentation. It's not. It's a video camera on a stand, no closeup of balls or puss. Second, it's five minutes long, which doesn't bode well for Max. Third, the zenith (or nadir as it may be) is the chick riding him and Max making a sound like a baby goat learning it has a voice. *Maaaa.* Awful. That sound haunts my house like a dead relative.

***

Morality in combat is worthless. There's no place for it. We exit a compound in northern Baghdad and a car drives through an Iraqi police (IP) officer toward our convoy. We're taking a left, so I don't see it, but I hear shots from the gunner behind me and in the turret. Seems legit. Who cares? We're shooting so many cars at this point, I don't bother to care if it's a good shoot.

Dean's driving the follow vehicle and his turret gunner's a softhearted Special Forces guy. The IP's bleeding on the ground as we drive off. They're not impressed. He must've been in the crossfire. Probably a ricochet. Who knows? We shoot and scoot like Ron Jeremy. Stopping to assess a threat is the worst-case scenario when protecting someone as their safety is paramount. Shoot. Scoot. Assess after…or never. Who cares?

We don't normally have an AAR after a run on the QRF, according to big boy rules, but Dean and Soft Heart get on the radio to gather us. They're livid. I'm oblivious. They assume we meant to shoot the IP. No one else has a clue the IP was shot. No reason to cry over spilled milk.

Dean: Who shot the IP?
All: ?
Dean: The lead Hummer shot. Someone opened up on the IP.
Top Gunner: I lit up the car.
Back Gunner: Me too.
Softy: Someone shot the IP.
Top Gunner: We shot a car.
Softy: Someone hit the IP. We can't go around killing innocent people.
Dean: Why'd you shoot?

Top Gunner: First off, Dean, you've killed more people driving than anyone has shooting. Don't give me that high and mighty shit.

Softy: We shouldn't kill innocent people.

Back Gunner: Agree. We shot at the car pushing past the IP. If he got hit in the process, that sucks. We had no idea.

Top Gunner: (Getting pissed.) If you were so worried, why the fuck didn't you stop and drag his ass in your vehicle? Were you worried about him? Fuck off.

Softy: This is shit. Be more careful.

Top Gunner: Fuck you. We shoot if we feel threatened. Sit in the back and shut your cocksucker.

We break the AAR without another word. It's too heated. No one likes their split-second decisions questioned. No one wants to figure out the morality of it. The truth is a moral person can flip into a killer within minutes then switch back. One person can assess a shoot to be moral and another interpret it as corrupt. I wish it were black and white. We operate in gray.

Plus, there are no repercussions. Aside from us, no one has a clue when we shoot or not. We're supposed to call it in to the TOC but why? So someone can conduct an investigation and find evidence that no longer exists? Iraqis lie about everything. We can't be court martialed because we're not military. Nothing good can come from calling in a shoot, and the honor system isn't compelling.

***

Ah, the elevated highway. We meet regularly but I miss you when I'm not on you. You have a special place in my heart. I'm not sure it's love, lust maybe. Blood lust? Lust regardless.

I hear a commotion and see an orange and white car fly off the highway like it's in a *Dukes of Hazzard* episode. It's airborne and not in my field of fire so I shouldn't be looking but I can't help it. It's loud and not like the movies. Scraping metal and no cool sparks or fire pouring off it. Disappointing.

Rewind thirty seconds: I hear an M-240 Bravo laying down hate from the follow vehicle. Full auto, 7.62 rounds. Rampage is killing it back there. He puts thirty rounds down in seconds.

Rewind sixty seconds: Rampage stands in the gun turret of the follow Hummer. He's attempting to halt traffic. We're descending the offramp to leave the highway. Rampage gestures for them to stop, yelling, "Halt! *Imshi!* Stop!" The vehicle doesn't obey. Rampage bends over his 240B and fires warning shots.

Rewind ninety seconds: Rampage is in the rear turret watching an orange and white car careen toward the convoy. He stands up so the driver can't miss him. The guy's huge. Helen Keller couldn't not see him.

Real Time: The machine gun fire's deafening. We move down the off-ramp. I hear scraping and have no choice but to watch as we die because a car broke our security. The car launches off the highway to the ground fifteen feet below. The impact is earsplitting. The driver is dead, no doubt. What is wrong with these drivers?

CHAPTER 23

I t's July 2005, around noon on a Baghdad summer day, and we're hauling ass down a random street. I'm baking in this sauna we call a Hummer. We try to move in the morning or evening to avoid having our internal organs cook while we drive in this steel oven. Not today.

The Hummer has air conditioning. I'm sitting in front of it but can't feel cool air because the windows are down and there's a hole in the top where our gunner stands. Even if the windows were up and we closed the hatch, the AC isn't equipped to cool much more space than a mailbox. The engine would need to divert energy from lugging around armor to run an AC. It's working overtime for minimal output. It's as worthless as my absentee father. Fuck this AC and fuck that guy.

I sit next to an ammo can holding six hundred rounds of .556 linked ammo for an M-249. It's held down by a bungee cord. It's a precaution should we find ourselves in a situation where we must hold in place or need resupply. It's a necessary evil. We never use it but can't be without it. Mostly it sits blocking my comfort. But today it serves a purpose.

We enter an intersection and a white car's closing in. I shoot. My bullet hits the ground in front of the vehicle. Smoke pours from the tires as it skids to a stop. No reason to shoot the guy if I can avoid it. I'd rather scare him than take away his mobility. I'm becoming tender-hearted.

In my moment of morality, I don't see the blue bongo truck adjacent to the pickup, which doesn't stop. Jacob pulls the wheel hard left and we smash into it. We've been in a lot of collisions but this one's exceptional.

I lurch forward, hitting my head on the roof. My neck compresses. It hurts. I feel bad for the old guys I made fun of when I drove over the

IED hole on Route Irish. The top-gunner damn near flies out. I grab his legs to keep him in. I feel skin. He's wearing shorts. I grab leg hair. He's Mexican and lacks in the leg hair department. His hairless legs flail in an attempt to keep the rest of him in the Hummer.

I'm contorted like a circus freak-show actor and wonder if this is how Satan learned to suck his own cock. With a bald leg in my arms, I smash into my seat. It's occupied. Fucking ammo. My left hip bone crashes into it and pain explodes through my torso. Why the fuck didn't I secure that with something other than a damn bungee cord? That's right, because I'm an idiot. Combat is unforgiving. Small efficiencies make a huge difference.

The gunner stands on his box. It's adorable. He's too short to see over the armor so he has a box. Hairless legs protecting me. All's right in the world. Jacob apologizes for the impact. I apologize for not seeing the bongo truck. We're all sorry, but the Hummer's sluggish. It's not driving right. We must've popped a tire.

The vehicle behind us has a dash cam and later, I watch the video. For as intense as the crash felt, it looks anticlimactic. I hear a tiny pop, a puff of dust where my bullet hit the ground, and the car stops. The Hummer bumps into the bongo truck. The violence is calm to watch compared to being in the nucleus of the collision. The gunner looks like a dancing air puppet on a used car lot. I regret making fun of Max's sex tape. Nothing's as cool on amateur video as when it's professionally produced.

Jacob and I go to KBR to have the Hummer fixed. Fuck KBR and the horse they rode in on, Vice President Dick Cheney. We drop it off inside a huge hangar where contractor vehicle maintenance is done. It holds twenty vehicles, tools to fix them, and vast numbers of overpaid fat asses talking about how hard they work.

We park and walk to the maintenance office to sign paperwork stating the time and date we dropped off the vehicle, as well as a detailed explanation of how it got in this condition.

Me: We hit a bongo truck.

We return the next day and our Hummer hasn't moved so we find the mechanic and he gives us a detailed explanation as to why it's still in this condition.

Mechanic: We haven't looked at it.

This is how modern wars are fought.

We return to let the team know we're out of commission. The team has to improvise so they conduct missions with no lead Hummer. I'm out of a job until it's fixed. We return to KBR with a bottle of Jack Daniels because sitting around sucks. Miraculously, the mechanic finds time to look at the Hummer and tells us to return tomorrow. We do.

Mechanic: The Hummer's dead. You can't drive it.
Jacob: What? We drove it here.
Mechanic: The engine runs but the radiator's busted. It'll overheat. The frame's bent so we can't put on a new radiator. It's going to need to be scrapped.
Me: Would another bottle of the devil's honey help?
Mechanic: It'll help me but the vehicle's dead.

This feels like losing a family member. First Dumbledore and now this. Summer of 2005 is one to forget. I'm not crying, my eyes are sweating from the heat. I swear.

Jacob: Can we use your tools to take our armor off?
Mechanic: My toolbox is over there. Make sure you put them back when you're done.

We walk to the Hummer to assess how to take off the armor. We need a vehicle to haul our stuff. We can't leave the midget box our top gunner stands on.

Max tells us to stash the armor in storage at the compound until we get a new Hummer. We grab a Suburban, drive to KBR and unload it: mosquito net, Groucho Marx glasses, the gunner's step stool. We use ratchets and sockets to dismantle the armor like doctors peeling out organs for needy Hummers. I'm on the top removing armor when a KBR manager comes over, fuming.

KBR: What do you think you're doing? You're stealing our equipment.

Jacob: This is armor we got outside of KBR. We're taking it off this one so we can put it on a new one later.

KBR: This is mine. It's on my books. You're stealing it.

I get down from the Hummer.

Me: Fuck you, man. Get the fuck out of here.

KBR: What's your name?

Me: My name is Hugh G. Rection. Sound it out.

Jacob: Sir, we work for Blackwater. We got this armor from the Army. We're not stealing anything. We're going to get a new Hummer and put it on it.

KBR: I'm the shop manager. I own everything here. Where'd you get the tools?

Jacob: From the mechanic. He said we could use them to remove our armor. We'll return them.

KBR: They aren't his tools. They're mine.

Me: What the fuck is your problem, man?

He pulls the ratchet from my hand.

Me: You get near me again, I'm going to grab that rachet and beat you with it.

Jacob: Calm down. We'll take our stuff and leave the armor. Can you check the serial numbers to see this isn't on your books?

I'm furious. I'm scheduled to go on leave in a week and the stress of the last four months has me on edge. Jacob just returned from leave so he's cool as a cucumber. Cucumber. Our safe word.

At our team meeting later, Max tells us we're fired. Great. This day keeps getting better. Max is fired too. The KBR pussy ran to the State Department and told on us like a bitch. No questions asked. We're terminated.

Our only hope comes from Crop Duster, who asks for an appeal. It's granted but we can't work until the investigation ends. We write a report about what happened. Our leadership takes it to DoS. We're innocent. After a two-day investigation, KBR verifies the armor isn't on their books. We've been absolved.

Not to get deep into the bureaucratic garbage of working for a government entity, but DoS hires independent contractors because we're expendable. We're not employees. Blackwater's the contractor and we're subcontractors, which gives DoS the latitude to tell Blackwater to hire or fire us at will. Thankfully, we're vindicated.

They fire us anyway. There's no justice in Iraq. We're sent to the team house and told we'll move to a non-DoS contract and stay in country. We have two options. Kirkuk or Ramadi. Kirkuk's calm. Jacob and I have been there, and the chow hall's great. It has a good gym and a volleyball court where they play the *Top Gun* theme song as Maverick and Goose dominate. Ramadi is a real war zone. There's no better place to test my mettle. I'm scared to go, but I trust the people there and I may never get a chance to have this adventure again. I need a peach to think it over.

The team house has private guards from Jordan, a nice kitchen, and a local lady as a cook. They get local produce at the market, from Iran. At this point, eating local food is like playing Russian Roulette with my anus.

I walk to the kitchen and grab a peach from a fruit platter. I return to the living room where Jacob sits. The blinds are closed to keep the sun out. The AC vent is above us, which feels nice. I sit on the couch but leave a man-barrier between us.

The other couch has two Jordanian guards waiting for a ride to the airport. I take a bite of the peach. My taste buds ignite. The flavor dances around my tongue and the juice drips down my chin. I slurp to pull in the maximum amount of juice before chewing. Holy fuck. Each time my lower jaw moves, flavor blasts through my body. I take a second bite to confirm I'm not deceived. The second bite equals the first. This is the best peach I've ever had. Boner time.

Me: Jacob, you have to take a bite of this peach.
Jacob: No, thanks.
Me: You have to. I've never had a peach this good.
Jacob: Serious?
Me: Serious.

Jacob grabs the peach and takes a bite. He's astounded, flabbergasted, amazed by the flavor. He makes an "mmmm" sound. The Jordanians are looking at us. I don't care. He takes a second bite and I reach over to grab the peach before he devours it. I take another bite and pass it back. We share a peach. It's a moment.

Me: We should hit Kirkuk.
Jacob: Why?
Me: Chow Hall. Gym. That place is badass.
Jacob: It also has a snow-cone maker.
Me: I have a buddy in Ramadi, and he says they get a ton of trigger time.
Jacob: Sounds awesome.
Me: I'd rather have a solid gym and food.

I'm pussin' out and handing him a branch to puss out with me.

Jacob: Let's do it.

We're going to Kirkuk. This peach though. I go back for a second one and it's not as good. The first one had the magic bugs from *James and the Giant Peach* embedded in it. The Jordanians look at us funny.

Jacob and I tell the team house leader to send us to Kirkuk. I remind him I'm on leave in a week.

GUNS, GIRLS, AND GREED

Team Leader: Go to Kirkuk and drop your shit to ensure you have a spot there when you return.

Me: Isn't Kirkuk a DoD contract?

Team Leader: It's DoD now but transitioning to DoS. You can jump on the DoD contract and we'll hold you over when it switches. There's no oversight so you'll blend in. Plus, DoD contracts pay six hundred a day.

The lack of a tracking mechanism is shocking, but it works in my favor. I'll be Tony for a few weeks and fall ass first into some extra cash.

The team house medic walks into the room and yells at the Jordanians. They recoil as he walks to the kitchen. I look at Jacob, who shrugs his shoulders. The medic walks back two minutes later and yells at them again. They recoil. Not my house. Not my problem.

Twenty minutes later the medic comes and sits down on the couch in the spot I left as a dude-buffer. He yells at the Jordanians. He's an asshole.

Me: Why do you yell at them every time you see them?

Medic: Fuck those guys. We're sending them home.

Me: So, you yell because?

Medic: Because they keep fucking each other in the ass.

Me: Why's that a problem?

Medic: I'm the medic. They keep giving each other anal warts. I have to look at that shit. I've cured these guys three times and they keep fucking each other in the ass. Then they complain about it and I have to look at their wart-filled assholes and put cream on it. They stink. (Looking at them.) That's right. Fuck you.

Me: That makes perfect sense.

Medic: These two can't come back. They keep fucking each other on the night shift.

Me: Anyone think of putting one on the day shift and one on the night shift?

Medic: Doesn't matter. They all fuck each other.

Maybe this is why they looked at Jacob and I as we shared a peach. My ass itches. My scalp itches. I'm glad I sat on this couch. My ass itches more. I need to find an AC unit to hang it over like Tony to cure my osmotic anal warts.

***

They fixed the Casa Bird and we're taking it to Kirkuk. I'm not excited. It has precious cargo—me. We make a stop in Tikrit, Saddam's birthplace.

We corkscrew in. The landscape is a dustbowl. Iraq's a desert so you'd think it would be sandy like a beach. It's not. It's dirt with the consistency of talc. When the wind blows, it feels like baby powder thrown into a fan pointed at my face.

I see the words, "Welcome to Hell" carved in the earth as we descend. Each letter's a hundred meters tall. I'm amazed at the ingenuity. A US soldier carved this, knowing every plane would see it as they circle in. Tikrit sounds lovely.

We land with the normal fanfare of a gunner on the back hatch. He's no longer badass in my mind. He'll never fire his weapon so he's a castrated show dog. He may win an award but he'll never breed awesomeness to another generation. The pilots don't bother to turn off the engines as we drop off passengers. We lift off to Kirkuk with Mr. Best-in-Show sitting on the back hatch.

Kirkuk was inhabited by Kurds, but the oil was too valuable for the regime to leave it to them. Saddam, via Chemical Ali, started Ba'athification to push the Kurds north and insert Ba'ath party Sunnis from 1968 to 2003, when we invaded. This allowed Saddam to retain oil revenue and keep his regime afloat. He did the same in the south. It's ironic he was Sunni since they inhabit the middle of Iraq, which has no oil. Control the oil, control Iraq. The man knew how to dictate.

Kirkuk's the fault line between the Kurds and Ba'ath party Sunnis. Kurds want their land, oil, and houses returned from the Sunnis. No middle ground. No sharing. That would be asking them to share a meal with the men who raped their sisters. Bad blood.

The REO is located in northern Kirkuk and the Kirkuk Regional Air Base (KRAB) is in the middle. We don't go south of it for two reasons. First, it's where the American-hating Sunnis reside. Second, why would we pass up the snow-cone maker?

De-Ba'athification is the US policy to return what Saddam and his regime took dating back to 1968. The Kurds want us to kick Sunnis out of houses they've lived in for generations. Sunnis aren't keen on the idea. The new government we're propping up can't have Kurds own Kirkuk because the oil produces the revenue the new government needs to be viable. If Kurds control it, they can declare independence. The new government needs this money, to steal it, and stash it in Syria for the impending civil war. The complexity is confounding. It's like playing Chinese Checkers with guns in an earthquake.

Considering all this, it's safe. The KRAB has a PX where kids don't sell porn and, did I mention the amazing snow-cone machine? It's the closest thing to paradise I can ask for in a desert war. We land in Kirkuk and I'm home.

CHAPTER 24

Nick, my former team leader in Sulay, is the head of the teams in Kirkuk. I wonder if he's mad at me for calling him out on talking to his wife while squeezing his meat? Naw. No grown man in this profession can have soft skin. Nick may have looked homeless and smelled like the ass of a menstruating skunk, but he's no pussy-wussy.

Jacob and I walk off the plane. Our people are easy to identify, guys standing around with long beards, Land Cruisers, or Suburbans. Nick walks to greet his new team members. We're not expecting him. He's not expecting us. We run to each other. My sundress flaps in the wind. We embrace with a kiss as he squeezes my ass. That's a joke. He's not happy to see me. He has a well-kept beard and smells great, though. Progress.

We drive to the REO, and Nick tells us to meet in his room at six p.m. We're assigned rooms so we unpack before we walk the REO to get an idea of the compound. Old habits.

It's small. Fortified T-walls surround it with look-out posts on the perimeter. It smells like burnt oil, which reminds me Kirkuk's an inhabited oil field burning natural gas. We walk to the entrance and see flaming tubes standing like candles in the desert. I want a cigarette.

The State Department personnel live in the main building, which has the gym and a recreation room. Across from that is the chow hall. A small building to the west is the KBR area where we can drop laundry. A volleyball court with two picnic tables completes our tour. Forty people live here. I'm getting island fever.

This compound was owned by Chemical Ali along with a house that looks like a golf ball north of us on a hill. It was his house during the

Anfal Campaign and a US spy organization now inhabits it. The compound is convenient because it was fortified before being taken over by US Forces. It makes a cozy base.

We grab dinner and head to Nick's room in the embassy. It's massive: six hundred square feet with the floor covered in weapons. He has AK-47s, Dragunovs, a US made .50 cal. Where'd he get them? Why does he have them? What is he going to do with them? We sit on a bed next to him and, to his credit, he clears the air.

Nick: We worked in Sulay together, and you guys left. Not a big deal. No hard feelings.
Jacob: Okay.
Me: Okay.
Nick: I want to make sure we can work together up here with no problems.
Jacob: Okay.
Me: Okay.
Nick: Morgan's on team one and Jacob goes to team two. I'll send your team leaders to find you.
Jacob: Okay.
Me: Okay.

We leave his room.

Me: He hates us.
Jacob: No, he hates you.
Me: Fair. He just dislikes you. Think it has to do with the mutiny? I didn't start it. I only made the joke about him having phone sex with his wife.
Jacob: That was funny. I bet he doesn't remember that.

We laugh knowing that's the only thing he remembers about the mutiny. Word on the street is Nick went on leave to see his wife. She had gained a little weight since moving in with her mom and eating home-cooked meals. He loved her chunky ass and they spent a month together as he spent lavishly on her and her family. As he got ready to leave, she told him she was pregnant with another man's baby. Brutal. Not only did she cheat on the guy, but also let him blow his money on her for a month and let him have sex with her while she was pregnant with another man's baby. Women only want one thing—phone sex.

***

Jacob and I receive our weapons from the armory. They're used like a Fort Lauderdale hooker. I miss the rifle I was forced to leave in Baghdad. We're taken to the range to zero our weapons at the Northern Oil Company. It hasn't rained in weeks, but puddles cover the ground. The dirt around them is bone dry. The driver swerves around them, while the child in me wants to splash through them.

Contracting is like prison: the first guy to introduce himself is the guy you least want to hang out with. He wants to be your friend because he has none. He's a sack of garbage in human form. I'm stuck with him in the lead vehicle. Hank's talking my ear off as we pull in the range. Shut the fuck up, Hank. Cucumber.

We zero our weapons and I offer to drive back. I remember routes by driving them. If I drive it once, I'll remember it forever. It's an odd gift to have, but it's all I've got. I near a puddle and the TC tells me to slow down.

TC: Open the door and look at the tires. Keep the tires on the dirt.
Me: Dude, I'm going to romp that shit.
TC: No, man. It's oil.

I open the door and look at the puddle.

Me: Holy shit. That's oil. On the ground.
TC: It's a pain in the ass to wash off.
Me: This is some *Beverly Hillbillies* shit. Black Gold. Texas Tea.
TC: Yeah, stay off it.

GUNS, GIRLS, AND GREED

I watch my tires roll over the dirt areas covering the puddle. Oil at the surface of the earth. It's crazy. Hank's talking in the back of the Suburban. Fuck Hank.

We pass the Eternal Flame monument. This is where Shadrach, Meshach, and Abednego were thrown in the furnace after they refused to worship a golden cow or something. I can't remember the details, but the punishment was death, so they were thrown in a furnace.

This is the first manifestation of Jesus on Earth, as witnesses saw four individuals in the furnace instead of the three condemned. They left unscathed, minus the fourth person. Think of how freaky that looked: dudes chilling in a fire and then walking out.

Me: Do you think their clothes burned off?
Hank: Huh?
Me: Imagine the people watching. Four dudes in a fire and three walk out naked.
Hanks: This monument's sacred to Muslims because they believe Jesus was a prophet but not a deity.
Me: That's fine but imagine if you saw three naked dudes in a fire getting a tan. Then they walk out with char marks. It'd freak you out, right?
Hank: It's the second eternal flame. The first one was over here.

He points to another crater.

Hank: It went out in the eighties. They pumped too much oil out of the ground, strangling the fuel source. When it went out, Saddam had them dig this pit and relight it.

My fault. I made Hank think we're friends. Now he wants to give me a history lesson.

This is a sacred place for Christians because it's where Jesus, in human form, presents himself and proved he's the Son of God by saving the three men. I always interpreted the furnace to be a stove like the one we had growing up to cook beans. I'm disappointed.

209

***

I go on leave for two weeks. It's a mistake. I should've stayed in Iraq. Instead of going to the US, I go to Belize with my wife. We meet at the airport in Houston. Getting through customs takes so long, my flight's about to leave without me. Don't these TSA agents know who I am? I have a diplomatic passport. They don't care so I stand in line with the mortals.

I get to the gate with minutes to spare. My wife's there. She smiles. I'm in no mood for smiles. She's wearing a sleeveless shirt and her arms are seven pounds fatter than they were four months ago. I'm not impressed. I'm pissed she's been eating Cheetos for the last four months.

A private island in Belize is her idea. She's spending my money as fast as I can make it. The island reminds me of the confined bases, complete with sand, a small hut to live in, and a trash can where we're asked to put toilet paper, so it won't clog the pipes. It makes me stir crazy. The island's too small to go for a run and there's no gym so I'm left with my thoughts and no way to ignore them. Me. Alone with my thoughts. Stuck on an island with someone I'm certain I don't like.

I eat seafood for a week and I'm over it. The trip's a mistake. She's a mistake. I can't wait to send her back to my Land Rover, to get back to Kirkuk. Every life decision I make outside of combat bites me in the ass. I'm ready to get back to my comfort zone. This indifference is likely due to PTSD but that diagnosis isn't in vogue so, I assume I'm an asshole.

I fly from Houston to London. I have a sixteen-hour layover, so I take the train from the airport to the city. I find a pub and have a beer. It's amber in color, has a bird on the tap, and it's warm. I ask the bartender if warm beer is normal and he looks at me like the asshole I am. Apparently, they don't like foreigners questioning their taste. I'm tempted to remind him how we saved their ass in World War II after dominating them in 1776 but I don't. I finish my tepid beer and walk out unsure where to go.

I walk past a small brown circular sign, which says this is the building where penicillin was discovered. There should be a shrine with the drippy penis of a sailor thanking the doctor for curing his clap. Around the corner I see a bus stop and a cute girl holding a tourist sign. She tells me I can take a tour of London for a fee.

A red double decker bus arrives, and I jump on. I'm exhausted but since I'm in London, I may as well check it out. I have enough time to do a full tour of the city, grab lunch, and get back to the airport. I notice the guide has a slight British accent as she tells us where to look and the history behind landmarks. Big Ben. Check. Winston Churchill statue, electrified at his request so pigeons don't poop on his head. Check. A castle. Check. Tower Bridge.

Me: Where are you from?
Tour Guide: Kansas. I was an exchange student and decided to stay.

Ugh. My tour guide isn't authentic. My luck is terrible. Then she points out a building and I see a McDonalds. Hell yes. I get off at the next stop, walk back to the golden arches, and order a two-cheeseburger meal with a Coke and large fries. Damn. That's good. I should have skipped Belize and just flown to a Micky D's.

I jump back on the bus and take it to Paddington Station where I catch the train to the airport, clear security, and wait for my Royal Jordanian Airlines flight to Amman. I don't get a room in Jordan because there's a flight to Baghdad leaving as I arrive at the Bristol Hotel. I smell exhausted. Oh well. May as well get in country and start to recoup the cash my wife decided we needed to spend. Such a waste.

CHAPTER 25

I return to Kirkuk thankful to be away from real life. The primary effort for DoS is to shake hands, kiss babies, and hand out tons of money in the form of contracts to rebuild the economy and infrastructure. The military and local police are being rebuilt from scratch because the previous ones were Ba'ath party members. The provisional government disbanded the Ba'ath-controlled military, and the new soldiers need weapons, training, and so on. Uncle Cheddar hands out money like candy to refurbish military barracks, police stations, and government buildings, hoping to put people to work and keep them from siding with the insurgency. In reality, the contracts are convoluted, and local contractors make a ton of cash employing friends and family. Today we're going to the new police station to close out a contract.

The building's new but looks dilapidated. It comprises four walls and a concrete floor with holes for windows. The contract states it needs running water, sinks, and toilets for the police to occupy it. Our principal has a meeting with the head of police, a local elder, and the contractor. I'm stuck on principal duty because I'm the new guy and, rightfully, no one trusts me. I'm sure Nick poisoned the water while I was on leave.

We walk to a meeting room. The principal sits on one side of a long table covered with a white cloth and the locals on the other. Shelves line the wall behind the man I'm sworn to protect. I look presentable and sit silent in a chair next to the door to ensure no one enters. I size up the inhabitants deciding which one to kill first. The police chief first since he's armed. Then the local elder, who's wearing a white robe and cloth on his head held on with a cord. I'll strangle him with the cord. Always have a plan.

The conversation begins with the normal pleasantries. Yes. We're happy to work with you. Yes. We appreciate you telling us we liberated the Iraqis. It's excruciating because each sentence must be translated. It takes three times as long as a normal conversation.

> Police Chief: We want the police station opened. We want to train and live here.
> Principal: I want it open. We want to help the people of Iraq be safe and …

He blathers on with the normal ass-kissing stuff.

> Town Elder: We can open it tomorrow.

He claps hands once.

> Principal: We can't release the buildings to you until we have sinks and toilets installed to close the contract.
> Police Chief: Where are these sinks and toilets?
> Principal: That's why we're meeting today. They were installed last week. When we came to inspect the building, they were gone. We had to order more.
> Town Elder: (Looks at contractor.) Where are the sinks?
> Contractor: I never received sinks.
> Principal: We delivered them to you last week.
> Contractor: This isn't true.
> Principal: This was the third delivery of sinks and toilets. We stayed to watch them be installed.
> Contractor: Where was I?
> Principal: Here with us.
> Contractor: No no no. It was not me. It must've been my foreman.
> Principal: Either way, we watched them being installed. When we returned to inspect, they were no longer on the property.

Police Chief: They must've been stolen that night.

Principal: We have a contract with your police force to protect this building so there should've been a guard.

Police Chief: No. Not stolen under my watch. Maybe a worker stole them.

This conversation goes on for fifty minutes. I've killed these fuckers and saved my principal seven times in my head. My back hurts from sitting in body armor. I'm not privy to all that's happened but I can tell the DoS principal is begging them to let the inspection happen and then, for all he cares, they can loot the place. He needs a completed contract. I'm holding the severed head of the town elder by the hair.

The locals know if toilets and sinks disappear, new ones appear. Combat magic. There's no repercussion for the loss to the contractor, police chief, or anyone else. The US Army doesn't care about this dump, so they refuse to post guards for porcelain thieves. No one gives a crap except for the poor DoS bastard, who likely has completion of this contract as one of his annual goals. It's an amazing analogy for this country writ large. Everyone's out for their own interests and no one cares if it's stable. I love it. It's the same reason I'm here. That and the ability to imagine killing people because my back hurts.

A week later, it's D-Day for toilets and sinks and police station completion. We run our principal to the station and stay on site as the fixtures are installed at a furious pace. It's agonizing. I'm tired of smelling the locals' body odor. I hate him for acting like a general contractor. I want to grab him, toss him in the Suburban, and drive off.

I'm also jealous of these nice American toilets. Why are American tax dollars going to shitters and not holes in the floor? Because it's in the contract, dang it.

Once the work's done, we return to the REO and plan our run to the police station the next morning. We'll grab a KBR employee on our way to sign off that the contract is completed. I'm stuck watching the principal again, which makes me feel like the jock whose mom is forcing him to take an ugly girl to prom. It beats being in a Suburban with Hank for a couple hours, I suppose.

We load up early. I walk to the embassy to get my date. He's wearing a red dress and his hair is pulled up in a bun with curls on the sides. I'm wearing a tux with my nice John Deere hat. (If this is a fantasy, I get my hat back from Amsterdam.) We walk to the limo.

In reality, I wear a shitty brown t-shirt. I don't want to look nice or talk to him. I knock on his door.

Me: Ready to roll?
Principal: Please let this be the day we close the contract.
Me: Agreed.

I answer his questions with one word. Open-ended questions? I pretend not to hear those. If he likes me, he'll request I stay his babysitter. We're not friends. I may die for him but that's not friendship. I hate my life as we drive to the police station and park.

I get out and stand in front of the passenger-side rear door, reach my left hand behind my back, pull the door handle, and open it. My body between the principal and any threat. He walks next to me as we're surrounded by the team. They peel off as we walk in the building, return to the vehicles, and relax. I walk with him.

Principal: Fuck.

He hangs his head. The toilets and sinks are gone, stolen overnight. I want to laugh but watching his frustration is sad. This young man came to Iraq to make a difference, to help the people rebuild and be part of the solution. He probably went to a fancy school (not Bowdoin) and joined DoS to serve his government. I see his resolve drain from his body and flow down the hole in the floor where a toilet sat yesterday. Been there buddy. Welcome to the club. Membership's free.

***

The compound gets a new mission so the old guard's leaving. The leadership, from the regional security officer, who heads the local DoS mission, to the contractors are all being swapped. Hank and I embrace in a tearful goodbye. I'm so glad to see him leave, I cry. He's probably a great person but watching him get the fuck out is spectacular. Why am I pissed off all the time? I used to be caring.

The former mission of assisting the government has been changed to diplomatic operations in Kurdistan. I'm the only person with experience in the region, so I'm promoted to tactical commander. The majority of the missions will be long-range.

Nick's leaving so he can't torpedo me. The current team leader leaves soon so I'll take over in a week. I've snatched victory from the jaws of defeat. I choose Jacob as TC since he has time in northern Iraq. Fuck the other team. They can learn like we did.

We drive to the airport to get the new team members. George walks from the plane to grace us with his presence. It's great to see him. The rest are unknowns.

Dog Handler: He's tiny with little man syndrome. Blond with a large forehead. He's skinny-fat, which means he's out of shape but not obese. Before he was a contractor, I imagine him yelling at kids on the playground for not using the swings correctly.

Dog: He'll sniff for bombs because I'm terrible at it. Small with white short hair. An odd type of dog to have as a bomb sniffer. Most are German shepherds. Fuck it. I'll pet any dog after Mr. Mittens broke my heart.

Rodeo: New kid. Infantry Marine. Lived as an out-of-the-closet cowboy. He feels the need to talk about his fancy belt buckles and bull riding.

Bald Ranger: Former Army, not tabbed, which means he didn't go to Ranger School. Too young to be bald. He's portly with freckles covering his face and pate.

Red: Army Ranger, tabbed, which means he completed Ranger School, red hair and beanpole skinny. He loves being a Ranger but not enough to stay in the Army. He tells us every chance he gets how tough Ranger school is. I tell him Air Force boot camp was harder.

Ranger 2: This one has hair, not tabbed, a small goatee and is chubby. He's not a bad guy but seems a bit immature, which is an odd statement considering you've read this far and I can't imagine anyone more juvenile than me.

Fancy Marine: Tall, blond, and bland. Not handsome but not ugly. Fit but not physical. A guy with no specific quality.

This ragtag group of misfits is perfect for the job. Fancy Marine worked at an embassy while in the Corps, so I make him the principal handler. It's the worst job but his time in an embassy trained him to deal with DoS people. The dog handler and dog will switch between teams depending on the mission. This sucks a fat dong. I want the dog so I can pet him.

The FNGs go through the process, zeroing rifles at the shooting range at the Northern Oil Company and marveling at the oil on the ground while getting little particulates of it absorbed in their bodies that will one day lead to cancer. By the time they're finished, I'm team leader.

I spend the day planning our first run. We know where we're going, but it's a new team and my first time overseeing well, anything. Not bad for a Lazy Air Force Fuck. I'm ready. I'm twenty-four and getting ready to tell former Navy SEALs, Army Rangers, Special Forces soldiers, and Recon Marines what to do and when. It's absurd.

The team meeting is after dinner. I print our route and pin it to the wall for the mission brief. We're heading five miles south to a ministry building where the police, military, and civil servants go to get paid. We've been here. A good, easy run for a new team.

The meeting starts. Nay, I start the meeting. I'm in charge. I'm so nervous my hands shake. I hear my voice quiver as I go through the mission brief. Jacob talks through the route, then I do a quick intelligence assessment of the area. Moderately safe but an IED exploded a block north of the building last week. I ooze weakness as I set RP and we break. I know I can execute the duties of a team leader but I'm positive I'd rather screw the fat girl Andrew described than speak in front of people. Public speaking's scarier than OTW.

Nick's packed and ready to leave. His arsenal sits on the ground next to a couple bags and a box. It's a sight. I wonder how he got all the weapons and so does the new regional security officer. He walks to the Blackwater leadership to inquire why the man with the beard has enough weapons to take over Ghana. They take Nick into the embassy to ask him why he's hoarding guns like David Koresh. Nick walks out dejected, loads his bags in the Suburban, sans weapons, and jumps in.

This is a grandma-died scenario. When my great-grandmother died, her house was full of stuff she cherished but the rest of the family didn't. We had to go through the house, sell the stuff worth something, and get rid of the rest. It's a hassle because Nick's weapons are now our responsibility. We can't hand them to an Army unit because they aren't on their books. His parting gift is aggravation.

***

Children test their limits and so do contractors, who are basically highly trained, lethal children. I learn this on our run.

We arrive at the Ministry of Who Cares and Fancy Marine walks the principal in. We set security and I walk the compound pretending to know what I'm doing. An Iraqi police vehicle drives to the front of the building and unloads stacks of plastic-wrapped cash that make a pile five feet tall and two feet wide. It's pay day so throngs of workers will arrive to be paid. I relay this over the radio.

Me: It's going to be busy so stay alert. You see the dough being carried in?

Jacob: Roger. I got a picture of them lugging it on their shoulders.

I'm kicking ass at this leadership shit. I walk to our convoy and both Rangers are asleep in the front seat. Mouths open. Sunglasses on. What in the flying fuck? New guys are sleeping? *New guys?* I want to teabag them but decide that's not leader-like.

I jump in the follow vehicle and George has his body armor off, hanging out and schmoozing like he's at a cocktail party. The others, of course, followed his lead. No one's wearing body armor.

Me: Put on your fucking kit and go relieve the people standing watch.
Them: Roger.

They look disappointed as they gear up and walk out. I'm fucking livid. New guys are eating me like I'm melba toast. These guys don't deserve to sniff my jockstrap. They don't know the mission, never cut their teeth in Baghdad, and are clueless to the processes. This is what Sergeant Major must've thought about me.

Me: Jacob, come see me when you're relieved.
Jacob: Roger.

In a few minutes, he gets in the driver seat. He's so handsome. I want to have his babies but that's not the focus of this conversation.

Me: Dude, the fucking Rangers are sleeping in the first car. The assholes in this truck took off their body armor. What the hell?
Jacob: You serious?
Me: Go wake your Ranger brothers.

Recon Marines and Rangers have a competitive relationship so calling them his "brothers" is a nice dig.

Jacob: There was an IED right there.

He points to a busted-up sidewalk outside the fence seventy-five meters from us.

Jacob: We talked about it before the run.
Me: Lot of people coming to get paid.
Jacob: This is bullshit. We have to chew their asses when we get back.
Me: Agree.

I'm furious. Mostly, I'm disappointed like a dad who finds his son getting a hand-job from a fat girl at the park. I call a team meeting on the drive back to the REO. We're going to meet after we park. No, you don't have time to drop your kit. Right after the run.

I wait for the team to enter the shack. I walk in last and slam the door like a teenage girl. All my public speaking fears vanish.

Me: What the fuck? We go on a run and people are taking their kit off? You two fucking new guys (pointing at the Rangers) are sleeping in the fucking front seat of the Suburban where everyone can see you. Mouths hanging open like you're getting ready to take a cum shot.

Laughter erupts.

Me: No. Fuck that. This is fucking bullshit.

Jacob stands.

Jacob: There was an IED seventy-five meters from where we were parked, and people were taking their kit off. We're in a war zone, right? On what planet is it okay to fucking fall asleep in a war zone on a mission?
Me: Get your shit together. This isn't going to happen again. Un-fuck yourselves before our run tomorrow. Same place. RPs at 10 a.m.

Jacob and I walk out, and I slam the door. I learned this trick from my high school wrestling coach. We were screwing off before regionals. He yelled at us then walked out slamming the door. We sat in shock.

We could've left but decided to run practice ourselves. I now understand why he was so mad. I'm fuming as I grab lunch.

I have a burger and add bacon to make sure it's unhealthy. I sit alone and eat, seething. George sits down. I'm feeling anti-social, especially to a guy who knows better than to take off his body armor.

George: Hey, man.
Me: Yep.
George: Sorry I dropped kit.
Me: Yep.
George: Won't happen again.
Me: Can you line out the Ranger shitheads, please?
George: I'll talk to them.
Me: Thanks, man.

Just like wrestling practice. No idea why this works. I'm thankful for George. He's a solid dude and good in the pocket. We never have this problem again.

***

Did you know you can reuse a condom? You turn it inside out and shake the fuck out of it. This is the concept of the pocket pussy. I've never used one but they're popular here for obvious reasons.

George has one. It has multiple fittings so he can choose a feature (mouth, vagina, butthole), insert it in the tube, lube it up, and masturbate vigorously. Allegedly this is better than using one's hand. It's also dishwasher safe. (I, however, have a strong preference to use The Stranger technique. I sit on my hand until it goes numb and try to jerk off before the feeling returns. Feels like a stranger's beating me off.)

We hear all about George's pocket pussy after volleyball one day when we congregate at a picnic table near the court to have a drink and tell one-up stories: A person tells a harrowing tale, followed by a person who endeavors to tell a more harrowing tale. These sessions can last hours.

The topic du jour is masturbation. We all do it. My most risqué story is when I was in the ground offensive in Iraq. My buddy Tony and I had a bet on who would be the first to achieve the combat whack, the first to beat off in Iraq.

It was March 2003 in southern Iraq and combat operations were moving north at a rapid pace. I was in Al Nasiriyah starting an air base. Thirteen of us lived in a tent filled with cots. Between each cot was a stacked barrier of A-bags—large military duffles. Mine were near my head and a poster of the Olsen Twins was taped above them. Everyone was waiting for them to turn eighteen. There was even a website counting down the days, minutes, and seconds until their birthday.

The person above me, Mott, had my A-bags at his feet and stacked his at his head so we had bags, cot, bags, cot, bags, cot. Cots lined the sides of the tent with a narrow hallway between. On my second night, I woke at two a.m. I couldn't get back to sleep so it was time to win the bet. I grabbed a large green sock, beat my meat like I was tenderizing a flank steak, and went back to sleep. Babies don't sleep that well. The next morning, we got ready for our shift.

Mott: How'd you sleep?
Me: Pretty good. Except at two. I woke up and couldn't get back to sleep.
Mott: Yeah, I noticed.

This was awesome news. I asked Tony if he'd beaten off. Nope. I proclaimed victory. Tony refused to believe me until Mott confirmed I woke him with my gyrations. Winner, winner chicken dinner.

Back to the picnic table. After my story, George jumps in. The man's full of stories so I know mine will be beaten handily (sic).

George: I have a used pocket pussy.
Rodeo: Used like you used it?

George: Nope. Got it from Beans before he left Baghdad. He was going to throw it out. I couldn't stand the idea of letting it go to waste.

Me: You're jerking off with another man's jerkoff toy?

George: It's washable.

Me: Yeah, but that implies you washed it.

George: He washed it before he gave it to me. I washed it again.

Rodeo: Why didn't you order one online and have it shipped?

George: Because this one was free.

Jacob: We know how much you make.

George: So?

Jacob: So, buy one, for the love of God. You're messing with us?

George: No. It's dishwasher safe. Why would I buy one?

Jacob: You see any dishwashers here?

George: He washed it. I washed it again in the sink. You can turn the mouth inside out to wash it easier.

Me: I can't right now. You win.

George: It's not about winning. It's about free.

This is George. When people pack to leave country, he wanders to their room and takes anything of value. He asks me for my back scrubber when I leave Kirkuk. He's a scavenger. Highly intelligent. No morals. It's invigorating.

***

I don't like the dog handler. He's small and spends the majority of his day exerting ownership over his dog. We can't pet him. I understand this to a certain extent, but the dog must be bored as he only works an hour a day. This gives us twenty-three hours of petting.

The dog has behavioral problems. He's chewing through his kennel. It's not surprising. He rarely goes on missions because the locals don't like dogs and see them as vermin. It's a hassle to take him so the dog handler sits in his room playing video games with the dog in his kennel.

On a day off we use the dog to train around the REO. My team hides different types of explosives to see if the dog will be able to sniff them out. I stuff a short piece of yellow wire explosive under a pool table. The dog sniffs around like a 1980s Wall Street broker snorting cocaine. It's anti-climactic. The moment the dog smells an explosive, he sits, and the handler finds it. It takes five minutes.

> Dog Handler: The olfactory glands on a dog are so acute they can sniff out explosives easily.
> Me: How's it compared to human noses?
> Dog Handler: Think of a cake. As humans, we smell cake. A dog smells the cake and each of its ingredients separately, flour, sugar, baking soda and whatever else cake is made of.
> Me: Hell yes. Cake.

After training we take the dog on a mission. The handler takes him around the compound to clear it. He's an asshole to the dog. He pokes, prods, and kicks him to make him smell certain areas. I worked with dog handlers in Baghdad and Sulay and none of them treated a dog like this.

> Me: Do you need to do all that?
> Handler: Do what?
> Me: Kick him and yank his leash around?
> Handler: He's a high energy dog. It's hard for me to keep his attention.
> Me: I understand. Do you walk him to get the energy out?
> Handler: His exercise time is when he works. I keep him in his kennel at all other times so he's ready to work.
> Me: Makes sense. However, he seems to have too much energy to effectively work.
> Handler: I'm the dog handler.
> Me: Go forth and handle, sir.

After the run I'm pulled aside by Bald Ranger. He tells me the handler lifted the dog by the choke collar, off the ground, until it lost consciousness. He looked over and said, "You know you're doing it right when it pisses and shits itself." That's enough.

I email Patrick, who I worked with in Sulay. He leads the dog handlers in Iraq. I ask him to fly up for a welfare check of the dog. He agrees and the next day, we drive to the KRAB to get him along with new contractors. The mission's expanding so we're adding a team. I invite the dog handler to go but forget to tell him his boss is on the flight. Patrick and I shake hands, and he walks to the handler. The new guys are:

Stain: No one can remember if his name is Steve or Shane, so we call him Stain. He's bald in the back with a tuft of blond hair in the front and a wit that can cause laughter to the point of tears or frustration to the point of violence. He should be doing comedy roasts.

Michael: A cop from the Midwest. He has a sweet goatee and laughs like the happiest man on Earth. So much happiness. I'm not sure I can trust a cop but this one seems pretty great.

Aaron: A cop from New Orleans with the thick accent and gut I associate with NOLA. He's not a cop I'll trust.

Evan: The new dog handler.

The new dog handler?

Fifteen minutes after seeing the dog and talking to the team, Patrick relieves the dog handler of his post. Evan's our new handler and has a German shepherd. Every time George walks past, he says, "Clean it up," in a deep German accent. I thought we left that in Baghdad.

Evan's solid. He's been in Baghdad for a few months. He's genuinely nice but keeps to himself. His moral compass points north so I can't trust him, but he lets us pet his dog, which makes him an American hero in my book.

At six p.m., I'm called to the site leader's office in the REO. What have I done? I've been team leader for two weeks and can't figure out how I fucked up. Michael's sitting in a chair. He's a great guy with a salt and pepper goatee and smiles. I can't help but fall in love. Fuck. He's going to break my heart. I brace my anus for the fucking I'm about to receive.

The site leader received a call from Baghdad and was told to relieve me. DoS tracks each team, its missions, and its leadership. Mostly it's a roster showing the team, its location, and its TL. They have no way of tracking our movement. Someone saw my name and asked if it's the same Morgan who was fired. The site leader assured him it wasn't. Morgan's a common name for a man, right? The Baghdad guy called Kirkuk and told them to demote me to avoid questions. Michael will be the new team lead. It's better to be demoted than unemployed.

I call a team meeting over the radio. Yes, I know you're playing volleyball. Just come to the planning room. Jacob's also moving to another team. I want to tell him before he hears it from someone else. He's fine with it. Not that teams really matter here. We borrow from other teams daily. I walk into our planning trailer and cut to the chase:

Me: Gentlemen, this is Michael. He's the new team leader.

Everyone looks confused.

Me: I was fired off the DoS contracts while I was in Baghdad. Having me in a leadership position isn't going to fly, but I'll remain the TC.
Michael: Hey, guys. (Big smile) I want everyone to know this is Morgan's team. I didn't ask for this. Morgan has the experience and understands the area more than I do. He should be team leader. He deserves to be team leader. It is what it is at this point so I'm going to lean on Morgan until I get up to speed. Any questions?

There are no questions.

Me: Jacob's moving to the other team. The run to Arbil tomorrow stands as planned. See you in the morning.

I'm bummed to no longer be a team leader but there's not much I can do about it. I no longer need to look presentable, so I decide to grow out my hair and beard starting today.

CHAPTER 26

A fun fact about armored Suburbans: the windows don't roll down. Some allow the front ones to roll down four inches but none of the other windows move. It makes sense because a regular quarter-inch thick window is replaced with a two-inch-thick one meant to withstand a gun shot. Due to an inability to quickly ventilate, farting in the Suburban is a no-no.

George is the first to call out people. He's refined. Every so often a new person comes along, eats too much cheese, and blasts a big one. We're left with two choices. The driver and passenger can roll down their windows and risk being shot in the face or we can soak it in. My preference is to crank the heater and let the fart absorb into my skin.

George: Who farted?
Stain: Me. Ha ha.
George: No, dude. Not funny. Not cool.
Stain: Ha ha.
George: I'm serious. Don't fart in the Suburban.
Stain: What am I supposed to do?
George: Hold it.
Stain: Ha ha.
George: No one wants to smell your farts because you're a pig and
      can't hold it in for a few minutes.
Stain: (Awkward laugh) You're serious?
George: Yes.

Me: I agree. I'm not risking my life to roll down the window because you're lactose intolerant.

Stain: Okay. I get it.

We're on a long-range run to Lake Dukan at dusk for a meeting at the resort. This is where soldiers go for R&R. I'm sitting in the front passenger seat and George is in the back with Stain. Bald Ranger's driving.

We're already sixty minutes behind schedule because the principal was late, then George asks if we can stop. This is odd.

Me: No way. We're not stopping.

George: I'm going to shit my pants.

Me: Hold it. No farting in the Suburban. No shitting in the Suburban.

George: I'm serious. How long until we get there?

Me: Forty-five minutes at least.

George: I can't make it.

Me: You're serious?

George: Yes. If we pull over, I'll shit on the side of the road. Five minutes.

I call back to the limo.

Me: Hey, Mike, we have an emergency in the lead vehicle. Can we pull off?

Michael: No, we're late. What's the problem?

Me: George is going to crap his pants.

Michael: Serious?

Me: Yes, it's a full-on emergency.

George: (Getting on the radio) I can't hold it, Michael.

Me: (Laughing) We need to stop.

Michael: Can he go in an MRE bag?

George: I can try.

We're driving seventy mph and George is rummaging through the Suburban to find a bag to shit in. Based on the conversation, the speed we're traveling, and lack of firmness of the pending download, there's no chance this ends well.

George opens an MRE, dumps its contents, and pulls his pants down. With both hands firmly holding the side of the bag he squats, attempts to keep his balance, and aims his anus toward the bottom of the bag. He's about to blow mud when he spots his savior.

George: Whose cooler?
Me: Not the water cooler.

The cooler's red and white, sixteen inches tall and sixteen inches wide. He eyes it like a starving dog looking at steak.

George: You want me to try and shit in an MRE bag while we drive
　　　more than you want to save the cooler? Whose cooler?
Me: It's the team cooler.
George: I'll buy a new one.

He looks at the other team members.

George: Okay if I shit in the cooler?
All: Go for it.

George empties the cooler of warm water bottles. We laugh as a grown man uses it as a toilet, his back straight and neck craned hard against the ceiling.

Michael: How's it going up there?
Me: George is trying to poop in our cooler.
Michael: Ha ha. Serious?
Me: Yes, it's amazing.

The contractors in the limo are holding back laughter at this absurd situation. This is a test of strength because our laughter is audible over the radio. I have no idea how they manage it.

Splashdown. My sides hurt from laughing when I hear screams from the back. The smell slithers from the cooler and makes its way to the front.

Stain: My God, that smells awful. Roll down the windows.
Me: No way, man. I'll crank the AC.
Stain: I'm going to open the door. I can't…
Me: No, hold on.

The stench hits me like a pimp slap backhand, so much stink in a confined space. I dry heave. The driver looks at me as his eyes water.

Bald Ranger: I have to roll it down.

I say nothing. I refuse to open my mouth and taste his shit for a week. I lower my window, pressing my face against it with my mouth and nose aimed at the crack. Bald Ranger does the same. This is hell. Stain's holding his door three inches open by hanging on the door handle, his sole ventilation.

Michael: You okay up there? I see the door open.

I tuck my face in my shirt to answer.

Me: It's bad, Mike.
George: I'm almost done.
Michael: (Laughing) Button up the door soon. The principal's going to ask why it's open.

It smells like Satan's breath. I imagine the contractors in the limo listening and trying to keep a straight face while elevator music plays over the radio.

George: Stain, hand me the TP from the MRE I opened.

Stain takes a huge breath near the open door, closes it, and hands the TP to George.

George: Thanks.
He's always courteous. Stain opens the door again and hangs onto the door handle.
Stain: My pleasure.
Me: Close the cooler? Cucumber, man. Cucumber.
George: I'm wiping. Relax.
Me: Close Pandora's box.
George: Done.

I don't want the shit box in the vehicle, so we have to open a door and throw it on the roadside, but we can't let the principal see. We devise a plan: the follow vehicle has to take our place, we follow behind it and toss the box, then move back to resume our convoy order.

Me: Hey, Michael, can we swap spots so we can toss the cooler out?
Michael: No.
Me: There's no way we can keep it in the vehicle for forty minutes.
Michael: How are we going to swap places without the principal asking questions?
Me: We tell him we're doing a defensive maneuver or something. He won't have any idea what it means.
Michael: So, we're going to practice a defensive maneuver going seventy in the safest part of Iraq with the principal in the convoy, instead of doing it without him in training?
Me: Yes.
Michael: No.

Thankfully, the cooler's watertight which makes is almost airtight. George ties it down in the back so it doesn't tip over. The smell subsides as we keep the windows down. It's a crisp night. The wind hits my hair and face. For a moment, I feel normal. I'm back in Northern Arizona, driving with my windows down on a fall evening. If I ignore the smell, the pain in my lower back, and the thirty pounds of gear I'm wearing, I could be home. I leave the window down to soak it in.

***

Lake Dukan's more dam than lake. I suppose the dam makes the lake. Water levels are low based on the above-the-waterline stain on the rocks. We park and walk the principal inside. Whoever we're meeting is important based on the Apache helicopter parked near the entrance. I radio back to George.

> Me: Get rid of the cooler. No washing it. It's not a pocket pussy.
> George: Where?
> Me: I don't care. Look for a garbage can or walk down the road and throw it in the bushes.
> George: Want to look at it?
> Me: No.
> George: Come on.
> Me: Let me get my camera.

I walk to the Suburban and grab my camera. George opens the lid and I take a picture without looking in. The stench pushes into my nose and face. I recoil and walk off to look at the picture. It's awful. It's like looking at an eclipse through a camera lens so it doesn't burn my eyes—if the eclipse were brown and black sludge inside a cooler.

George throws the cooler off an embankment next to the hotel. Hearts and minds. Stain and George watch it tumble fifty feet.

> Me: What're you doing? George: Getting rid of it.
> Me: Next to the hotel?
> George: Come look.

I walk over expecting to see a lone cooler with sludge pouring out, but it sits nicely in a pile of trash. Even at a resort, they throw piles of trash next to buildings. George and Stain are merely adding to the ambiance. I'll never understand this country.

On the radio:

Michael: They asked the principal to stay the night so we're getting rooms.
Me: None of us packed go-bags.
Michael: Neither did I. He wants to stay. We'll take off first thing in the morning.

The plan is to get up at seven, wait for the principal to finish breakfast and leave. We gather in the lobby and I grab room keys for the team. All our rooms are next to each other on the second floor. The beds are terrible, I can feel the springs poking my back, but each room has a toilet so that's nice. We make a roster to stand shifts outside the principal's room. One-hour each. The person on first shift is furthest from the principal's room. The person in the subsequent room takes the next one. Shifts start at nine p.m. and go until breakfast. The handler (Fancy Marine) gets the night off because he's been stuck with the principal all day.

Mike and I take the worst shifts since we're team leaders. I get the coveted two a.m. shift, which means I get to sleep a couple hours before and a couple after. It sucks. I stand outside the door looking at my Casio Sea Pathfinder every three minutes. It doesn't help. When my shift's over, I'm wide awake so I stand an extra fifteen minutes, so the next guy doesn't have to suffer so badly. I'm a gentleman.

I set my alarm for six-thirty, crawl into bed, and lie awake with my mind racing. I think about nothing but am unable to stop thinking. I get an hour of sleep before light blasts through the window at six a.m.

No go-bag means no deodorant, so I wash my pits in the sink. Not much I can do beyond that. I slop water on my greasy hair and strap my Glock on my leg before leaving. I talk with the guy standing guard for a couple minutes and then head to the lobby.

I stride onto the back patio, which offers a view of the lake. It's beautiful by Iraq standards. I stand in the fresh, clean air and feel invigorated.

An empty swimming pool sits between the lake and the patio. It fits the décor of seen-better-days. The wait staff cater to my every move. They love Americans. I'm offered coffee and they show me the breakfast buffet. It's filled with fresh fruit and pastries.

There's one other person on the patio, who's eating fruit and drinking coffee. It's the President of Iraq, Jalal Talabani. Damn it. I shouldn't be here. Our eyes meet. I say, "Good morning, sir." No wonder the wait staff's so helpful.

He waves me over to his table and points to a chair. His security, posted inside the lobby door, watches my every move. The guy clearly likes to eat. His stomach protrudes from his suit jacket. He's wearing a tie and has a tidy mustache. He looks like Tweedle Dee from *Alice in Wonderland*.

In fluent English, he thanks me, as the face of America on the patio, for liberating Iraq. It's odd. In my head I'm not part of the war effort. He talks about the beauty of the lake as he puffs a cigar. I'm not sure what to say so I keep my answers short. It's better to say nothing than to say something stupid. The waiter comes with coffee and Jalal invites me to get a plate. I get up and grab food slowly to avoid going back. I have nothing to say. Plus, I smell.

Me standing is a cue for his entourage and hotel workers to filter to the patio. The principal needs to get his ass down here. I take my plate into the lobby, eating with my hands like an animal. Michael's posting our team around the lobby, which means our principal's ready to move. I get on my radio and let the team know to hang back. No need to do a full escort with the president's security present. Fancy Marine can grab some food.

We leave ninety minutes later. On the way home I'm exhausted, but Stain's chatty. It's fun banter until he starts talking shit.

Stain: Morgan, do you think your wife's cheating on you?
Me: Shut up, Stain. I'm not in the mood.
Stain: You'll be back in two weeks. Think she'll tell you?
Me: Okay. I get it.

Stain: Do you think his name is Johnny?
Me: That's enough, motherfucker.
He's getting a reaction so he can't stop.
Stain: I hope his dick's small.

I turn in the seat and lean my head forward so I'm inches from Stain. My face feels hot and my fists are clenched.

Me: When we get back to the embassy, I'm going to beat the fuck out of you.
Stain: Like Johnny is beating up your wife's pussy?
Me: (Yelling) Fuck you. Don't bother taking off your kit. Just get out when we park and be ready. I'm going to stomp your fucking skull in.
Stain: That's your comeback? If you wanted my come back, you'd have to wipe it off your wife's teeth.

The vehicle goes silent. He's crossed a line. In thirty minutes, I'm going to kick the crap out of him.

Stain: Sorry, man. Just joking. You know she swallowed it.
Me: Be ready, motherfucker. I'm going to walk around, open your door and beat your fucking face in.
Stain: I apologize.
Me: Too late, motherfucker.

When we drive through the REO gate and park, I get out and go to my room. I'm pissed but I know if we fight, my career is done. I go to the gym to work off the anger. I like Stain even if he has no idea when to quit.

At eight p.m. I go to Stain's room. I have no idea what I'm about to do but I know I have to do something. I knock and he answers. I assume he has no idea it's me or he wouldn't be so inviting. The room's dark and he's in bed. He sees it's me and moves.

Me: Hold on. I wanted to say I'm sorry.

Stain: Huh?

Me: Don't get up. I'm sure you're naked and I don't want to see that Irish inch.

Stain: I took it too far.

Me: I overreacted. I apologize.

A bag of cherry sours sits on his desk. I pour some in my hand and pop a few in my mouth. If I'm swallowing my pride, it may as well taste good.

Me: I think the world of you. I lost it. Rough night of sleep. No excuse.

Stain: Girls are off limits. I get it. No hard feelings. I shouldn't have gone there.

Me: No shit. Either way, I don't want you to think I'm going to try to fight you tomorrow. It's done.

I finish my cherry sours and leave, not sure how I can go from ready to beat a man to death to apologizing to him. Grandma would be proud even if I'm not.

***

My contract ends in two weeks. I've been here over a year and need to go home. All my relationships have deteriorated but I think they're salvageable. I don't want to be the contractor who throws away relationships for money. Absolute power corrupts absolutely, and money is power. I'm realizing the physical and emotional distance between my family and me makes me powerless.

I haven't put much thought into what comes next. I have a job waiting at Sam's Club in Flagstaff, Arizona. Sweet gig at ten bucks an hour. I have my GI Bill so I can go to college, work at Sam's Club, and try to live a normal life. I ponder life with our medic.

Medic: Headed home soon?

Me: Yeah, it's time.

Medic: I have no reason to go home.

Me: You're married.

Medic: We just filed for divorce. Twenty-seven years. She wants me to come home but I'm trying to make us a better future.

Me: Twenty-seven years? Go home.

Medic: This is my only chance to make this kind of cash.

Me: At what cost?

Medic: She's going to take half my military retirement, so I have to stay.

He's decided to throw away his marriage for contracting. He's listening to sirens luring him to decimate his life for a song. The money's intoxicating. The adventure's addictive. We become slaves to the combination.

**

I need to see a doc for my back and Evan, the new dog handler, has some medical issues. I'll run the mission to the KRAB to give Michael a day off. Evan and I will see a doctor, and the rest of the team can go to the base exchange. (The Air Force equivalent of a PX. Since the Air Force is a beautiful, unique snowflake, they call it something different.) It's an opportunity to get haircuts, cash checks, and eat snow cones. Jacob joins for the snow cones.

My future is decided when Michael mentions they'll increase my daily pay by a hundred dollars to extend my contract anywhere from one to six months. With the 10 percent bonus, I'll be at six hundred and sixty bucks a day. Sign me up. School doesn't start till January and Sam's Club can wait. I extend for three months, which takes me through Christmas, so I'll get three thousand dollars each for Thanksgiving and Christmas Day. The relationship stuff will figure itself out later. Show me the money.

We drive to the KRAB. Evan and I are dropped at the medical building. My diagnosis is fairly simple. Sciatica from wearing body armor. I'm prescribed ice and heat. If that doesn't help, they'll send me to Germany for a better diagnosis. Where am I going to get ice in this hellhole? I don't make shit in Germany. I vow to stop going to the doctor.

Evan sees the doctor after me. I'm in the waiting room when he walks out.

Me: What's the verdict?
Evan: I'll be fine.
Me: Need a prescription?
Evan: No.
Me: Let's get out of here.

I call over the radio for a pickup and we head to the morale, welfare and recreation tent for snow cones. Today they're red. They could be brown, and I'd eat one.

I go find George, who's getting a haircut. His red curls are in a pile on the ground. He went in an animal and now looks almost human. He looks good, but the woman cutting his hair looks better. I decide to wait for George and sit next to Jacob in a black faux leather chair, which the supplier undoubtedly decided to deliver so he could charge the government more than for a plain old metal one.

Due to my haircut strike to mark my demotion from team leader, my hair is now flowing across my shoulders. I'd look like Fabio if he were in worse shape, grew a beard and looked homeless. My whiskers are oddly red, which I'm proud of. I suppose the red is because I'm one-eighth Irish. I'm also surprised how much water is retained in my beard. It stays wet for hours after I shower. (Why don't people don't talk about this?) I'm twenty-four but I look like a forty-year-old living in an alley.

The lady barber bends over George, shampooing his hair. She has a tight little ass shown off by her jeans. Her black hair flows to her shoulders. Thin arms. Filipina, I assume by her skin color. A content smile is plastered on George's face as she massages his scalp and shampoo runs down his neck. It's a Vidal Sassoon commercial. He's a lucky man. Last time I was here, only guy barbers inhabited the shop.

The lady lifts George upright in the seat and towel-dries his hair. I see her face and realize the lady ass I'm admiring is a dude's lady ass. Maybe Andrew's on to something? I laugh.

Me: Does that dude have the nicest lady ass you've ever seen?

Jacob: Yeah, full on lady ass. I want to grab it.

Me: But she's a dude, right?

Jacob: Yep, but with a total lady bottom. Skinny legs. Lady butt.

Me: I think we've been in-country too long.

Jacob: No way. That's one of the nicest lady asses I've seen in my life.

George: You guys talking about his lady ass?

Me: Yes, so at least we agree it's a lady ass.

George: Totally. We talked as he cut my hair. He's gay. Loves it here.
  Make better money then in the PI. All the hot GIs.

Me: George is seriously comfortable with his manhood and sexuality.

George: Who cares? It's good for him. Good haircuts. Everyone wins.

Me: Why the short cut on the noggin?

George: Once a year or so I chop it off and clean up. Feels good.

Jacob: You look great.

Me: Yeah, you clean up real nice.

George: (In a Buffalo Bill-*Silence of the Lambs* voice.) I'd fuck me.

Me: Me too and that dude with the lady ass.

George: I tipped him twenty dollars. He did a good job.

Jacob: On a seven-dollar cut?

George: Yes. I tip based on service and he did a great job.

Jacob: I ain't tipping that much.

George: You're cheap.

The irony's thick. George will take a used pocket pussy but is a great tipper. As Jacob moves to get in the chair, George and I walk to the BX. I have to leave before I go home and profess to my family the Filipino lady-man in Iraq turned me gay.

CHAPTER 27

We train in first aid so if our medic goes down or is working on a casualty, we can keep each other alive. Repetitive training gives us confidence to trust one another when the shit hits the fan. (Why do we say that? Has shit ever hit a fan? I suppose the intent is how messy it would be if fecal matter actually hit a rotating fan.)

Today we're training to handle gunshot wounds (GSWs) and set up IVs. Our medic is a former Special Forces 18D and knows his craft. He explains stuff so we can understand it. Per SOP, we don't take it seriously.

A gunshot wound needs to be packed to stop the bleeding. Ideally, one applies pressure on the artery between the wound and the heart while another stuffs the wound with gauze. If bleeding doesn't slow, apply a tourniquet above the wound but below the closest major joint to save as much of the appendage as possible. I'm starting to think this type of situation isn't normal for most people.

I'm the victim. The medic informs the Ranger twins I've been shot in the upper leg. They race over and one applies pressure with his knee to my femoral artery near my hip. It hurts like crazy, but I'm shot so I can't feel pain. The second one takes a role of gauze and begins to unroll it. He simulates an open wound by making an O with his left hand and stuffing the gauze in it with his right. Unroll a little. Stuff. Unroll a little. Stuff. The SF medic stops them.

SF Medic: What the fuck is that?
Bald Ranger: I was packing the wound.

SF Medic: Really? He bled out and died. Stuff the whole fucking role in if it'll fit. If not, throw the roll over your shoulder to unroll it.

Bald Ranger: But it will get dirty and contaminated.

SF Medic: (Looking at me.) Do you prefer clean gauze and dead or dirty gauze and alive?

Me: Dirty gauze. I'm a dirty boy.

SF Medic: We can deal with contamination once he's stabilized. We have antibiotics. We can't bring the dead back to life.

He gets down next to my wound and starts working.

SF Medic: First, take the gauze out of the packaging and try to stuff the whole roll in.

Me: Stuff it in like I do to your mom!

SF Medic: You're zero help. Take the end of the gauze and hold it with your non-dominant hand. Take your dominant hand and throw that shit over your shoulder as hard as you can.

The gauze unrolls across the floor behind him.

SF Medic: Take your dominant hand, grab the gauze, and stuff it in the wound. Deep. He can't feel it.

Me: I can feel it.

He increases the pressure on my leg.

SF Medic: Shut up. You have endorphins running through your body. Stuff it in the hole like you're fingering a pussy. Two fingers. Three fingers. As many as will fit. You can get two or three rolls of gauze in a GSW.

Me: Give it to me, daddy.

SF Medic: Once it's stuffed, have the other person let off the artery. If it begins to bleed through the gauze, apply a tourniquet.

He puts a tourniquet over my leg and tightens it down. Tight. It hurts. He takes joy in watching my face crinkle. I can't blame him since I've been joking the entire time. Never fuck with a medic.

> Me: You're going to cut off my circulation. They're going to amputate my leg.
> SF Medic: You'd rather be dead?
> Me: Mmmmmm?
> SF Medic: Why'd we pick him to be the patient? Tighten the tourniquet down as tight as you can. Tie it off so it can't loosen. I've seen appendages saved after being in tourniquet for six hours. We can try to save a leg or arm. We can't save dead. This is why you tie the tourniquet below the nearest joint. No reason to lose an arm if they're shot in the hand.
> Me: Don't take my arm, daddy. I'll give you the nub of love.
> SF Medic: Ha. That's funny. Try to remember to put tourniquets below the joint or as close to the wound as possible.

I loosen the tourniquet and feel warm blood rush to my toes. I'm healed so it's time for IVs. IV training happens in two places. The medical area in the REO or near the hooches when we're drinking and don't want to be hungover the next day. One drunk gives another drunk an IV.

The giver's wasted and takes four tries to set the needle in the arm. With blood thin from alcohol, the receiver has blood pouring down his arms and legs. But hey, if you can give an IV when you're drunk, there's a good chance you can give one in a stressful situation. We've been tested for HIV, so we pretend there's no reason to worry about swapping fluids even after all the hooker stories we've heard.

Today we use Fancy Marine as our pin cushion. He's gotten out of it so far because, being the handler, he'll be the one giving the principal an IV if things go bad. We feast like mosquitos on his veins. IV needles are thick. I make a joke about how it looks like a McDonald's straw as he sits in the chair.

Jacob pulls on purple gloves, sterilizes Fancy Marine's inner elbow with an alcohol swab, and goes in for the kill. Perfect hit. He tapes the tube onto the arm, removes the needle, and sets the IV drip. Fancy Marine is about to be super hydrated. He's ecstatic. He's so happy he turns white. His head bobs and he passes out. Holy shit. He's pale as a ghost and falls limp like Hugh Hefner's dick.

The SF medic goes into medic mode and revives him. He regains his senses and stands with the IV still in his arm. This concludes medical training for the evening. We break for dinner and volleyball.

After we play best-of-five volleyball, we settle in at the picnic tables as darkness falls. It's a lively night with fifteen of us. We get lawn chairs to accommodate everyone.

Fancy Marine never hangs out but he's here tonight. Maybe he's feeling good from the extra fluids. We turn on flood lights so we can see. Coronas and bottles of hard alcohol spread across the table with mixers. It must be Thursday. I choose Captain Morgan and Coke. Jacob has a Corona. Fancy Marine sips a martini because he's so fancy. Okay, it's a Corona but it looks fancy in his hands.

Aaron, the cop from New Orleans talks about Hurricane Katrina. Cops are hard to trust because they do stuff by the book. We have no book here so I don't trust him, but I want to know about the hurricane. We've seen reports of the carnage on TV. It looks bad, but I can't figure out what the fuss is about.

Me: Hey, Aaron, with all the flooding, are there places where I can buy land on the cheap? Nice neighborhoods. May as well try to make a buck off this.

Aaron: You don't want to buy that land.

Me: They're going to rebuild. I'd buy the land and try to get the government to strip it, then sell it in five years.

Aaron: No, dude. It's gross. Everything is mildewed. It's a biohazard. Crime rates are out of control. I was waiting for my call to start training at Moyock when the hurricane hit. It's a war zone. You'd be better off buying land in Iraq.

Jacob: Why didn't people fill up their bathtubs and sinks with water before the hurricane? Looks like they just sat on their roofs waiting to be saved.

Aaron: I have no idea. Most of the neighborhoods I worked were filthy before the flooding. After the hurricane, we went from call to call for looting.

Me: They were trying to get supplies?

Aaron: Not unless they needed TVs and Air Jordans to survive. They stole everything. It wasn't worth trying to stop them. They were animals. We would go to a call and wait until they stopped looting. We wouldn't even get out of the car. No point in confronting them. There was more chance of it turning bad if we went in.

Me: So, you hung out?

Aaron: Not at first. We initially went in but kept getting shot at. We had a guy holed up in a store who shot at us from behind the counter. We took cover, then my partner popped over the counter and shot him with a shotgun. Killed him. Then we had to do paperwork. Easier to let them take everything to avoid paperwork.

Jacob: They waited for rescue? They could have left or stocked up on food and water.

Jacob's getting fired up. He's on his second Corona. I continue the conversation with Aaron, who's drinking his ass off. I'm on my third drink when I hear raised voices behind me.

Jacob: What the fuck happened today?

Fancy Marine: Me?

Jacob: Yes, you. How do you pass out getting an IV?

Fancy Marine: (Laughs awkwardly) I don't like needles.

Jacob: Fuck that. You pass out because you're afraid of needles?

Fancy Marine: Yeah, never liked them.

Jacob: How'd you make it through boot camp?

Fancy Marine: I don't pass out getting shots, only large needles. (Laughing.)

Jacob: Don't fucking laugh. You need to figure out how to get over that shit. We can't have you passing out when you have to get an IV.

Fancy Marine: (Low awkward laugh.)

Jacob: I'm serious. You need to get your ass in the medic area every day and get IVs until you're over that shit.

Me: I agree. You can't pass out.

Jacob: Let's go. Let's give you an IV right now.

Fancy Marine: No, thanks.

Me: All right, Jacob. We get it. He gets it.

Jacob ignores me.

Jacob: I'm serious. You need to get over that. Get stuck until you can do it without passing out.

Jacob's ruined the party like a husband slapping his wife at the dinner table. Fancy Marine leaves after finishing his beer. I realize guys like Jacob and me, who've been here for over a year, are the Old Guard and we intimidate others. I can't speak for Jacob but I'm edgy.

***

Contractors come and go. Unless we specify a date to return, we're expected to take our crap when we leave. After the initial six months, most choose to do three-month contracts, go home to blow their cash, get the itch to return, and sign for another three months. At that point, we're needs-of-the-company and can be sent anywhere. It's an odd paradigm. We can be best friends for a month and then never see each other again. It's a business.

Aaron's leaving tomorrow. He's fired for getting drunk and kicking in the door to his room. His leg punctured the plastic, which reciprocated and punctured his calf so badly he was rushed to the hospital for stitches. DoS fired him. It's for the best since he can't walk.

Red's headed home. We need to give him a proper sendoff since we don't know when or where he'll return. We have a party at the volleyball courts after our nightly five games. It's a total sausage-fest, bulky dudes playing volleyball bare-chested and wearing short shorts. I'm wearing a pair of shorts I got from Jacob. They have his name on them. I'm his prison bitch and personal property.

After the games we sit around the picnic table as it gets dark. Replacements are here. I don't care to know them. I listen to their backgrounds and stories but tomorrow I won't be able to pick any of them out of a police lineup. I go home in three months and plan to work at Sam's Club.

I hear a deep sound in the sky and freeze. Everyone's silent. It's a rocket. Maybe not. It's menacing and gets louder. Too late to react. We're all dead. The new guys haven't had the time to build a cash surplus. Sucks to be them.

No explosion. I'm disappointed. It must've been a coalition aircraft flying low. My adrenaline's pumped and this is likely the closest the new people have been to being attacked. They laugh awkwardly. Everyone should spend a few months in Baghdad to harden up. Kirkuk's a luxury they don't deserve.

I take this opportunity to grab two rolls of duct tape. I nod at Jacob, so he knows it's fucking on. Jacob stands and walks behind Red. We've been feeding him hard alcohol, but he's still spooked. He looks like a gazelle trying to figure out which way to run as the hyenas close in. It's too late. Jacob's on him before he can make a choice. We walk him to the sand. I point to the new guy.

Me: Get a case of water.

Red's fighting like a wounded bear.

Red: No.
Me: Yes, go get it.
Jacob: Don't fight it. It's natural. Accept it.

247

Me: Let it happen, Red. No reason to fight.

Five of us hold him and tape his legs and hands together. We put tape on his arm and leg hair, so it'll hurt when he rips it off. We put a strip around his mouth and head for good measure. George hands me the water bottle. I'm out of breath so I take a quick sip before pouring it on Red.

Me: Refreshing, isn't it?

We douse Red and bury him in the sand like a cat turd. He flops around like a fish struggling for oxygen. We kick sand in his mouth and nose as he gasps. We pick him up and stand him against the volleyball pole and tape him there. Then we pose for pictures.

The new guys are stunned as we walk off the court and leave him there. If he's there in an hour, we'll send out the medic to cut him loose. The medic is sacrosanct. No harm can come to him, so we send him out knowing he won't get beaten. He can check to ensure no bones were broken in the melee. We jump in the shower to wash off the sand.

Out of the kindness of my heart, I walk out after twenty minutes. The new guys haven't cut him down, which is best. I tell Red we'll miss him as I free him. He's small so the idea of reciprocation is limited. Cold beers must be consumed so Red cracks one. We sit and BS for an hour.

Red, having a drunken epiphany, decides it's time to go out in style. He strips off his shirt, pants, socks, and to my surprise, underwear. Why in the hell does he wear underpants? He's on a mission to run through the US embassy naked. We encourage it as we get our cameras. He sprints through the hall, arms up in the air like an Olympian. He runs out the back door and to his room to shower. Victory is won.

***

Evan lives across from me. I see his door open one day a couple weeks after we went to the doc, so I knock and ask to pet his dog. He agrees. I sit on his bed and play with the pooch. There's not an Iraqi worth the life of this dog, as far as I'm concerned.

Me: Did you get cured from the doc?

Evan: Yeah.

Me: What was it?

Evan: Promise not to tell anyone?

Me: Absolutely.

Evan: I was having pain in my groin. The doc asked me if I was masturbating.

Me: I'm intrigued. Please continue.

Evan: The doc said being in country increases testosterone levels and sperm count. I needed to release the testosterone.

Me: You gave yourself an STD by not beating off? That's great.

Evan: Yeah. You can't tell anyone.

Me: Promise.

Evan's going on leave in a month, but he's on his first contract so he'll be back. Plus, he's too nice to fuck with in the name of esprit de corps.

Evan walks his dog that evening around the compound, which serves a dual purpose; the dog sniffs for explosives and takes a dump. I call him over.

Me: Tell everyone how you gave yourself an STD.

Evan's eyes get big with embarrassment.

Evan: What?

Me: I told you I wouldn't tell anyone so come over and tell them yourself.

He sighs heavily.

Evan: Thanks, Morgan. The doc told me I need to masturbate more because I was blocked up and it was causing me pain.

George: Nice. A prescription to jerk off. I have a pocket pussy if you need it. It's dishwasher safe and has different inserts.

Evan: No thanks.

Me: The man has opposable thumbs, George. He's all set.

George: Let me know if you change your mind.

Evan's one of us. Poor bastard. He drinks a beer as we rib him for his STD and pet his dog.

***

I go to the gym after a run but before volleyball. I need to slim down so I'm doing cardio wearing tiny shorts and no shirt. I grab a jump rope and jump like I'm in grade school.

I must be having a big penis day because my manhood's flopping around like it's on a pogo stick. I understand why sports bras were invented. I need one for my penis. It's out of control. The cleaning lady walks in the gym. We make eye contact. I watch her look down. I don't blame her. It's a lot of motion to ignore. She takes a look at my man bits flopping around and leaves. I keep jumping.

Volleyball starts so I walk out of the gym and continue jumping rope on the sidewalk near the court. Since the game started, I can't get in until the next one so I may as well keep jumping. One of the new guys, a cop with a mustache, clamps his foot on the rope to stop it. It slaps against the back of my leg and leaves a welt that burns like chlamydia. I lose it.

Me: Hey, fuckhead, what're you doing?
Cop: Ha ha.
Me: Don't fuck with me while I'm working out. I'm not going to your room and slapping the dick out of your mouth while you're working.
Cop: Calm down.
Me: Fuck you. We're not friends. I don't know you.
Cop: Sorry. Jeez, take it easy.
Me: You better fucking figure it out. I'm not your buddy. Don't fuck with me.
Cop: Okay, Jesus.
Me: Are you shitting me? Do you not get it?
Cop: Fine. Fine. I'm sorry.

I skip volleyball. The fuck is wrong with people? I take a shower to calm down and walk to the volleyball court thirty minutes later. The cop's there.

> Me: Sorry I blew up. Don't fuck with me when I'm doing my thing.
>   I won't fuck with you.
> Cop: That's fair. Sorry.
> Me: No worries.
> Cop: Your beard and hair, you look like Jesus.
> Me: What?
> Cop: You look like Jesus. Hello Jesus.

He smiles. I want to jump across the table and choke him. I walk to my room and grab the electric shaver I use to shave my body hair, including balls and ass crack. As I shave off my beard, I smell sweaty balls on the razor head. It's unpleasant. I shave my head next and jump in the shower to shave my face and wash the butthole smell off my upper lip. This dude ruined my day. I lie in bed angry until I fall asleep.

***

What do an Ivy League graduate and a tampon have in common? They're both stuck up cunts. We're headed to Arbil for a meet-and-greet with an Ivy League diplomat who's here for a couple weeks. She brings her helper, a young guy, to the meeting with other tampons near the airport.

Arbil opened an international airport in 2004. I remember it because the pictures outside the bathrooms were odd. Each sign has a blacked-out sideview of which sex can use the bathroom. The male bathroom has a picture of a guy with short hair. The female bathroom has the same picture as the male but with a mullet.

I'm the TC and guide us to Arbil. Andrew taught me that the Arabic language doesn't include the letters O, C, P, or E which is ironic as it spells OPEC. This is why it's spelled Arbil and not Erbil. If a map spells it with an E, it's a giveaway it was created by a non-Arabic speaker.

Andrew's off in Syria studying to become a doctor while I'm critiquing bathroom signs.

We pass a Christian church on the way to a walled compound. The cross is displayed prominently on the building. This is what I hope Iraq becomes: a place where all religions can worship without the fear of being blown to bits. Heck, a place where people can walk around and not be blown to bits would be a good first step.

We meet with a local diplomat and go on a sightseeing tour of the citadel in downtown Arbil. It sits on a large mound thirty feet above the street. Walls rise out of the mound like a castle made of mud. It's an amazing sight. The street has lots of shops with huge handwoven rugs. I check the back of the rugs like Dave taught me. So many knots. I explain rugs to Bald Ranger, but he couldn't care less. Uncultured fuck.

We go on a tour of the citadel, which is three stories tall. We're told it's the oldest continuously inhabited citadel in the world. I assume that's a lie because that's what Iraqis do, lie. The guide shows us a door with a metal locking mechanism from seventeen-million years ago. I'm bored so I walk around giving myself a tour.

I reach the second floor and walk to a balcony to see Bald Ranger below taking pictures like a Chinese tourist. Really, dude? You take pictures of this but don't care about my rug knowledge? I pull my dick and balls through the zipper of my pants and whistle at him. He looks up to see me securing the compound with all two inches of my manhood flopped out. He takes a picture.

We return to the street and see a donkey cart with the Kurdish flag draped over it. It looks like Jerry's Kids made a float for the Rose Bowl Parade. I jump in the donkey harness and a couple people jump in the cart. I pretend to pull as they brandish their pistols and rifles like we're racing to battle. We load up and drive to the compound for an hour meeting before we head home.

The hour meeting turns into a wine mixer so we settle in the living room. There's a TV and plenty of DVDs. I put in a horrible Bruce Willis movie. His daughter in the film is his actual spawn. She's fourteen in the movie and in real life. I'm on the couch with six of the team lounging in different spots. I look at a new guy on the floor. I'm going to fuck with him.

Me: That girl's so hot.
Him: Seriously? She's fourteen.
Me: In the movie. Still hot.
Him: She really is fourteen.
Me: Doesn't make her any less hot. Do you think there's a countdown on the internet for when she turns eighteen, like for the Olsen twins?
Him: You're fucking with me.
Me: No way. It's not illegal to go to the junior high and sniff bicycle seats. It's only frowned upon.

I notice movement. I look up to see one of our principals exiting the room. Fuck. I sit up.

Me: You let me say that shit in front of our principal?
Him: I thought you knew he was here.
Me: Seriously? You thought I knew and wanted to let him know I sniff bicycle seats at the junior high?

Silence.

Me: Fuck. You guys have to learn to watch out for each other.

I walk to the kitchen pissed. It's my fault. I should've looked around or, better, not made jokes about being a pederast. That said, I've never been on a team where we didn't watch out for each other.

We stay the night because Tampon got drunk with her friends. The new plan is to return the next morning. We sleep where we can, couches, old mattresses, rugs. It's a long night.

Our principal sleeps in and goes to brunch with her friends. We take showers but none of us has a change of clothes or deodorant. There's a bar of Irish Spring in the shower so I smell like an Irishman minus the beer breath. Without deodorant it's a matter of time before we stop smelling like Ireland and started smelling like Bigfoot's dick. It's time to go.

The principal wants to stay another night. To his credit, the team leader pushes back. We've been eating MREs and smell terrible while she's been eating chef-cooked meals and getting wasted on red wine. He tells her we can come back after we go get clothes. She floats the idea of her staying by herself. This isn't an option. It may be safe here now, but that's a relative term in a living, breathing combat zone. She has to come with us.

We return to the REO and before the sun sets, the horrible bitch writes an email to her supervisor stating she has no confidence in the team leader. He's removed and on a plane in three days to a new location.

Thankfully, she's gone within a week. I hope her superiors learned she was getting drunk with friends and relieved her. We should've left her up there and told the insurgents her location so they could chop off her head. A new team leader's flying in from Baghdad to take over. The old team leader will be on the return flight.

We arrive at the airport early so I hit the chow hall and get a plate of fresh fruit. I eat it like a starving monkey. I sit across from a guy I recognize from another life. Master Sergeant Harmon. We served together in the Air Force. It's a small world. He doesn't recognize me. I've put on thirty pounds of muscle since I last saw him in 2002. I have to fuck with him.

Me: Harmon?
MSGT Harmon: Uh, yes.
Me: You live in Arizona, right?
MSGT Harmon: Yes, do I know you?
Me: You should.
MSGT Harmon: (Trepidation in his voice.) How should I know you?
Me: You dated my sister in 2002. You got her pregnant and she had an abortion. You refused to pay for it.

I stand up and look angry.

MSGT Harmon: You have the wrong guy.

Me: I don't think so. You were at the 161st Air Refueling Wing next to Sky Harbor Airport working with security forces.

Now the table's looking at us because I called out their military unit.

MSGT Harmon: Yes, but I don't think…

Me: I'm messing with you. It's Staff Sergeant Morgan Lerette.

MSGT Harmon: No shit. How've you been? I didn't recognize you.

We spend five minutes catching up. I ask where he's located. The next time I come to the KRAB, I'll bring him a case of beer. I go to the airport terminal and wait for our new team leader as Harmon complains about the bruise on his pear. He has the life here.

I come through on my promise. On my way out of Kirkuk, I track down Harmon at a small building and drop off a case of Corona. A couple years later I learn he was caught with alcohol in Iraq, a big no-no for military, and got demoted.

***

The day is upon me. I'm twenty-five. It's crisp in Kirkuk in October. We make a run to the local ministry building and I relax, work out, and bask in my quarter century of life by telling no one. I have a strong preference to avoid being beaten.

I walk to the recreation room in the embassy and watch a bootleg version of *The 40-Year-Old Virgin*. The audio's terrible. Some guy in a movie theater recorded it. I give up and use it as background noise as I nap on a couch. It's my second birthday in Iraq and I'll never see birthdays as a special occasion again. They're lonely and dumb. I'll reiterate this to my children.

We play volleyball. I have no idea which team wins. Maybe that's the point. It doesn't matter. I stay afterward and have a couple beers. The party moves to our living area and I drink more. There are quite a few of us drinking for a Monday night. I have a Captain Morgan and Coke, my kryptonite.

It's eleven-thirty p.m., and we're about to give each other IVs.

Me: My birthday's almost over.

Fuck, I slipped.

George: What? It's your birthday?
Me: No, a random Monday.

I sprint to the nearest bathroom and lock myself in as George starts giving orders.

George: Go get Jacob and tape.
Me: I'm staying in here until midnight.
George: Doesn't matter. We'll get you after.
Me: Nope, the rule is on the birthday.
George: We still got thirty minutes.

There's a small window. No way I fit through it, but it's worth a shot. I take apart the hinge and get my arm through. Not even close. I'm going to have to Butch Cassidy my way out. I have no chance of survival.

I open the door. They look at me. I look at them. Everyone pauses waiting for someone to make the first move. I lunge forward. Red rover, red rover, send Morgan right over. I break through one level. I'm free. The second level descends. I'm not free. I'm on the pavement kicking and punching. I hear duct tape being pulled. I submit.

I hold my hands to my face. They grab my hands to tape my wrists. Suckers. Submit my ass. I grab the nearest hand and bite, hard enough to leave a mark but not hard enough to cause bleeding. No one deserves a rabies shot because I'm an asshole.

Jacob: Hold him down. I have an extra bed frame in my room.
Me: Bring it, bitches.

Jacob: Yes, we're bringing it over.
Me: Well, that backfired.

Guys return with a bed frame, place it over me, and put their weight on it. I'm smashed against the ground like a frog. They tape an arm and a leg to the bed legs. Leaving their weight on it, they pry my other arm and leg free and tape them to the other legs. I attempt to catch my breath, hugging the headboard and begging my dominatrix to stop without saying the safe word. Thanks goodness the medic's here. They tape my mouth by looping duct tape around my head, including my hair.

I now know what a pig trussed for a barbecue feels like as they lift the bedframe. It hurts. I can't reduce the weight on my forearms. They're on fire. I make fists to flex them, pushing blood to the muscles in an attempt to shield the bone from metal. Pure pain. I hear the medic say, "I'm leaving before you break his arms." Great, dude. Thanks. I'm walked to the volleyball court, doused in water, and sand is kicked in my face. Fucking animals. How can they treat their fellow man like this? Cucumber, fuckers. Cucumber.

They free my mouth to take pictures. I smile for some and spit for others as I try to get the sand out of my mouth and nose. After pictures, they cut slits in the tape and disperse. The slits allow me to free myself. I run to multiple doors trying to pick a fight. They locked themselves in. Fuck it. I take a shower.

Getting sand out of my scalp takes four shampoo sessions. When I'm done, I walk out and have a beer. The unwritten rule states that when shit's over, it's over. It's over and I lost.

***

I'll be going home in a couple months, so I need to train the next tactical commander. No one wants the job. I can't blame them. It's more responsibility for the same pay. Bald Ranger reluctantly accepts, but I don't think he can handle it based on his sleeping habits. I begin driving the lead vehicle while explaining to him routes and what to tell the convoy.

I gas up the Suburban and stage it near the embassy. George tosses his kit in the back and walks to the chow hall to grab a snack for the road. I'm alone in the car so I turn the radio to the US forces station which plays a hot mix of popular songs. Gwen Stefani sings "Hollaback Girl," and I'm fucking jazzed. She sings about bananas and I jump in.

Me: B. A. N. A. N. A. S!

I'm getting into it. Singing my ass off and shimmying my shoulders to the beat. It's just me so why not? My soul is merging with Gwen's as I sing. We're alone. She sings to me like the sirens Odysseus encountered. I yearn to hear more. She has control over me. I hear a knock on the window and snap out of it. It's Bald Ranger.

Bald Ranger: Hey, you have a hot mike.

I look at my radio. It's not on. For me to have a hot mike, my radio would need to be on, and the talk-button pressed.

Me: My radio's off.
Bald Ranger: We can hear you singing.
Me: The fuck?
Bald Ranger: The compound can hear it.

I turn my radio on and put in my ear bud. I hear Gwen. Someone has a hot mike. I look in the back seat and see George's ammo magazine pushing his radio button. This is bad. His radio is tuned to the channel the embassy monitors.

Me: Fuck! Goddamnit, George.
Bald Ranger: We can hear that too.

I reach back, pull his radio out of his kit, and turn it off.

Over the Radio: Can we exercise a bit of professionalism? Between the cussing and singing, are we playing a game of who can have the dumbest radio conversation at the embassy?

Me: My bad. I got it fixed.

Over the Radio: Thank you.

We start the convoy to meet Ambassador Khalilzad for the ground-breaking of the American University of Iraq in Sulay. Many Kurdish and Iraqi dignitaries will be in attendance. Our principal is obligated to go, get on both knees, and suck any dick needing a good sucking. I feed Bald Ranger what to say over the radio since he's in training.

Me: We're going to go in the roundabout at six and out at nine.

Bald Ranger: In at six, out at nine.

Me: Good job, champ.

The TC's job is to relay info such as potholes and possible IEDs on the roadside to the convoy. On night missions, the priority is to pass a vehicle and radio back when the next vehicle in the convoy is safe to pass. This is important because Iraqis drive at night without headlights because they think it increases gas mileage. I'm serious. We have a ton of near accidents because of this, like the time when we can't see a car coming straight at us when we overtake a fruit truck on a two-lane road.

Me: Trash on the road, right.

Bald Ranger: Trash on the road, right.

He's absentmindedly repeating me. I start calling out everything I see and making up some stuff.

Me: Rocks on the road.

Bald Ranger: Rocks on the road.

Me: Sheep at three o'clock.

Bald Ranger: Sheep at three.

Me: Village on the right.

Bald Ranger: Village on the right.

Brian: (Team leader via radio) Thanks for the riveting commentary up there.

Bald Ranger: Why are you telling me to say all this crap?

Me: Wanted to see if you'd catch on.

Bald Ranger: What do I actually need to say?

Me: You've been in convoys for three months listening to the radio. What did we say on the radio?

Bald Ranger: I don't know.

Me: Christ almighty. Pretty much tell the convoy where we turn, and how far we are from the location.

Bald Ranger: I don't know any of that.

Me: You've got two weeks to learn. We're getting ready to pass Chamchamal on the right. We're thirty minutes out. Pay attention. What have you been doing in the back seat?

Bald Ranger: Not much.

We're ten minutes south of the new university. It's outside the city on the road to Kirkuk. The back gunner opens the door to stop a vehicle. The vehicle doesn't stop. He fires at it.

Me: Whoa. What are you doing? What the fuck?

Back Gunner: He wasn't stopping.

Me: Fuck. We're in the safest place in Iraq. You don't shoot vehicles here. (On the radio) Brian, we shot a vehicle.

Brian is silent.

Me: We need to let the REO know before it gets back to them. (To the back gunner) Come on, man. We're going to a fucking groundbreaking with the US Ambassador. You think you need to shoot at a car? Never shoot in Kurdistan.

Back Gunner: I didn't know.

Me: Use your fucking head.

I've taken over the TC role at this point and Bald Ranger's fine with it.

Brian gives a heavy sigh.

Brian: I let the REO know.
Me: Bam. International incident because you got all trigger happy. Damn it. Go tell Khalilzad when he arrives.

We arrive and park. After thirty minutes, I tell my team to take off their body armor. No reason to have pictures of a groundbreaking with Neanderthals walking around in full kit. A helicopter arrives with Ambassador Khalilzad and three Blackwater contractors. The ambassador starts schmoozing. The Blackwater guys see our Suburbans and come over. They're new to country. I tell them they can relax in Kurdistan. They refuse.

Them: Is this OTW?
Me: Technically yes, but it's safe here. You guys can drop kit. It's going to get heavy.
Them: So, we're outside the wire?
Me: Yes, but you don't need to be locked in. It's actually better if you're not because of the diplomats and news cameras.
Them: But we're OTW.
Me: Sounds good. Do your thing.

After a couple hours, the groundbreaking ends, and Khalilzad returns to his helicopter. Everyone feels good about a new university. Well, everyone but the dude who had his car shot. He's at the REO saying his car is destroyed and his wife is clinging to life at the local hospital.

It's horseshit. The guy called his cousin or brother or friend to pick him up and drove to Kirkuk to ask for compensation. We're driving home when Brian jumps on the radio.

Brian: Hey there, Back Gunner. The guy in the vehicle you shot is at the REO and claims you shot his wife.

BG: What? No way. He was the only one in the car.

Brian: Yep. We'll need to file an incident report when we get back.

Me: (Not on the radio) See fucker?

Brian: We'll have a quick debriefing and then walk over together.

Me: (Not on the radio) You're fucking with my volleyball time, wife-killer.

BG: Copy that. (Not on the radio) Shut up, Morgan.

Me: Shooting the women and children of Iraq. Feel like a real man, BG?

The gentlemen are at the REO when we arrive. We fill out an incident report. Mine's short. I'm glad I'm not in leadership. Bald Ranger can take it from here.

My report: BG opened the door. BG yelled at the vehicle to stop. I heard a round fired from BG's area. BG's a fucking idiot and should be dick-slapped by everyone on his team for making them miss volleyball. He committed a modern-day war atrocity equal to My Lai.

BG, Brian, and Bald Ranger give sworn statements. The truth is, BG's an idiot and should've kept his door closed. In Baghdad, his shot would be justified, but this isn't Baghdad. The driver was the only occupant and unharmed. Knowing the US will pay for any incident, he drove to the REO and lied his ass off. He concocted a story to make it seem terrible, so we'd pay. He's scum. A normal guy.

I'm positive DoS paid to get his vehicle fixed and gave him a little extra to go away. After this, we receive a standing order to not open doors or stop traffic while traveling in Kurdistan. This war is getting touchy-feely. This, ladies and gentlemen, is why it's easier not to call in a shoot.

CHAPTER 28

Elections are upon us. Again. For this election we have to deal with DoS and reporters from major news organizations. The media is our enemy. Blackwater has a shit reputation and giving a reporter access to us is bad. I tell everyone to keep their mouths shut.

They arrive three days before the election. The next day we travel around Kurdistan to allow them to look at election sites. It's the same public relations stunt I witnessed in Baghdad a year ago. It's a load of shit landing in my lap two weeks before I leave. I'm more than ready to go. Bald Ranger is doing fine in his TC training. He understands routes and distances. I'm replaceable.

Our first run is to Sulay. One reporter looks familiar, but I couldn't pick a journalist out of a lineup if he raped me. For all I know he's Tom Brokaw or Mickey Mouse. I didn't grow up watching the news. Current events consisted of being featured in the *Verde Independent* if you caught a fish. I couldn't give less of a fuck who they are.

Each election site gives a tour to the journalists to show the voting process. I sit in the Suburban and nap while Bald Ranger sets up security. Revenge is sweet. We do this all day. One voting site after another.

As evening approaches, we drive over a mountain to the private residence of Iraqi President Jalal Talabani and get rooms in his mansion. I'm rooming with George. I pray he didn't bring his pocket pussy. Around ten o'clock, he goes to the room and I sit on a couch with a reporter next to me in a chair. A small table sits between us. My glass sits on the table and the reporter pours me Johnnie Walker Green Label.

Reporter: Green Label is a malt blend with notes of oak because of the fifteen-year aging process.

Me: I have no idea what that means.

Reporter: It's a midrange scotch. Like it?

Me: The more I drink, the more I enjoy it.

He pours me another. I have to drink it. I'm soon slurring my speech, and he takes his shot.

Reporter: Who do you work for?

Me: Myself. I'm a private security contractor. White Thunder LLC.

Reporter: And you contract under?

Me: The State Department.

Reporter: Via?

Me: Blackwater.

Reporter: How do you like it?

Me: It's great. I make a bunch of money and drink Johnnie Walker Green.

Reporter: I'm a reporter with the *Washington Post* and would love to do a story about your experience. How old are you?

Me: Just turned twenty-five.

Reporter: Were you prior military?

Me: Air Force.

The reporter picks up a notepad.

Reporter: What did you do in the Air Force?

Me: Security Forces. I was in the ground offensive in 2003.

Reporter: What's your name?

George: (From the room) Morgan, get your ass to bed. We have an early morning.

Reporter: Your name's Morgan?

Me: Got to jam, brother. Have a good night.

Reporter: I'd love to talk more.

Me: Early morning.

Reporter: Here's my card. Email me. The *Washington Post* is sympathetic to your cause and we report without bias. We keep things down the middle.

I take his card.

Me: Thanks. I'll be in touch.

I walk down the hall. My head spins from the booze. I'm paranoid I said too much. Hell. I'm an idiot. Nothing's changed in fifteen months.

George: You don't talk to reporters. They're the enemy. You know this.
Me: I know. Fuck, man. Did I say too much?
George: Go to bed.
Me: Thanks for looking out for me.
George: Good night.

I can't sleep. I lie on the floor, fully clothed, drunk, with my pistol next to me. My mind races trying to remember what I said. I'm an idiot. I'm on two days without sleep because I can't get out of my head. I don't sleep as well as I used to. I'm always alert, especially when I mess up. I throw the reporter's card away. Thank goodness for George. He's solid.

We drop the reporters at the airport the next day so they can go who-knows-where to see polling stations for an election no one cares about to elect a government no one listens to. The US government's pissing up a rope it will climb later and complain about the smell. Is that ammonia?

I return to the REO ready for sleep. Exhausted, I walk into the chow hall. I see Dale, the dog handler who's replacing Evan while he's on leave. That means a new dog to pet. Hell yes. Dale was on Templar 12 in Sulay. His mustache is eating a burger and fries. It's great to see him. Based on his eating habits and chain smoking, I'm surprised he's alive. I grab food and sit next to him.

Me: Dale. The man. How's the mustache?
Dale: Morgan. What the hell? I had no idea you were here.

Me: Yeah. I try to keep it on the DL.

Dale: DL?

Me: Dick licker. Down low man. You're not that old. You're a dog handler now?

Dale: After my first contract I put in for a dog handler job and got accepted. Spent eight months in training.

Me: I hope you jerk off more than that, dude.

Dale: ?

Me: Ignore me. We play volleyball every night. Come on out. We can catch up afterward. I've got a bottle of Captain Morgan in my room I need to polish off before I leave.

Dale: I'll be there.

I catch a nap and go to volleyball. It's erotic, dudes in short shorts pretending to be Maverick and Goose from *Top Gun*. I'm wearing my Jacob shorts. Dale watches, chain smoking Marlboro Reds. Viewing physical exertion gives him heart palpations. I go for a spike and soft tap over the blocker. I'm so cool. Dale notices.

I'm hung over from the reporter's heavy pours, so I only play one game and call it a night. I tell Dale to meet at my room in twenty minutes. He took over Evan's room.

I walk to the chow hall and grab six Cokes for the rum. Dale knocks on my door five minutes later like he's stalking me.

I crack open two Cokes, take a chug out of each and fill the empty space in the can with Captain Morgan. I hand him one and we toast. It's great to see him. I'm stoked he got the dog handler position he wanted. Good for him.

Me: You got your dog, huh?

Dale: I put in for it once we hit Baghdad. Got picked up after my first six-month contract. This is my first gig in Iraq with him.

Me: You went back to Moyock and did the handlers course?

Dale: Yeah. I hadn't seen my wife in a year except for a couple weeks.

Me: That sucks. You met her in the Army, right?

Dale: Yeah. We've been married twenty-two years.
Me: Holy crap. I was three when you got married.
Dale: Fuck you.

We drink. I start to chain smoke with Dale, which is a sure sign I'm wasty-facety.

Dale: Last time I saw you was in Sulay, then you went back to Baghdad.
Me: We left you old farts behind. I went to Baghdad and was on the QRF for a bit. That was nuts. Then I got fired and came here.
Dale: How's it here?
Me: Calm. Nothing crazy. Do runs, play volleyball, make money.
Dale: That's the plan. But not the volleyball part for me.
Me: Don't want anything to get in the way of your smoking. You retired from the Army, right?
Dale: That doesn't pay shit. My wife spends that every month.
Me: Well, soak it in up here. It's a cushy gig.

The bottle's almost gone. My teeth are numb along with my face and toes. I'm fucked up and dirty from volleyball. I jump on my computer hoping Dale gets the hint it's time for bed. We have a half-assed conversation where he talks, and I give one-word answers.

Me: I'm going to email my wife.
Dale: I'm drunk. I emailed mine earlier.
Me: Yep.
Dale: Been happily married for over twenty years.
Me: Indeed.
Dale: It's been great catching up.
Me: Agree.
Dale: Can I suck your dick?
Me: What? No.
Dale: Yeah. I want to suck your dick a little.
Me: I think you have the wrong guy. I'm married.
Dale: Me too. But I want to see …

Me: Time for you to go to bed.

I'm freaking out. I need to stay calm. I've got my pistol and rifle. I can beat this old man to death if necessary. He doesn't have a pistol. I'm good.

Me: Okay, dude. Bedtime.
Dale: Can I jerk you off? I want to see you cum. I'm not gay.

I stand up, acutely aware I'm almost naked except for some shorts which say Jacob.

Me: Time to go.
Dale: I'm not gay. Just want to…
Me: Get some sleep.

I walk him out my door, close it in his face, and lock it. I'm full of fluids so I grab an empty water bottle and piss in it. I put it across the room, so I don't drink it in the morning. I'm freaking out. What the hell happened?

In Blackwater, your word is your bond. I'll never tell anyone Dale's a peter puffer, but does he know that? Is he going to come in and try to shoot me tonight, so I don't tell everyone? Is he gay? He's married. Maybe he likes to see dong blowing a load in his face, on his mustache. Fuck. This is a horrible position to be in. I refused the advances of a fully armed man where he has no reputation. He's got to be scared his secret's out.

I grab my Glock, open my door, go to the toilet, empty three water bottles, close my door, lock it, and wait. I put my Glock under my pillow facing the door. If he kicks in my door, I'll kill him. I'm drunk so I'll shoot myself in the temple if I try to shoot lying down. I grab my gun and sit in my chair. I'm full of caffeine and adrenaline. *Bring it, Dale.*

After thirty minutes, I push my chair against the door and get in bed. I set my Glock facing the door under my pillow and place my hand on it. I'm certain I'll be accosted tonight. He's either going to come in and kill me or blow me. I'm not comfortable with either option. His mustache is coarse. No way I can pretend it's Christie Brinkley with that handlebar. I fall asleep with my hand on my Glock.

The next morning, I'm hungover. I wake with my hand on my pistol and piss bottles all over my room. The Glock has no safety, so I'm shocked I didn't kill myself. I jump in the shower wondering how I'm going to approach Dale. This place is too small to avoid him.

As I shower off the dirt from volleyball, I try to put a positive spin on it. There are twenty extremely fit people on this compound. Of all the people he could have asked to suck off, he chose me. He chose my amazing penis to go in his mouth. Hell yes. In Dale's mind, I'm the cream of the crop (pun intended). My dong stands above all dongs on this compound. My dong is the chosen one. He's going to kill me.

I put on pants, strap my Safari holster to my leg, drop my Glock in it, and walk to breakfast. I'm twelve feet from my door when I see him. He's up early. Hell. Here we go. I'm transported to Tombstone, Arizona, 1881. I'm Doc Holliday getting ready to shoot outlaws. Okay, I'm Morgan Earp since the name fits. No, I'm Doc Holliday. "You're a Daisy if you do." I wait for him to draw.

Dale: What happened last night?
Me: We drank a bottle of Captain Morgan.
Dale: I woke up in my bed. I don't remember leaving your room.
Me: We got pretty loaded.
Dale: I didn't do anything stupid, did I?
Me: No, you were fine. Hammered but fine. I was right there with you.

I move in to kiss him on the mouth. Not really. I'm deflated. He's pretending he didn't proposition me. I feel used. This morning I was cock of the walk because my dong was the chosen one. Now he's pretending nothing happened. I've done this to girls. I'm going to write apology letters to them.

My stride of pride devolves into a walk of shame as I slog to breakfast. This is the only way it could've ended without bloodshed. I'm relieved he's pretending nothing happened. I'll do the same. I vow to never tell a soul unless I write a book about it later.

It's December 2005. The elections are today and the Army's piggy-backing on our convoy. We meet them in the morning and do a mission brief. My heart's happy to see an up-armor Hummer. I volunteer to jump in it and direct them to polling stations.

An Army major comes over to give a pep talk to his troops. I'm intentionally disrespectful. He's a dude with an orange flower on his shirt as far as I'm concerned.

Major: Be safe out there. Are you directing the convoy?
Me: Yep.
Major: We're counting on you to know where we're going. Keep the convoy informed of where we're…
Me: No, I'll tell your driver where to go. They can relay. I'm not play-ing with your radios. I'll call back to my people. Follow them.
Major: Okay. (Looking at his troops) Remember, every run we need to decide if we're going to make friends or enemies. Do your best to make friends with the Iraqis today.
Me: Ha ha. Come on.

I walk away so he can tell his soldiers not to be like me. I've made my point. He's a turd. In his defense, all Army majors are turds. His troops know it.

We jump in and set out to a polling station. It's brisk. I drink in the smell of burning diesel fuel pumping from the Hummer. It smells like history, like Baghdad, like QRF. I miss this.

We enter a roundabout. In at six, out at three. We're on the inside lane with a white and orange sedan on the outside. The driver moves into both lanes and plows into the side of the car, demolishing it. I love it. I find absolute joy in this for no reason. It feels right. Does the major think we made a friend?

We drive north where there's a driving ban. The only vehicles allowed on the road must post a sticker on its windshield. All others are considered a threat. Once we break the line to Kurdistan, I go into relax mode.

The lead driver's maneuvering his vehicle like Mad Max. He runs a truck off the road. I tell him, "Calm down. We're in Kurdistan. These are good people."

We pull into the polling station. Diplomats and Army officers walk around like they're interested in the democratic process. This is my third election and Iraq's in tumult. I'm here for me.

I see an election poster of an old woman walking to a voting station with the Kurdish flag above her. I begin to peel it off the wall. An Iraqi police officer walks over to stop me. The nerve. I want a piece of history. I'm taking it. The Iraqi policeman is certain I'm not. He says something in Kurdish. I tell him in English, "I'm taking this, bro." He's five-foot-five. I'm six-foot-two. He gets an officer.

The IP says something, and I rip the poster. Fucker. Leave me alone. He's explaining to his officer that I'm stealing. He looks at me. I look at him. He looks to his subordinate and motions for me to take it. I get a picture with it as I finish removing it. Maybe I'll sell it on eBay with proof I stole it from the source. Let's be honest, I don't care about history when I can make twenty-five dollars.

We go to the next polling stations. We see a truck with passengers in the bed but no sticker. The driver runs it off the road.

Me: Dude, enough. Don't push people off the road. They're the solution.
Driver: I didn't see a sticker.
Me: I don't give a fuck about a sticker.

The driver is quiet. I laugh as I say:

Me: Are you making friends or enemies? Seriously, these are good people. Stop pushing them off the road.
Driver: Roger that.

I can't go back to Sam's Club. I need to get back to Baghdad or any other location to get more adventure. I miss it. I'll go home for a few months but, after today, being in this Hummer, I know I'm coming back. I sign a contract to return in two months.

***

After the election, we gather for a beer. I strike up a conversation with our medic. I'm feeling down. It's an odd discordance. I'm burnt out after eighteen months in Iraq but not ready to leave.

Medic: What are you going to do when you get home?

Me: No idea. Maybe I'll go back to school.

Medic: No vacation planned?

Me: No. I have a new dog. Would like to meet her. Decompress for a few months and decide if I want to come back.

Medic: I went to Prague on leave. Holy shit. You have to hit Prague.

Me: Are there good museums there?

Medic: I have no idea. The hookers are amazing. Dark hair and blue eyes.

Me: I'm not in the hooker-buying business.

Medic: I went there with a buddy. We each got a hooker in the park. He didn't wait to get back to the hotel. I looked over and he was fucking her over a park bench.

Me: In daylight?

Medic: No. It was night. I yelled to him, "Use a rubber." He yelled back, "Too late, man. I'm exposed." I'm shocked he didn't get HIV.

Me: No way.

Medic: Serious as a heart attack. I was supposed to spend seven days there. On day four I bought three hookers. We did a bubble bath with candles. They start pouring wax on each other and me. I took three Viagra. We fucked all night. I woke up the next morning and changed my flight to leave early. I couldn't have any more sex.

Me: Sexed out? No way.

Medic: Yeah, man. My dick was so swollen. I flew to Jordan and got to the Bristol two days early. Bought Ambien and slept for twenty-four hours.

Me: Sexed out.

Medic: I didn't know it was a thing until it happened. I couldn't take any more.

My liver can't take much more. I walk to my room and pack. I put my personal stuff in one bag to go home and filled the second with the stuff I'll need when I return. I'll leave it in Baghdad.

I haven't had a drink since election day and don't plan on drinking my last day. I'm packed so George hits me up for my stuff. He's visibly agitated when I tell him I'm taking my back-scrubber. He rummages through what I'm leaving.

It's December 23. I fly to Baghdad tomorrow, stay for Christmas to get my bonus, and catch a flight to Jordan. My completion bonus is eleven thousand dollars so my final check will be twenty-eight grand. I haven't told anyone I'm coming back to Iraq, including my wife. Surprise. I don't love you enough to stay.

After dinner I hear a knock at my door. Dale's coming to suck me off. Nope. It's my team. It's my last night and I have to have a drink. I relent. My birthday's fresh in my mind so I tell them no goodbye-beating as a condition of my presence. Plus, I'll be back in two months. They agree.

George pours Johnnie Walker Green and sips it like a sophisticated adult. I can't imagine being refined. I sip my Corona like, well, it's a piss beer. Each team member pours me a shot over the course of ninety minutes. I'm on shot five with two beers in me. I'm done.

Me: Okay, gentle people of the earth, I'm going to piss in the embassy one last time and go to bed.

Rodeo: Pussy. Drink that vodka.

He points at a bottle of Absolut.

Me: I have to function tomorrow.
Brian: Do it. It's Christmas.
Me: Ah yes. Celebrate the birth of our Savior by chugging vodka.
Bald Ranger: You scared? It's like two shots.

I refuse to be ridiculed by Bald Ranger. I grab the bottle and chug. One gulp. Two gulps. Three gulps. My esophagus is on fire. The fourth gulp is small. I'm done. I slam down the bottle and walk to the embassy to piss. Take that, assholes.

I wake the next morning in bed as someone pounds on my door. I look at my watch. Fuck. I'm late. I open the door and it's the head DoS person.

Him: Hey, Morgan. It has been a pleasure working with you the last seven months. You've been great and you're always welcome back to Kirkuk.
Me: Thanks, I appreciate it.
Him: Jump in the convoy. Here's my contact information. If you ever need anything, don't hesitate to reach out.
Me: Thanks, I will.

I push everything not packed into my backpack. I don't have time to shower, which sucks because my back-scrubber is in the bathroom. George is going to be stoked when he rummages through my stuff later.

***

My flight lands in Baghdad. Blackwater has upgraded from crappy old vehicles to Mambas, which have armored V-hulls to deflect explosions. I notice dried blood on my right hand and a swollen area between my knuckles. I pick at it and pull out a chunk of glass. What in the flying piss happened last night?

I attempt to nap while we wait. The flight from Tikrit arrives and a gentleman with long blond hair joins me in the back. The driver fires

up the Mamba and we're moving. It's loud against my headache. The
blond guy taps me. I look over as he taps his left wrist and mouths, "Nice
watch." We both have the Casio Sea Pathfinder.

He has an anchor tattoo on his inner forearm. Must be a SEAL. I
smile and say, "Nice watch." I want to ask him if he bought concealed
throwing knives.

I unload my bags at the man-camp and get assigned a room for the
night. The camp's full so I sleep in someone's room. It stinks like cigarettes and sweat. Dirty clothes litter the bed and floor. I push them off
the bed and crawl in to sleep off my hangover.

There's a knock on the door that evening. I open it. I'm summoned
to the phone. It's Brian in Kirkuk.

Brian: What happened last night?

Me: You tell me. Last thing I remember is chugging vodka.

Brian: You came back after that, sat down, and talked shit to everyone before we put you to bed. You were ruthless to Bald Ranger.

Me: I don't remember any of that.

Brian: The embassy staff noticed today the bathroom mirror was
broken. Someone said they went in after you, and the mirror
was shattered.

Me: Fuck. I must've punched the mirror. My hand's fucked. Been
picking glass out of it all day.

Brian: Come on, Morgan. Why?

Me: No idea. I don't remember anything. First time I've blacked out.

Brian: The RSO wants you fired.

Me: I don't blame him.

Brian: Nothing's going to happen until after Christmas because no
one's in the office for DoS or Blackwater. Enjoy Christmas
in Baghdad.

Me: I'm on a flight to Jordan on the twenty-sixth. Should I take
both my bags?

Brian: People are pulling for you. I think we can get you back. Leave
your gear bag there.

Me: Good enough.

I walk back to the filthy room. How does anyone live like this? I crawl into bed and wonder how Santa will get in. I leave out cookies and carrots next to a huge CD case. I recognize the CD case full of porn. This is Jason the Porn King's room. What a pig.

Fourteen years later I see Jason. Fourteen years later I recall how nasty his room was.

Me: I got stuck in your room for two nights on my way out of Baghdad in 2005. You're disgusting.
Jason: That was you? Ha ha.
Me: Yeah. The only reason I knew it was your room was the porn collection.
Jason: That collection was awesome. I purposely left that place filthy. I figured someone would come in, see it, and refuse to stay. I chain smoked in it for weeks before I went on leave.
Me: Your plan almost worked. I felt dirty in your bed.
Jason: I didn't wash the sheets for a month and left my smelly clothes all over. I can't believe you didn't ask to be moved.
Me: It was a rough couple days for me.
Jason is full of pride.
Jason: That porn collection. I had it all. I was like the Blockbuster of porn.

We laugh. Jason's a good dude.

***

I fly to Amman on December 26, 2005 and spend the night at the Bristol. The next day I'm called to the phone in the lobby.

Blackwater Guy: What happened in Kirkuk?
Me: No idea. I drank too much, and someone said I beat the shit out of the embassy bathroom.

Blackwater Guy: We worked together in Baghdad. I know you're a
    solid guy, but you know I have to fire you, right?

Me: I know. I fucked up.

Blackwater Guy: Go home and call me in a month. We'll get
    you back in.

Me: I need a couple months off, but I'll keep in touch.

Blackwater Guy: That's fair. We want you back, but we need the
    waters to calm.

Me: I get it. I'm an idiot. I don't blame you if you never want me
    back. I deserve what I'm getting.

Blackwater Guy: You finished your contract, so you'll get your bonus.

Me: I'm not worried about the money.

I hang up, disappointed in myself but can't figure out why I care. I
never planned on making this a career, and I can return to contracting
anytime, either with Blackwater or another company. Still, leaving as a
pariah wasn't my plan.

It's for the best. I'm yearning for a "normal" life, but I have no idea
what that means. Hopefully, marriage will ground me. I need to return
to Earth. I've been treated like a god, a hunter, for too long. It's time to
do what warriors did when they came home after World War II, settle
down and build a real life.

I never received an exit package from Blackwater. What if I had combat related injuries? A traumatic brain injury or PTSD? No one cares.
PTSD isn't in the public vernacular in 2006 so the soldiers and contractors who come home must figure out life sans help. I'm pissed at everything and can't figure out why. I have PTSD but my only support system
is a MySpace page of other contractors. Facebook eventually took this
role. I need to put contracting behind me so I ceased contact to focus
on college.

EPILOGUE

Back in Arizona a week later, I receive my bag from Baghdad. It's been rat-fucked, and all my good kit's gone. They took my Safari drop-leg holster but sent home my smelly workout shirts.

I return to the love of my life, an amazing black Labrador named Shelby Southern Belle. My wife got her from a shelter while I was gone. She's the sweetest dog. I give her the life I wish the dogs in Iraq had. I take her everywhere. She lays her head on my lap as I drive, and I pet her. She's a fetching machine. It's cathartic to throw a ball and have her retrieve it. Every time I come home, no matter how bad a day I've had, she's happy to see me. I'm not sure I've felt love like this. I don't deserve it.

I start classes at Northern Arizona University as a buffer between Iraq and assimilating. I haven't decided if I'll return to contracting but know I need time to decompress. The stress of the last eighteen months followed me home. I'm angry and alert. When I drive, spikes of adrenaline hit me when cars don't stop at a red light. My eyes dart at the movement and I reach for the rifle I don't have.

I'm lost but I have my GI Bill. My income goes from fifteen thousand dollars a month to twelve hundred, enough to pay the mortgage. Savings covers the rest. I'm broke, alone, and mad at everything. This sucks.

I'm isolated sitting in classes with children. They can own a gun and buy cigarettes but aren't adults. They're sheltered. I'm a combat veteran devoid of emotion.

I'm in a class on law enforcement when the Virginia Tech mass shooting happens. I'm livid the shooter committed suicide. The professor attempts to gauge the emotions of the students.

Professor: It's a horrible massacre, a tragedy. Anyone want to talk about it?

The class sits silent. I feel anger. Blood rushes to my cheeks. I've been here before. I can't stay silent.

Me: He's a fucking pussy. He wanted to be notorious but he's a joke. I'm sad no one got the satisfaction of killing him. Only a coward kills himself after slaughtering innocent people.

The class is shocked and silent at my comments. My fault. I gave them a glimpse into my reality. They weren't ready for it. The professor wanted to talk about gun control, but for me, it's personal. Everything's personal. I'll never adapt to college. Later in the day a female student, who knows I was in Iraq, asks about the shootings while we're working on a class project.

Her: How was he able to kill thirty people?
Me: Luck. He expended 174 rounds but only killed thirty. If he was trained, he could've had a body count near seventy-five.
Her: Are you serious?
Me: I think I could've killed ninety people with that many rounds.
Her: You're an asshole.

I'm too old, too jaded, to emotionally disconnected to relate with her. After class I buy a New York strip steak, head home, do homework, and grill it. I pour a Captain Morgan and Diet Coke and play fetch with Shelby. I wouldn't say I have a drinking problem so much as a desire to distance myself from war and civilization. I don't bother to cook for my wife. She'll come home and eat chips and salsa. It's our roommate routine.

My wife's spending money like a drunken sailor and I'm going broke trying to pay the bills while she buys purses. Thankfully, she leaves me in November 2006 and asks for my Land Rover. Before we finalize the divorce, I take it four-wheeling and romp the shit out of it. A fitting goodbye. I doubt many Land Rovers see the woods, much less get driven up a dirt hill backwards. I keep the windows down so it's filthy when I hand it over. I need to get back to my roots—the redneck who's happy surviving. Anything more's a blessing.

I spend time and money in therapy trying to save my marriage in 2007. PTSD isn't mentioned but it's what I work through with my therapist as she explains my marriage's over. I'm broken. A divorce is for the best. I'm an asshole and she's a chunk butt. No way this'll work. My life's shattered like the bathroom mirror in the embassy. I busted both to pieces and can't recall why. I'm a loser. Failing at marriage is the last straw. I may as well go back to contracting until I die. No amount of money will replace the thrill of combat. I have an anchor at home now with Shelby but can't adapt. She's my Service Dog though neither of us know it.

If I take a normal class load, I can graduate in two and a half years. My goal is to be the first person in my family to get a college degree. No idea why. I've made it this far without it. It feels like a competition I want to win. Nothing less than straight As will do. If I'm going to do something, I'll be the best at it.

The economy's tanking and job prospects are limited even for people with quality degrees. I'm on track to get a less-than-quality B.S. in Criminal Justice but have no desire to become a cop. I'm lost. Where do I fit into society? I don't.

I email my Blackwater buddies to inquire about contracts. I talk to the team house leader in Baghdad and sit on the couch, mentally preparing to go, when Shelby puts her head in my lap. She snuggles me. As I scratch her belly, I cry, wallowing in self-pity. Snot and tears roll down my face as the weight of a broken marriage and broken life hits me. I can't leave Shelby. She's the first thing in my life I've felt responsible to keep alive. She's the one relationship I can salvage.

This leads me to the Northern Arizona University ROTC. I speak with an amazing LTC (who knew good ones existed?) about scholarships and career paths. There's comfort in talking to someone who has a combat deployment. Hell, I yearn for adventure but for the first time in my life, I want stability. It doesn't feel right but doesn't feel wrong. I sign a contract to become an Army helicopter pilot.

I complete my degree in a year and a half by overloading classes. I have nothing better to do. College is torture. I find refuge in the ROTC building but not familiarity. Talking to cadets willing to put on a uniform and serve is refreshing, even knowing many will become incompetent majors and retire having nothing but their rank to prove their worth. I graduate with a 4.0 GPA.

Unknown to me when I signed my ROTC contract, the service agreement for helicopter pilots is seven and a half years. I don't know much, but I know I'll hate the Army. I commission as an intelligence officer so I can leave in three years.

The Intelligence Officer Basic Course is in Fort Huachuca, Arizona. My brother's stationed there, which allows me to take Shelby. I'm stuck in a dilapidated Army hotel on base, so I leave her with my brother and visit her daily. On weekends, I sneak her in my hotel room, put the Do Not Disturb sign on the door, and let her on the bed for unlimited cuddles.

I meet an amazing woman in my intelligence class. I immediately offend her when I tell the class I don't like working with women in combat operations. She hates my guts. I don't blame her, but I'm smitten. Later in the day I talk to her.

Me: You have beautiful blue eyes.

She gives me a look that says "lay off, asshole" but she's polite.

Her: Thank you.
Me: I'm serious.
Her: Thanks.

We don't talk after that. I've cultivated my reputation as the class bully and she's not into assholes.

Halfway through training, we have a class barbecue and I bring Shelby as my date. Everyone loves her. I show off her tricks and ignore the group. Shelby's my priority. Another student offers her a chicken wing and I slap it out of his hand. She can't eat it because it might splinter in her esophagus and kill her. I'd murder everyone at this party to save Shelby Belle. A while later, I'm wondering where Shelby went and spot Ol' Blue Eyes petting her. This is my chance to turn things around. I fast-walk over so she can't leave. She looks up smiling at me and says, "What a great dog." Bam. I'm in.

We talk often and she asks when Shelby will hang out. We go on a date to Olive Garden, the classiest place in Sierra Vista, Arizona.

Me: Two weeks ago, you wouldn't give me the time of day.
Her: You're an asshole at work. When I saw you with Shelby, I realized you're a decent human. You love her.
Me: (Holding back tears) Just because I rock doesn't mean I'm made of stone. More breadsticks, please!

I have zero desire to find love after a divorce and joining the Army. I have no time for it. I'm not capable of it. And yet, I find myself falling for her. Ugh. We begin to date. We both know this will be a slog.

She deploys for nine months to Afghanistan. We spend six weeks together before I leave for Iraq. It's the best six weeks of my life. She's Prometheus giving fire to man. I can't get enough. She's a drug, beautiful, intelligent, driven, and super-hot. I'm addicted. She reminds me I want a normal life, outside the military, and outside combat. She replaces my addiction for adventure. I don't know what a normal life is, but I know I want it with her and Shelby.

To cement the deal, we get her a Labrador puppy named Callie before I deploy. Callie's a hot mess of a lab with crazy eyes and the best heart. Callie accompanies us to send me off to Iraq. The soldiers adore her and she howls as the bus leaves. I see Ol' Blue Eyes tear up as we leave. God has a sense of humor because the bus breaks down before we can leave the parking lot. We offload to start the horrible process of saying goodbye again thirty minutes later. Callie reminds me of the book *Marley and Me* but I don't mention it. I'm off to travel the world. Having a puppy is worse than going into combat as far as I'm concerned.

I arrive in Baghdad in 2009. I leave my four-hundred-and-fifty-thousand-dollar military life insurance policy to Shelby. The Army's not impressed, and I must jump legal hurdles to ensure that if I die, Shelby gets it. My battalion commander must sign off on it. He looks at me like I'm crazy. I look at him knowing his first love's the Army, so he'll never understand.

***

Between the Air Force, Blackwater, and the Army, I saw the evolution of war, from the ground offensive, to the peak of fighting, to the drawdown. I can't tell if we lost but I know we didn't win. As an Army officer, I'm stationed at the base we drove to in Blackwater for the Regime Crimes Liaison Office, where the gallows are located. Okay, God. Cucumber.

I'm sitting in a clam shell helicopter terminal with three of my soldiers after visiting our leadership at the Perfume Palace. There is a shelf of books near the back and I see *Marley and Me*. I've read most of it but never finished because I know the ending. I sit next to my soldiers as we wait forty-five minutes for a bird. As I read the last chapters, my nose starts to run. I'm going to cry. I close the book and walk to the back of the hanger so my soldiers can't see me. Tears hit the pages as I read and think of Shelby, Callie, and Ol' Blue Eyes. I finish it, walk to the port-o-potty, and look in the crappy metal mirror. Fuck, I'm an ugly crier and there's nothing to freshen up with unless I want to dunk my head in the blue water that smells like someone ate twenty pounds of cinnamon and crapped it out. I put on sunglasses and walk back to the terminal.

I leave the Army as a captain, the last respectable rank before giving my soul to the staff-gods who contribute zero to the military. As I suspected, I hate every minute of it. It did little to change my perspective on the caliber of humans trying to win a war from the comfort of a palace.

In its defense, the Army led me to my love, so I forgive it for usurping three years of my adulthood. I can't bear the thought of asking her to sacrifice her ambitions to follow me as a career officer when I ask her father for his permission to marry her. She accepts and I apply to Tufts

University where I'm accepted to their graduate business program. Go Jumbos! I'm still not sure what the fuss is about snooty schools, but I'll try to send our kids to one all the same.

I get a desk and a cubicle in Corporate America. I wonder how many people have had badass adventures like me only to sit in a cubicle and become a slave to a paycheck. If I met current me when I was twenty-three, I wouldn't be impressed. Older me is a weakling.

I assumed my days filled with adventure are over until we have a daughter. Don't tell my Blackwater buddies, but seeing her for the first time was better than the moment I got my unused rifle in Baghdad. So pure and innocent. In that moment, all I want is to be a good father to make up for my garbage dad. We have a son two years later.

After each of their births, I put a beanie on them to get their scent. I take this home for Shelby and Callie's approval before we brought them home. The dogs accepted both. Had they not, we would have put our kids up for adoption.

Being a parent's a hoot. Watching my children take their first step, eat their first Cheerio, and slop food on the floor for the dogs is utopia. I have a life I don't deserve, a life I assumed would be cut short in Iraq. How did my worthless father give this up? I feel bad for him. If I see him again, I'm going to yell, "Billy Joel's gay" and punch him in the face.

I have cool war stories to tell my children and grandchildren but I'm not sure I will. I want to protect their innocence. They won't be allowed to read this book.

AFTERWORD

Daniel Krug, a former soldier and contractor, wrote a story about giants that sums up the profession of arms. "This world creates these giants in order to send them off to guard the gates. But then when the giants are done, nobody wants the giants. They're too big, they break things. They can't fit. They loved the giants when they were guarding the gates but nobody wants them back... They make giants and say 'Okay. Don't be a giant anymore.' How do you do that? You took away their purpose and you expected them to be fine. And now they kill themselves and suddenly you're surprised?"

It's been eighteen years since I worked for Blackwater. Thankfully I made it out of Iraq and Blackwater didn't. They served a purpose in the GWOT because the politicians had no plan on how to move from combat operations to diplomatic ones.

I made lifelong friends at Blackwater. Sadly, some have taken their lives. It's a terrible feeling knowing we were in the same spot and their final outlet was suicide. It's difficult to transition to a normal life. Being a PMC is an addiction and some never transition. Blackwater never gave me a post-employment packet telling me where to turn for help. Facebook has filled the void with groups. That's sad. The people who profited the most are absent while former employees turn to Facebook for community support.

How do people work their asses off to make a living but never have cool stories? War's hard to leave for a soldier and harder to leave as a PMC who can go back on demand. I understand why some Blackwater brothers took their lives. I count myself as lucky.

Dave became a successful business owner. I'm proud of him. He's in the government sector which is flush with cash.

Andrew studied in Syria and went to Harvard for a graduate degree in foreign policy. He's driven and can take any opportunity and turn it into gold. He has two little girls he adores.

Tony and Eric fell off the earth. I've tried to find Tony repeatedly but have given up. Last I heard, he was living in the Midwest on a small farm attempting to avoid human contact. Vintage Tony. I hope he got the recon paddle I gave his mom in 2011. I've had to make the hard decision to let him live his life distinct from me.

Jason the Porn King is running a private security firm in the southeast. He's doing great. When we talk, he beams over his kids. He's a great dude and I'm proud to know him. I see him regularly when he teaches classes in Arizona.

George went into real estate and made enough money to retire. You'd never know it. I saw him in 2014 and he was living in a small house doing woodworking as a hobby. Out of spite, he went to Harvard so when DoS principals asked him where he went to school, he could throw the H-bomb at them.

Blackwater matured me. Hard to believe if you've read the book. I spent eighteen months of my formative years in a combat zone. I learned to be ultra-competitive and find humor in terrible situations. It's served me well.

I learned war is futile and PMCs are a mixed blessing. Don't get me wrong, I love war. It's the cornerstone of my life. The GI Bill paid for my college degrees, including one at Tufts University. My time as a PMC allowed me to stay out of debt. I love war.

The brotherhood of combat, the esprit de corps, can't be replicated in civilian life. These men were my brothers, my blood, and I'd cross the earth if one were in need. When I hear one committed suicide, it cuts to the bone. They are the knights who couldn't assimilate back to society.

Thankfully, Blackwater as a PMC is dead. They made their money and survive by selling the brand via licensing agreements. The vestiges of Blackwater survives by selling shirts, trinkets, and licensing the company's brand to weapon and ammunition manufacturers, who engrave the infamous bear paw logo on them and sell them as premium products. The brand's owned by PG Investment of Virginia LLC.

The contractors who died by their own hand would be national news if they hadn't been working under the Blackwater "bear paw." Blackwater's complicit in creating separation between the agencies who wage war and those who conduct it. Fortunately, lawyers are helping contractors get compensation for PTSD under the Defense Base Act. Blackwater hasn't facilitated this. It'd be nice if they had a link for people who worked under the "bear paw" to get assistance—but that might hurt their ashtray sales.

I miss combat. It lessens with time, but I still miss the adrenaline, the endorphins, the feeling of invincibility coursing through my body. It's a drug, and I long for that high. It's intoxicating and toxic. I feel bad for those who never experienced it.

We continue to find ourselves in wars we can't win regardless of how much we spend. The strategic benefit's minimal compared to the human toll. I've seen how war affects people, myself included. It leaves deep, irradicable scars and we, as a nation, don't understand how our military members, contractors, and the inhabitants of the places we fight are impacted.

Contractors are stuck in a precarious position. They carry scars of war, but aren't afforded public support given to military veterans. Yet contractors became critical in the Iraq war because no one planned for a protracted conflict.

Blackwater filled the void. With limited supervision and no repercussions, we became the epitome of mercenaries: highly paid men with a mission but no rules of engagement—Guns, Girls, and Greed drove us. Erik Prince stated repeatedly that we conducted over forty thousand missions with only two hundred shots fired. What he doesn't report, and likely never knew, is the carnage we wreaked by smashing into cars and the actual number of shots we took because we never reported them.

I don't blame Prince or Blackwater for how contractors acted, but future wars can't be fought using unsupervised PMCs. The repercussions for local populations are too severe. This is not to say private security contractors don't have a place in combat, but DoS and DoD need to get out of their ivory towers, get in harm's way, and be part of missions. Until then, private security contracts will be a net negative.

I've searched my soul for an answer to war and my conclusion is we must let local populations figure out their own paths. If we intervene, we need an exit strategy before we go in. Shoot and scoot isn't an exit strategy.

Americans see the world through the prism of American exceptionalism. We're proud patriots. We may disagree on goals and how to achieve them but agree on what we want to see the US achieve. This doesn't reflect Middle Eastern culture where sects (Sunni vs. Shia) and ethnicity (Kurds vs. Arabs) trump nationalism. This is the difference between US and the locations where we fight wars—the loyalty to a tribe, ethnicity, or religious sect trumps the desires of a "nation."

Someday war will be seen as a last resort instead of diplomacy by other means. War has transitioned from being state-on-state to state-on-ideology. No war can eradicate an ideology. I wish I had an answer, but I can't figure out what my kids want for dinner.

Maybe that's the answer. If we can figure out, as a nation, as a world, how to get children to eat vegetables, we should build on that. It's a better plan than Colin Powell and Donald Rumsfeld had going into Iraq.

Shelby died in 2018. I still miss her and can't bring myself to see her picture without crying. Callie died in 2020. She was crazy until the end and we miss her. Ol' Blue Eyes and I have been married for over a decade and didn't learn our lesson because we now have a yellow and chocolate lab we rescued.

While revising this, on December 4th, 2022 (fifteen minutes ago), I learned my father died and I'm not sure how to process it. I'll likely put on some Elton John and Billy Joel and see if their lyrics speak to me.

If you've read this far, I hope you enjoyed the book, had a few laughs, and got a look at the human side of Blackwater. Maybe I gave you a more nuanced view of private military contractors in Iraq, the good, the bad, and the offensive. My guess is the opinion you had prior to reading this hasn't changed. That's fine.

APPENDIX

The first edition of this book is intended to show the insanity and the human side of life as a Private Military Contractor (PMC) for Blackwater in Iraq as the company expanded the number of its employees to protect diplomats in combat.

The book is about catharsis. The stories are based on a hilarious, depressing, and terrifying chapter of my life—surrounded by the best trained, smartest, and most lethal people on the planet. Yet, we're perceived as knuckle draggers who enforced our will upon locals in the name of diplomacy. I've been called a murderer for hire, a sex trafficker, a terrorist, and a litany of even deplorable things which illustrate the gap between the mystique of Blackwater's mission and how the public perceived us.

The Blackwater contractors killed in Fallujah in 2004 changed the public paradigm of PMCs. Until their murders, few had heard of Blackwater and fewer knew what contractors did—myself included. The larger question is: Why did a single unarmored vehicle, woefully unequipped, drive through Fallujah when the Standard Operating Procedure (SOP) required no less than three vehicles? Who allowed this? Who had oversight; the Department of Defense, Blackwater, the employees? No one took responsibility. It was settled out of court.

This incident shows how lines between government contracts and combat operations blur. Terrorists dragging burned US citizens and hanging them from a bridge led to Marines fighting to regain Fallujah in November 2004 at the cost of eighty-two dead Marines with more wounded. This should have been a wake-up-call at the costs of having PMCs in combat operations. Instead, the use of private contractors expanded.

Do private contractors belong in combat? I doubt anyone entertained the idea until the US handed sovereignty to an interim Iraqi government, because we didn't want to be seen as occupiers. The toppling of one government with replacement by a hastily-created, propped-up interim government created a gray area where no one understood where wars end and diplomacy began. To fill the leadership gap, we threw money at the problem with private security companies happy to profit. Blackwater wasn't the only PMC—though it got much of the blame. There was DynCorp, Aegis, Triple Canopy, and the shitshow that was Custer Battles (the worst named PMC, considering what happened in General Custer's last battle). My position is PMCs should never be in a place where US troops are not. If the government doesn't have the balls to commit troops, they shouldn't' wage war by PMC proxy.

We can debate the catalyst for failure in Iraq. Was it disbanding the Iraqi military; Sunni, Shia, and Kurdish sectarianism; or the League of Nations forming Iraq after WWI? That's fodder. The US invaded Iraq with no post-combat plan.

Blackwater as a PMC has been dead since the government of Iraq kicked it in 2007. Triple Canopy took over the contracts and hired the Blackwater contractors on site. This was status quo when contracts switched companies.

Blackwater became Xe, then Academi, and was sold to Triple Canopy (TC) in 2010 once it became clear they wouldn't get government contracts. Constellis consumed TC and other PMCs, and then Blackwater as a PMC was officially dead. Kaput.

I reached out to the president of Blackwater—I'll call him "Predator"—before the book published. We emailed via LinkedIn, and I offered to send him the manuscript. We set up a time to talk. He couldn't talk because he was going to dinner. He promised to call later but didn't. I published the book under the title, *Welcome to Blackwater: Mercenaries, Money, and Mayhem in Iraq: a memoir.*

Predator wasn't happy and issued threats against me on the Blackwater Facebook page, the nexus of support for former employees, and railed to mutual acquaintances that he was going to "make my kids homeless." Classy dude.

I assume he was salty after his conviction for failing "to make and maintain or cause to be made and maintained adequate records specifying the actual location where firearms were stored on Blackwater's premises and failed to make and maintain or cause to be made and maintained required records with respect to registration of certain firearms,"[1] which resulted in four months of home confinement, a fine, and three years of probation.

In his defense, he received feedback my book was inaccurate, which is true. I told stories second-hand. Some were liars—a small but mighty minority in the community. I corrected them in this text.

Most of the Blackwater community were supportive of the book and agreed the experience of being a PMC in Iraq from 2004–2005 felt insane. Some were butthurt I used the term "mercenary" in the title and others told me I wasn't "real Blackwater" because my background wasn't as cool as theirs. None of the haters served with me in Iraq but acted like any deviation from the Blackwater official narrative or thoughtful analysis of being a PMC was blasphemy.

In the first go at this book, I added a story told to me by a person I trusted. The anecdote concerned the death of a Blackwater contractor and injuries to others. But making the story public hurt those involved, along with the widow of the fallen man. I'm sorry for that. I promised to fix it. I put my money where my mouth is and added the real story. I left the version of events as told to me in this text but clarified what happened to show how someone can take a terrible event and make themselves the hero. There are no heroes in war—only people who fight it, witness it, and live with the scars of it.

US Government agencies, including private military contractors, must be held to strict standards and accountability in combat zones just

---

[1] *https://www.justice.gov/usao-ednc/pr/previous-officers-corporate-entity-formerly-known-blackwater-plead-guilty-are-sentenced